Sourced from Within

Sourced from Within

A Practical Framework for Vibrant Freedom

Cynthia Lamb

Sourced from Within by Cynthia Lamb

Published by Vibrant Freedom
Austin TX

© 2021 Cynthia L. Lamb

All rights reserved. No part of this publication may be reproduced, stored in a retrieval system, or transmitted, in any form or in any means – by electronic, mechanical, photocopying, scanning, recording or otherwise – without prior written permission from the author, except as permitted by U.S. copyright law.

For permissions contact:
cynthia@vibrantfreedom.com

Cover by Florian Zimmer florian@soulbook.info
Book layout and design by Sarco Press

First Edition

ISBN: 978-1-7362650-0-0

Dedication

In Loving Memory of Dr. Frank Alper

Contents

Introduction 1

Chapter One: Our Source is Love 3

Chapter Two: We Are All Intrinsically Worthy 29

Chapter Three: Viewing Life from the Paradigm
of the Loving 54

Chapter Four: We Each Have Free Will Choice 97

Chapter Five: Taking 100% Responsibility 157

Chapter Six: Making the Paradigm Shift by Updating
Your Belief System 176

Chapter Seven: Judgment – A Natural Outcome of the
Right/Wrong Reality 243

Chapter Eight: Embracing Disowned Aspects of Self 271

Chapter Nine: Releasing Emotional Energy 311

Chapter Ten: Cultivating New Healthy Patterns of Behavior .. 371

Chapter Eleven: The Integration Process 391

Chapter Twelve: The Framework of Loving 410

Acknowledgments 425

Introduction

As the consciousness shifts upon the planet, more and more people are beginning to wake up to who they truly are as spiritual beings. They feel a pull to live in the place of peace and infinite Loving.

There are quite a few brilliant teachers out there who live in Loving, and many profound teachings of what this place of enlightenment has to offer. The question I hear most often is, "That all sounds great, but how do I *get* there?"

For years I struggled with the same question. Until one day, it finally clicked for me. Applying my new understanding of how to heal myself and create lasting change, I gradually went from experiencing tremendous misery and suffering to living in bone-deep peace and contentment on every level of being.

For the past thirty years, I've been supporting people worldwide to learn and embody an accelerated self-healing process, using the principles and tools that worked for me. Most of my clients and students have experienced deep, soul-level healing as well as profound changes in their daily life, including notable improvement in their self-care, relationships, parenting, careers, finances, and more. Like me, they've gone from residing in fear and suffering to living vibrant lives of joy, inner peace, and deep fulfillment. Freedom is available, and best of all, it's totally doable if you have the right tools.

The purpose of this book is to make the tools for 'getting there' available to those who are genuinely ready to move into the new paradigm of Loving.

This book will take you through the foundational understandings necessary for creating true and lasting personal transformation. Each chapter includes an experiential exercise designed to help integrate the information from *understanding at the brain level* to *knowing at the cellular level*. Take your own time with each exercise as you integrate these foundational understandings from philosophical ideas into the reality of your own daily life experience.

One suggestion: As you read this book, please take what rings true for you, leave what does not, and place anything that you do not understand on a shelf in the back of your mind. It may be useful sometime in the future.

My deepest desire is that my words will support you on your journey into the Loving.

CHAPTER ONE
Our Source is Love

Do you feel ready to live in peace, joy, and love in every moment of every day? If so, then you are ready, as Gandhi said, to "Be the change you wish to see in this world." If you want to fully experience freedom, truly *be* free, you must take your knowledge of what it means to be free into every single cell of your being. In this way, you will literally *become* the freedom and peace that you seek.

To begin the process of transformation at the cellular level, the number one priority is to begin to make the paradigm shift from living in a fear-based life to living a life of Loving. Accepting and claiming your Loving Source is the integral first step toward creating a life of joy and freedom.

Our source is Loving. We come from and are an intrinsic part of a vast, infinite, ever-expanding, and evolving source of pure love. This love is ever-present and all-encompassing. To feel this love, know this love, and have a tangible connection to this love, all we need to do is claim it as our birthright.

The truth is that we are sourced from infinite Loving, and we are all born Loving beings. There are no unloved beings from our Source's perspective. We all come from the Loving, and we are each always loved by our Source, no matter what happens during our lifetime.

For some of us who were raised with images of a judgmental God, punishment, ideas of sin, and threats of going to hell, this idea that we actually come from pure love may take a little while to assimilate. If you have any resistance to this idea, I encourage you to simply observe your thoughts, see what comes forward for you as you sit with this concept. Do your best to stay open minded as you explore this new possibility. Let's take a deeper look at the mechanics of coming from a source of infinite Love.

Humans run on electromagnetic energy that travels through our nervous systems. Science can now take pictures of the HEF (Human Energy Field); the emissions of energy of most living things are visible through Kirlian photography, a kind of photography that can pick up energetic emissions that are not within the normal parameters of human vision. These energetic emissions are measurable and taken as fact by our modern science. We are all 'plugged in' to a source of electromagnetic energy through an invisible cord. We, as humans, have an electrical circuitry; we are wired, for lack of a better word, with nerves throughout our body. Our spinal column is like the heavy gauge wire, and our tiniest nerve endings are like very fine gauge wire. Our circuit board and circuit breaker switches are located in our brain. The spinal fluid and water in our body act as a conductor for the electrical impulses. We receive electricity that runs us, and that is part of what makes us alive.

A Soul in a Body, Plugged into a Vast Source of Consciousness

But there is more to human life than simply a source of electromagnetic energy; we are sentient beings. In addition to being plugged into a never-ending supply of electricity, we are also plugged into a vast source of consciousness, a co-creative force that gives us life, intelligence, creativity, inspiration, joy, and so much more. Besides having a physical body, a mental body, and an emotional body, we have an energetic spiritual body that is part of a much larger spiritual body called the soul, which exists beyond our reality's measurable levels. Our soul is a part of ourselves that is much greater than our four-dimensional experience can comprehend; it is intimately connected at a higher level to our source of Loving. By acknowledging our soul's presence, we can experience this connection to our Source to a much greater level than most of us have even begun to imagine.

We are all plugged into something much bigger than ourselves. We are plugged into a source of vast and unfathomable intelligence, a source of infinite creativity, brilliant imagination, and cosmic consciousness. I call this source of energy and consciousness the Loving, because this source provides instant access to the energies of infinite, boundless love as well as infinite compassion and every other quality you could possibly desire.

Everything in existence has a frequency. The highest level is infinite love. This Source of boundless Loving literally contains all that is. Not only are we connected to this Source, at the elemental level, we are actually made out of this Source. While Quantum Physics is getting clearer about how our energy bodies solidify into physical form through the power of our thought, we exist first and foremost at the energetic level. So, we are connected to our energetic Source, and we are made from our energetic Source. We are both individual and one at the same time.

There are many different names for the source of Loving that all point to the same idea. Some of these names are Source-energy, Infinite Intelligence, God, Goddess, the Divine, Oneness, All That Is, Universal Mind, Quantum Field, the Absolute, Cosmic Consciousness, and many others. To me, it doesn't matter what the Source is named; it is all the same Source – a source that, at its highest, is pure, infinite Loving.

From the perspective of the Loving, it does not matter if we believe in God or not; it does not matter if we are Hindi, Catholic, Jewish, Christian, Buddhist, Muslim, Spiritualist, Mormon, Agnostic, or Atheist. Regardless of our personal beliefs, we are each just as spiritual as the next person. We are all souls born out of and connected to the infinite Source of all that is whether we recognize our Source or not, and it is all the same Source energetically regardless of what we call it. The bottom line is that if we are alive, we are a divine soul in a body.

Our current science is on the verge of understanding our innate spirituality as it discovers the mechanics of manifestation from energy into physical level reality through quantum physics. Within a very short time, the concept that we are energy much more than matter will become the norm, rather than an outlandish idea. Just like there was opposition to the radical idea that the Earth revolved around the Sun rather than the opposite, many people will balk at the idea that we are not as solid as we might think. To help you integrate the idea that we are all really spiritual energy-beings, let's take a deeper look at the matter – the actual physics of our universe.

We, as human beings, are currently having a four-dimensional experience on a planet called Earth, which is the third planet out from the star named the Sun in a star system known to us as the Solar System, spinning at the edge of a spiral galaxy called the Milky Way, which is dancing through a larger body of galaxies and space which we call the Universe. And, there is much more yet to be discovered beyond this universe. Basically, from a purely physical standpoint, we are just a speck of existence in the grand scheme of things.

Outer space has always fascinated me. When I took stellar astronomy in college, the part that amazed me the most was how much distance actually exists between all of the heavenly bodies floating around in that inky carpet of darkness. My class would have a telescope set upon the roof of the college to view some local star system, and, if an over-anxious student happened to bump the scope, that star would just disappear, nowhere to be found. It was nearly next to impossible for one of us mere students to locate anything other than vast, absolute darkness on the viewfinder. We'd have to call the instructor over, who, by using specific coordinates, would then carefully find the little speck of light in the vast sea of emptiness of outer space.

Yet, when you look up at a starry sky, especially in an area that has minimal light pollution, such as a remote desert or mountaintop, it appears as if there are thousands of stars, layer upon layer of stars, right next to each other. Things are sometimes not as they appear to be. As I found out learning to find something through the lens of the telescope, there is actually considerably more space between the stars than I'd ever imagined.

You Are a Microcosm of the Macrocosm

Human beings have just as much space between their actual physical particles as our universe does – we are microcosms of the universe. Imagine a large circle or sphere, visualize it in 3D, and then place a random speck inside. This speck would represent physical matter, or lightwave taking particle form, and it would be zinging around in that ball of space like a ping pong ball. Then imagine many of these balls of mainly empty space, each with a teeny, tiny speck inside, and picture these balls all in a group together forming various different types of physical matter, forming everything from water molecules, to cells, to whole human beings. Look at the ratio of speck to space. That is a lot of space!

For our purposes here, it's not important to understand how the specks create matter in the physical level of reality. The idea that I do want to really sink in is that we are made up of over 99.999% space. There is a massive amount of room between our subatomic particles. We have mini universes going on inside of our bodies, tiny particles revolving around each other like moons, suns, and planets, with vast, unfathomable amounts of space in between.

You Are 99.999% Source Energy; Your Essence is Loving

That space is not empty. That space is actually alive and infinitely intelligent. That space contains the creative force that has given birth to all that is. That space is like the glue that holds our subatomic particles together so that we may take physical form and have the opportunity to experience human life. That space holds up our Sun, our moon, and the other planets that revolve in our solar system. That space holds up the stars and allows for a multi-dimensional experience to be made manifest in who knows how many other star systems. That space contains the energy of what we are made of, what we have come from, and what we as human beings are plugged into. That space contains the physical manifestation of the energy source that some call God and that I call the Loving.

You are not only plugged into the source of Loving/God/ All That Is, but you're also actually made out of Loving/God/

All That Is. You are, in fact, over 99.999% this energy of the source of consciousness. A very infinitesimal part of you is actually physical matter. Out of that small percent that takes physical form, you are mostly made up of water; even though you feel very solid, you are much more fluid than solid and much more space than anything else. Your essence is Loving, in its purest form.

About now, you may be wondering how I came into my knowing that our Source is indeed a Loving Source. Not so surprisingly, I had a little help from spirit! When I was eighteen, shortly before my nineteenth birthday, I had an out-of-body near-death awakening experience. During surgery, I was taken, led by the hand, up out of my physical, corporeal form, by a group of several beautiful energy-beings. Within seconds we had flown out beyond our solar system, and within moments beyond our galaxy, flying up into the center of the universe where I received download after download of teachings on many different subjects.

My Near-Death Experience was Steeped in Loving

To attempt to put everything I received into words may take me several lifetimes, yet the most relevant thing I can share in this moment is that my entire experience was steeped in the highest vibration of love-energy imaginable. Actually, it was unimaginable to me at the time. It was extraordinary, quite beyond anything I could ever have dreamed up. I was literally surrounded by love and beauty, filled by it, and protected by it. I felt not one second's hesitation or trepidation as my adventure unfolded, just a sense of delight and wonder, like a child in full discovery-mode. It felt as if my mind became the most absorbent sponge. I simply soaked in the information I was given about the Universe, our purpose as humans on planet Earth, our connection to our divine Source, the principles of physics and manifestation, the various realms of being, the principles of healing, universal law, my soul's purpose, and much more.

More potent than any information was the actual feeling of love and joy; the joyful feeling of flying through pure love, being the recipient of several radiant beings' pure loving gazes, along with gentle, caring, and respectful treatment in every moment is a profound, wondrous, tangible memory for me that I can viscerally recall each time I think of that experience. It was a feeling higher than any words can describe, more joyful than pure bliss, more delightful than ecstasy…and I felt the truth of it down to the tips of my energy body's toes.

We Each Have Equal Access to Our Source of Loving

As a result of my awakening experience and subsequent embodiment of the teachings I received, I can state with full, experiential knowing that we are sourced from a Loving Source, made out of that Source, and that we each have equal access to our Source. Because I have direct knowledge of access to Source-energy, I have had the joy and honor of assisting many people with connecting to our Source; I've delighted as they've discovered they are plugged into Loving and claimed their power to transform their own lives.

You are plugged in, too. The Loving is your birthright. We are, in fact, divine energy-beings having a human experience. This is quite a different idea from thinking that we are human beings that, if very, very lucky, can sometimes have a rare cosmic experience, get touched by spirit, or have a once-in-a-lifetime miracle occur. We are, each of us, a one-of-a-kind, miraculous, divine emanation of God/Loving. We are, each and every soul, a unique expression of divinity made manifest in a form we call human. Each of us is capable of daily miracles, infinite intelligence, and limitless creativity. We are each a vast reservoir of as yet mostly untapped divine potential. This is what the Bible refers to as made in the image and likeness of God. Each one of us is a unique child of God, a divine emanation of the Loving.

You Are a Unique, Divine Emanation of Source

A simple way to describe this is to picture a sun, how a child might draw the Sun, as a circle of light with many rays shining out in different directions. Label the sun 'God/Loving/Source of All That Is' and label one of the rays' me'. You can see from this image that you come from your source of energy. You are both a part of your Source and made from your Source at the same time. The Sun is your source of light, and you are the light that shines. You are literally the embodiment of light!

Since you are made out of the light of God's love, this means you have instant, 24/7 access to the Loving. You have access to the Source of all that is. You can access literally whatever qualities of this Loving energy you wish to experience just by tapping into your own ray of consciousness. This means you can feel love whenever you wish! You can also access compassion, joy, peace, gratitude, and more simply by connecting with your Loving Source.

To me, this was celebratory news. Do you mean, I thought, that I no longer have to seek love from other people? Do you mean I can feel love inside of myself whenever I want to feel love? Do you mean I don't have to remain stuck in misery and suffering for my entire life? Do you mean I could live a life of joy and freedom and liberation?!

The answer is a loud, resounding *yes*. Each of us is sourced from Loving. Each of us is made of Loving. And each of us, at any time, can return fully to living in the Loving, knowing that we are a divine child of God, simply having a human experience. The Loving is actually our soul's natural state, which is why we feel so grateful whenever we get to experience feeling real love. Our essence is Loving, and every part of us wishes to reside in the Loving where we can feel connected to our Source and each other as an intrinsic part of all that is.

Your body is made out of Loving. You are plugged into a vast source of energy that contains both electromagnetic energy and the infinite intelligence of the collective consciousness. You are plugged into the universal consciousness of God/the Loving. You are part of it, and made out of it. You are a unique expression of divine intelligence. Living a life of Loving is actually your birthright.

What this means is that from this moment on, you never have to seek love from outside of yourself again. You can experience all of the love you've ever needed or wanted internally, all by yourself. You can choose to share your love with others, and you do not need to 'get' love from anyone or anything outside of your own inner connection.

Many people think of love between two people as a 'give and take' kind of relationship. This is not an accurate way to explain what is really happening energetically. If you picture two rays of sunlight emanating from the Sun, one ray does not need to chop off some of its own radiance and give it over to another ray. It wouldn't even make sense. That other ray already has all of the light it needs and is perfectly capable of radiating all on its own. Both of the rays, after all, have equal access to their source of light. The word 'take' implies removing something from someone or somewhere and having it end up elsewhere. No ray of light has the need to take another ray's radiance for itself; each has plenty of its own radiance.

Love Can Only Be Shared

What is really happening with love-energy is that, just like sunlight, it can only be shared. People can share their own love, to whatever level they are accessing their own divine Loving essence. To the degree a person is 'plugged in' to their own Loving Source, they will have that amount of love-energy flowing through their energy body. Some people have the capacity to share a lot of love, and some people can only share very little, depending upon the current state of their energy field. While we all have equal access to our source of Loving, people can shut down, deny their own connection to Source-energy, sometimes operating in life on just a tiny trickle, maybe like a ten-watt bulb shining through their system.

Access to Loving Can Get Shut Down in the Heart-Center

Have you ever known someone who just seems to have no love or affection for anyone or anything? Someone who acts cold or hard as they go through life? This only means that they may have shut down energetically at the heart-level from receiving Loving from their Source. All humans need some level of Loving flowing through their energy body in order to survive. Still, it is absolutely possible to have that Loving vibration lowered and have the energy be directed to only certain areas, such as the mind, the will, or the sexual center. People who have experienced fear, hurt, trauma, or suffering will often react by closing themselves off from experiencing the flow of Loving into their own hearts. They make the irrational assumption, after feeling hurt by someone they love, that it hurts too much to love, or that it is unsafe to love, so they shut down their Loving source internally. Sometimes people do this as early as in their mother's womb, especially if they come into a highly challenging environment.

If a child is raised by a person with diminished access to love-energy at the heart level, that child may follow the familial patterning to become closed off and go through life desperately seeking just a very low level of love-energy from other people. For a child who has only felt brief glimpses of love, or no love at all, even just a few seconds of attention – even negative attention – will feel like manna from heaven.

Often, in this tremendously fear-based reality, many people are seeking just a crumb of attention, acknowledgment, or approval from their parents, their bosses, their spouses, and other relationships. It often never comes. This is because people cannot radiate something they don't have to share, and people cannot get something from someone that is not available in the first place. Since there is a universal law that states' as within, so without', the child who experiences a lack of Loving from the outside will not have the modeling of self-love. Therefore, that child will not understand that love comes from within or be able to feel access to Loving internally. A child who is raised with a low level of Loving modeled will likely grow up with a continued feeling of lack of love until the time the possibility for a different understanding of Loving presents itself.

Birth & Death can Cause a Heart to Open

Sometimes a person who has operated on a tiny crumb of love will have a heart-opening experience, such as the birth of a child or a death of a loved-one, that will energetically change their inner experience and allow more Loving to flow through.

Children are very close to their natural Loving essence when born, so a child raised in a nurturing environment will radiate love and light consistently. Just being around a laughing child's naturally joy-filled, Loving state can often assist adults in beginning to open up their own hearts. You will see this happen when people become grandparents. It may seem like the grandparent is choosing to love the grandchild more than they loved their own child; what is really occurring is they simply have greater access to their own Loving Source-energy, because they no longer have the same level of fear, stress, worry, or whatever pressures were present when they were in the role of the parent. Therefore, they can share more love now than they were able to share in the past when their own kids were young.

Other People's Level of Loving is Their Own

It is essential not to take another person's lack of Loving personally. Another person's level of access to their source of Loving inside of themselves is their own and actually has nothing to do with you at all. Each person is merely experiencing their own inner connection with Source to the degree that they are capable of at that moment, depending upon how they were raised, current life circumstances, beliefs they have made, how much fear they are experiencing, and more. This means that you can feel 100% loved on the inside, regardless of how anyone on the outside is relating to you at any given moment. If you can grasp this concept and apply it, you will become liberated.

Tragic Experiences can Cause a Heart to Open

Some people seem to just be going through life on auto-pilot, with no access to love at all. Then suddenly life will throw them a curve ball – an accident, an injury, an illness, a flood, a bankruptcy, a tornado, a fire, a random bombing, whatever – that will give them such a massive jolt of love-energy through their system that their heart-center becomes wide open. That previously seemingly disconnected person could become the warmest, most openly loving, compassionate person you've ever had the pleasure to meet. Just standing in such a person's energy field can bring on a smile. Have you ever known a person who radiated love like that?

When a person is openly flowing 1000 watts of love through their heart, everyone nearby will be affected by their radiance. And when we get touched by someone else's pure Loving, it will often resonate or strike a chord inside of us that will cause us to tap into more Loving inside of our own self, and we will experience a higher level of flow. What is happening energetically is that the Loving being who is more open is acting as a catalyst, a reminder if you will, so that others can get jolted or 'woken up' to remember that they, too, can feel, hold in, and radiate that much love and light.

Everyone Has the Power to Turn Up the Loving Flow

In the same way people can shut their heart-center down to receiving just a trickle of Loving, people can also choose to turn up their flow of Loving internally. Know that you have power over how much Loving you decide to access. If love is like the water of our spirituality or connection to our Source, you can imagine that you have a faucet on the inside which you can adjust to flow a little or a lot. You have the ability to turn up your own Loving flow, and you have access to an infinite source of Loving. You can have as much love as you desire.

Once a person gets a little taste of the Loving, they usually want more. Know that you can consciously ask to receive a higher level of Loving, and that you can set intentions to access a higher level of Loving daily. As you consciously set about to access more love, your heart-center will heal and re-open if it has been shut down. If you have always had an open heart, your heart-center, along with your entire energy field, will begin to expand to hold more love. Your body will start to recalibrate to contain the higher frequency. You can think of it like electrical circuitry, as if your nervous system is being rewired from fine 30 gauge wire, to wider 20 gauge wire, to even larger 10 gauge wire, and so on to expand on the inside to be able to contain and radiate more and more love and light.

What this means is that true love can only be felt to the degree a person is open to receiving their own flow of love inside their own heart-center. When a person has Loving flowing from their own heart, they radiate that love out to everyone they see, just like a 100 watt light bulb lights up the whole room. If two people are experiencing love inside themselves at the same time, they can share in the experience together and feel a profound connection; two bright lights make even more light when placed near each other. This is where the feeling of falling 'in love' comes from. It really means that two people have looked at each other from a place of Loving inside themselves and have had the beautiful opportunity to share in a mutually Loving moment.

The problem with this model of love is that if you can 'fall in,' you can also just as easily 'fall out' of that Loving state. For most couples who have had the experience of falling in love, after a few weeks or months of bliss, daily fear-based life begins intruding. Then one party drops out of their state of Loving and back into old patterns of fear, judgment, self-doubt, resentment, or whatever unresolved issues they might be experiencing. The other party immediately reacts by jumping to the erroneous conclusion of, "Oh no! They don't love me anymore. It is over!" based on the irrational idea that their love has to come from their partner. Since they can no longer feel any love-energy coming their way from the partner who is currently residing in fear-based energies once again, they now feel abandoned, empty, and unloved. Sound familiar? This is just one small example of a pattern that frequently shows up for people engaged in codependent relationships.

Out of Codependent into Interdependent Relationships

People who are operating on a very low level of Loving will almost always engage in dysfunctional, codependent relationships, where they are relentlessly trying to 'make' someone love them or to 'get' the love they need from another person.

Because they have been used to operating on just a small crumb of love-energy, they are often seeking very low levels of love in the form of attention, acceptance, acknowledgment, or approval from people outside of themselves. They engage in fear-based manipulations involving lies, threats, intimidation, coercion, guilt, shame, blame, jealousy, and many forms of abuse, all in the misguided attempt to try to get their need for Loving met.

Their endeavors are always unsuccessful. We can only share our love when we are residing in the energies of Loving inside of ourselves. Likewise, we can only share attention when we attend to ourselves first; we can only share acceptance when we accept ourselves first; we can only share acknowledgment when we can acknowledge ourselves first, and we can only share approval when we approve of ourselves first. 'As within, so without' is the law, so people who don't have access to Loving on the inside will only be experiencing the lack of it in their outside world. Our outer world experience is merely acting as a mirror to show us what is going on inside ourselves.

People who begin to see the light and get healthy become aware that they are sourced from within, and they discover that all of their needs can be met, independently, by themselves. Once a person has become completely independent and self-sufficiently self-Loving, from there, they can begin engaging in mutually supportive, interdependent relationships. An interdependent relationship – or conscious relationship – consists of two, whole, healthy people who understand that they each have the ability to meet their own needs for love from within in every moment, and they simply want to be together, to share love, friendship, affection, communication, and more.

The good news is that a healthy, mutually supportive,

conscious relationship is available to anyone ready to take full ownership for the amount of love they experience, how loved they feel internally, and how they choose to share their own Loving essence. The simple truth is that in order for continuous, ongoing Loving to be shared in any relationship, people must cultivate the ongoing flow of Loving inside of themselves, rather than holding impossible expectations that the Loving is going to come from outside of themselves, from another person.

This also means that people do not need to reciprocate or to 'love you back' for you to share your Loving essence with them. The sunlight doesn't dim its rays in the presence of a grumpy person who'd rather not feel the sunshine. People have gotten the irrational idea that they need to shut down the flow of their love-light in the presence of someone who isn't feeling or sharing very much of their own Loving nature. Nothing could be further from the truth. Feel free to radiate your light whenever and wherever, and shine to the highest degree humanly possible. And, yes, you might really tick someone off. So what! Be willing to act as a catalyst for their own highest good, knowing that their anger toward your Loving essence is an indication that they obviously have some growing to do in this area. Don't allow someone else's small-mindedness to cause you to keep yourself small. Be willing to shine fully. To the degree you hold the knowing that we each have access to infinite Loving, you make that knowledge available to everyone you meet.

Where Have You Been Seeking Love?

Who did you seek love from the most during your childhood? Your mother? Your father? A grandparent? A sibling? Did you seek to experience a high level of Loving, a moderate level, or were you just looking for a crumb of attention or approval? Most of us were under the illusion that someone else needed to love or care for us in order for us to feel loved, and, if and when they didn't, it usually meant in our young mind that we must be unlovable or undeserving of love, attention, acceptance, approval or even just the acknowledgment that we existed. Guess what? If you have ever felt that way, you were simply operating under a misunderstanding of how love really works. The simple truth is that you are loved, always.

Who do you seek Loving from in your current adult life? A friend? A boyfriend or girlfriend? A spouse? A parent? A child? An employer? Looking for love from outside of yourself is a futile endeavor. If you are still searching outside of yourself for any level of Loving – a crumb of attention, acknowledgment, approval, acceptance, caring, or infinite Loving – know that you can shift this inside of yourself, right here and right now. The truth is that you are your own source of Loving. You are already dearly loved. You come pre-approved and fully accepted. You have the ability to attend to yourself, to approve of yourself, to accept yourself, to acknowledge yourself, to care for yourself, and, most of all, to love yourself to the degree that both Source and your soul already love you.

All of the Love You Have Ever Desired is Already Inside of You

All of the love you have ever desired is already inside of you. This truth is absolute and immutable. You came from the Loving, were born loved no matter how you may have been treated until now, and you are always loved no matter what you have experienced or will experience in this lifetime. Whatever you have been seeking outside of yourself in the past has been inside of you all along. You have instant access to the direct Source of infinite love, the highest level of self-acceptance, all of the attention, acknowledgment, and approval you could ever want. All of your needs are already met from within. All you have to do is open your own heart and breathe love in. Drink it in. Bask in it. Steep in it. Radiate it. The love inside of you just is. Your love flows from inside, always. You have never had to do anything to feel loved except turn on your faucet. From here on, you can simply open to your own divine Loving essence and *be* the love.

Exercise: Claiming Your Source of Loving

To free yourself from old, fear-based, limiting beliefs, the energies of love and compassion must be applied liberally inside of your own consciousness. These two energies, love, and compassion, are the two ingredients that make up the experience known as forgiveness. The root 'for' means 'already' – so the word 'forgiven' means 'already given.' Forgiveness simply means that love and compassion are a given. Love and compassion are two energies that are always available to all of us. In order to actually experience the love and compassion that is our birthright as Loving beings, we must first actively connect with those energies.

Accessing the Energies of Love and Compassion

Sit or lie down in a comfortable position, breathing naturally and relaxing your body. First, create a Loving, protected field around your body by saying a short prayer and/or setting conditions to surround your energy field with love and light. A very simple, universal protection prayer such as this is fine: "The Light of God surrounds me, the love of God enfolds me, the power of God protects me, the presence of God watches over me. Wherever I am, God is. So be it."

If you don't resonate with the word 'God' as the name for your source of Loving, setting simple conditions is equally powerful. Example: "I set the conditions of love and light. I set the condition that all that occurs herein be only that which is in my highest and greatest good and in strict accordance with the will of the Loving. So be it." However you set the presence of Loving protection around you is up to you. Your intention here to create a safe, Loving space is what is most important.

Next, do a brief invocation to ask spirit to be present with you. A simple invocation would be: "I call upon the presence of the Loving." Or you could say, "I call upon the presence of Mother/Father God and my own soul."

After you have surrounded yourself with Loving protection, and invoked spirit's presence, set an intention inside yourself to begin to feel and experience the Loving inside of yourself at the cellular level. Example: "I set the intention to access the highest level of Loving that is available to me at this time." Then breathe it in. Imagine, sense, see, feel yourself breathing in the highest level of Loving energy that you can access at this moment.

Breathe in love. You can picture it like a golden ray of light pouring in through the crown of your head. Fill your heart until it is overflowing with this Loving energy, like a golden fountain. Continue breathing in love, breathing the overflow down to your toes. Picture and feel yourself filling up your entire body with Loving energy. Fill your feet, your ankles with Loving. Light up each and every cell inside of your body. Breathe in Loving, filling your shins and calves. Breathe in Loving, filling your knees and thighs, until every cell in your legs has been flooded with love and golden light. Breathe in Loving, filling up your hips and pelvis. Breathe in Loving, filling up your abdomen and all of your internal organs with Loving. Breathe the Loving up your spine, filling your whole torso with light and love. Fill up your chest, your lungs. Take the Loving down your arms to your fingertips, filling up your hands, your arms. Breathe the Loving up your arms through your shoulders, your collarbone. Breathe in Loving, taking the Loving up your neck, filling your chin, your whole face, and finally your entire head with Loving.

See, sense and feel your whole body lit up from within with golden light. Experience your cells all vibrating at a higher frequency. It may feel like your cells are buzzing or tingling. You may also feel warm, dizzy, or high. If it feels too high for you, set an intention to reset the energies to a more comfortable level so that you may stay present and fully engaged in the process.

Once you feel the Loving throughout your entire body and energy field, set an intention inside yourself to access the highest level of compassion that you can reach at this time. Breathe in compassion, knowing that compassion is the energy of the divine Mother. Compassion is the energy that says, "It is Ok. All is well. You are alright," when suffering is present. Speak the words that bring you compassion. Flood your entire being with compassion, taking it to your toes and filling up your entire body, just as you did with Loving. Wrap each and every cell in your body with compassion, paying special attention to any areas that need healing or feel tight or constricted in any way. Breathe in compassion until you feel yourself radiating this energy from every cell in your body.

Now, from this place filled with love and compassion, you are ready to begin. Repeat out loud any of the following irrational beliefs that may apply to you. Then, create a new, updated belief to transform the old one into something higher. Feel free to change the wording to suit yourself; my suggestions are only a guideline. Your beliefs will be uniquely wired inside of you, so choose the words that naturally come forward for you to maximize your healing.

Exercise (say out loud):

"I forgive myself for buying into the irrational belief that I was ever unloved." (take a deep breath and let this idea go)

"My new updated belief is, I now know I come from the source of infinite Loving, I am made out of Loving, and therefore I have always been loved." (take a deep breath and breathe in this new idea)

"I forgive myself for buying into the irrational belief that I ever needed to look outside of myself for love." (take a deep breath and let this idea go) "My new updated belief is, I now know I am directly connected to my source of Loving. All I need to do is breathe it in. I contain all of the Loving I have ever needed or wanted. I am sourced with Loving from within. I am love." (take a deep breath and breathe in this new idea)

"I forgive myself for buying into the irrational belief that my parents were my source of love." (take a deep breath and let this idea go) "My new updated belief is, I now know I am directly connected to my source of Loving. My parents were only able to share love with me to the degree that they were connected to the Source within themselves; I have always had my own connection to Loving. All I need to do is breathe it in. I contain all of the Loving I have ever needed or wanted. I am sourced with Loving from within. I am the love." (take a deep breath and breathe in this new idea)

"I forgive myself for buying into the irrational belief that my grandparents, sisters, brothers, cousins, etc. were my source of love." (take a deep breath and let this idea go) "My new updated belief is, I now know I am directly connected to my source of Loving. Other people could only share their own level of love; I have always had access to my own source of Loving. All I need to do is breathe it in. I contain all of the Loving I have ever needed or wanted. I am sourced with Loving from within. I am love." (take a deep breath and breathe in this new idea)

"I forgive myself for buying into the irrational belief that anyone else was ever my source of Loving, any girlfriend, boyfriend, lover, partner, husband, wife, teacher, minister, rabbi, mentor, etc." (take a deep breath and let this idea go) "My new updated belief is, I now know, I and I alone, am my source of Loving. All of the love I need is accessible within me. From now on, I know I can share love with someone else to whatever degree we both have access to at any given moment." (take a deep breath and breathe in this new idea)

"I forgive myself for buying into the irrational belief that I have ever had to shut down my flow of Loving or dim my own light in the presence of someone else who was feeling closed to their own Loving." (take a deep breath and let this idea go) "My new updated belief is, I now know it is Ok and fine for me to feel love all of the time, to experience my own Loving essence regardless of how others are feeling, and to shine my love-light brightly in any situation. I am now free to radiate my Loving, no matter what." (take a deep breath and breathe in this new idea)

"I forgive myself for buying into the irrational belief that anyone's judgment, unsupportive opinion, lack of acknowledgment, disapproval, or hatred has ever had the power to cause me to feel cut off from my source of Loving." (take a deep breath and let this idea go) "My new updated belief is, I now know I *am* the Loving. I come from the infinite source of Loving and have access to the Loving in every given moment. I have always been connected to the Loving, no matter other peoples' words or actions." (take a deep breath and breathe in this new idea)

"I forgive myself for buying into the irrational belief that I have to do something a certain way, act a certain way, or say a certain thing in order to receive the love I need from someone else." (take a deep breath and let this idea go) "My new updated belief is, I now know I am already loved no matter what I do, how I act or what I say. My love comes from inside of me, and from now on, I can simply relax and be myself, knowing I am loved in every moment." (take a deep breath and breathe in this new idea)

"I forgive myself for buying into the irrational belief that it serves me in any way to continue the pattern of trying to seek love, attention, acceptance, approval, acknowledgment, or any other level of Loving from any person outside of myself." (take a deep breath and let this idea go) "My new updated belief is, I now know I am sourced from within. My new pattern is that from now on, I seek all levels of Loving from inside myself. If I feel the need for attention, I attend to myself. If I feel the need for acceptance, I accept myself. If I want acknowledgment, I can simply acknowledge myself, etc. I meet all of my needs from within." (take a deep breath and breathe in this new idea).

End with Acknowledgment, Gratitude, and Grounding

When you have finished working your process around your beliefs, take a moment to acknowledge yourself for your own commitment, or whatever you would most like to hear, out loud. This can start with something like, "I acknowledge myself for _____" (example: taking the time to focus on myself, for my willingness to look at myself deeply, for my commitment to my own growth, or whatever is authentic for you)

Next, spend a moment in gratitude to make closure by giving thanks and blessings to each of the energies you invoked at the beginning for their presence during your process.

Finally, spend a few moments connecting to the physical level to ground your energy field at this new, higher level of being. You can connect with the Earth energies by visualizing sending a grounding rod down into the earth from your base; picture growing tree roots from your feet deep into the ground; doing down dog or forward-fold;, sinking your bare feet into the grass, dirt, or sand; hugging a tree; or any other method of grounding you may have to anchor your energy fully to the physical level of the planet.

Suggestions for Integrating New Beliefs:

Drink plenty of water, as water acts as the electronic conductor for your new beliefs to be delivered to all of your cells energetically.

I also encourage you to create a healing notebook or journal. Write down your new beliefs and read these repeatedly until they are a given. You do not have to use my words - these are just an example. Your specific outdated and updated beliefs will work best if you use words that are real and true for you. However you choose to update your beliefs, I encourage you to choose ideas that feel positive, inspiring, empowering, and freeing. Read them often until they are fully integrated. You will know this when they feel matter-of-fact, and no voice pops up to naysay when every part of you responds with "of course."

You can also use index cards to make belief cards, writing your forgiveness statement on one side and updated belief on the other. I used to take my journal or cards with me wherever I went. I read my new beliefs in restaurants, sitting in the car waiting for my children to get out of school, in moments between appointments, and anywhere I happened to have a free minute throughout my day. You could also keep your cards or notebook by your bed and reread your new beliefs in the morning upon waking or at night before bedtime. The more frequently you can run the energy of your updated beliefs through your mind-body system, the faster you will integrate your new beliefs at the cellular level. Once your new belief is integrated, you will literally be vibrating at a higher level of consciousness, and your life will change accordingly to reflect your new state of being.

CHAPTER TWO
We Are All Intrinsically Worthy

As a divine being having a human experience, you are already intrinsically worthy in every way. The idea of an unworthy being is laughable from your soul's perspective. How could a divine being ever be unworthy in any way? Source is priceless, and we are all made of Source-energy. God is invaluable, and each and every one of us is a unique, divine emanation of God, a one-of-a-kind, rare, and precious child of God. At the level of the soul, in fact, the idea of our inherent value as a being is such an inherent, immutable truth that it is simply a given: we are all intrinsically worthy.

If you visualize the sun again as the Loving source of light and picture yourself as one of the sun's many rays, you can see how irrational the idea is that one ray would be deemed 'worthless' - 'less-than' another ray from the perspective of the sun. The sun would see each ray as a part of itself; each ray would be equally valued and precious to the sun. Each ray is simply one part of the greater whole that is the sun.

Consciousness operates just like the sun. We are each simply experiencing one aspect of our Source, yet we are the same energy as our Source-energy; the sun and the sun's radiance are one and the same – it is not possible to separate the sun from the sunlight. Similarly, we are not separate from our source of Loving/God/All That Is. We both come from the Source and we *are* that Source. Therefore, your value is the same as the value you place upon infinite Loving/God/All That Is.

If you think of your source of Loving as God or the Infinite, how could you possibly decide to devalue God or the Infinite? It is, after all, all that is and encompasses anything that we could place value on in our human existence. If we, as energy-beings who take particle-form, are made out of this stuff that comes from God or whatever we want to call our source of energy, then how could we place a lower value on ourselves? How, for that matter, could we place a lower value on anyone else?

The truth is that from a spiritual perspective, we are all priceless. Our value is the highest value that could be given to anything. We are precious treasures, each and every one of us, regardless of age, ethnicity, gender, sexual orientation, nationality, socio-economic level, educational level, skill level, physical appearance, or any external factor. We are all simply priceless because we exist.

If you are born as a soul in a body, you are born intrinsically worthy, no matter what. Your worth has nothing to do with size, shape, or color, and everything to do with the fact that you and your Source are one and the same. Life is a precious gift; therefore, *you* are a precious gift. The very fact that you were born is a miracle. You are a beautiful, priceless gift, worthy beyond your belief.

As a result of all being infinitely worthy, you are automatically equally worthy from your soul's perspective. No being is more worthy or less worthy than another. It does not matter what sort of differences people have at the human level; all beings are equally worthy at the level of being. This means the homeless of the world are equally as worthy as the richest 1% of the world; abandoned orphans in China and India are equally as worthy as the pampered babies of the western world, and so on. All of God's children are equally worthy and equally beloved by Source, no matter what sort of circumstances may be present at the human level. This is a truth that every human – man, woman, and child – needs to understand and integrate to move out of creating a fear-based reality of separation and into creating a world of peace for all of humanity.

A feeling of low self-esteem, or a lack of self-worth, is hands-down the single biggest issue that people bring forward for healing. A sense of 'I'm not good enough,' 'I'm a bad _____ (fill in the blank),' 'So-and-so is better than me,' and 'I don't think I really deserve to have _____ (fill in the blank)' are some of the most common irrationalities I hear over and over again in my sessions with clients. I was personally afflicted with serious lack-of-worth thoughts and feelings for the first thirty-some years of my life, so I can really relate to these irrational ideas.

My unworthiness story went something like, "I am a pathetic excuse for a person, a horrible mother, a no-good wife, a bad friend… I suck as a dancer, I can't draw or paint for crap, I'm not good at anything I do – I'm worthless. Everyone is better than me, more attractive than me, funnier than me, smarter than me. I don't even deserve to be alive."

Take that small sample, multiply by about a hundred, and that would give you the gist of what my self-talk sounded like inside of my head about thirty years ago.

It is astonishing how incredibly stuck people can get in the irrational idea that they are worthless. Take me, for instance; I maintained the story that I was a useless, worthless, terrible excuse of a person even *after* I'd had an unfathomable, out-of-body, enlightening experience that showed me otherwise. I came back from having a mind-altering, paradigm-shifting, awe-inspiring experience of being taken out into the cosmos for a divine field trip into the Loving in order to prepare me for my purpose as a teacher of truth, and still thought I was unworthy of everything. How absurd is that?

While I was out there in the Loving, I was whole, radiantly healthy. I knew my intrinsic worth down to the tips of my Light Body's toes (my physical body had been left behind on a table during a major ten-hour emergency abdominal surgery for what turned out to be a ruptured appendix). The experience of myself as pure, Loving consciousness was like a beautiful homecoming. My energetic cells rejoiced. I remembered who I truly was and became one with everything. Time expanded; I journeyed in the cosmos receiving downloads of information for what seemed like months, while I was really only unconscious for about 30 hours. My blissful awareness of myself as a divine being lasted on a feeling level about as long as it took for the drugs to wear off, which happened only a day or two after returning to Earth-plane reality consciousness the day after my surgery.

During my excruciating recovery, it was challenging to remember the feeling of radiant wholeness, even though I recalled the experience and concept on a mind level. In the days and weeks following my remarkable journey, I began to forget the feeling of connection and knowing I'd experienced. I began to question my guides over and over. Why me? There must have been some mistake. Did the angels get the wrong hospital bed? Spirit must have gotten the name wrong or picked the wrong coordinates.

Whatever the mix-up, I was certain that there had been an error – *I* was not the one who would be teaching Universal Law to the masses; that part was for certain. Didn't God know I was a complete mess? Didn't spirit recall that a guy I'd been head-over-heels in love with had just left me heartbroken and that I was completely totally worthless in every way, unworthy of being loved, let alone teaching about love? The idea that I could possibly have anything to say about the subject was so absurd to me after I'd been back in my body for some months that I decided to just write off what I had been shown as some kind of bizarre joke. I had a constant stream of thoughts that went something like, "Who does spirit think I am anyway? Ha. What a joke. I'm worthless. I'd never be able to do any of that." In my mind, I was not one of the divine beings those beautiful emissaries of light had been speaking about during my out-of-body experience, that was for sure. Little by little, I talked myself out of allowing myself to believe in the totality of my experience, and I did my best to shut it out of my mind and heart. Lapsing back into my old, comfortable, unhealthy patterns of thinking, I decided that divinity was all well and good for everybody out there except for me; I was crap in my own mind, and there was nothing anyone could say or do to convince me otherwise.

Fortunately, everything happens in divine-perfect order, and I was guided to the right teachers and circumstances regardless of my lack of faith in myself. In my mid-twenties, I had a spiritual teacher call me out on my feelings of lacking worth, saying something like, "What makes you so special?

Why would every other being ever born be worthy, and you get to be different?" He had started by asking me how I felt about everyone else in the room, and of course, I had answered that they were all totally worthy and deserving. He then asked me what I thought of poor people or people who were mentally or emotionally challenged. I hotly defended them, saying that no matter anyone's financial status or birth circumstances, all people are worthy. He asked me what I thought of criminals; were they unworthy? I said, of course not; they probably felt unworthy and were acting out from that negative self-image, but I did believe that all people were inherently good and worthy of love. He finally asked me if there was anyone in the world besides myself I would say was unworthy or not good enough, and of course, I said no. At this point, he started laughing and said, "You see my point." Basically, he said, lack of self-worth is an entirely egotistical idea, this nonsensical idea that somehow people get stamped 'good' or 'bad', and we have decided we have earned the special 'bad' stamp. At the same time, we believe everyone else is innately 'good'. While a part of me really understood what he was saying, I was so far into my own unworthiness story at that time that my personality simply glommed onto the idea that I was even worse for being self-centered about my unique level of unworthiness. Now I was bad, completely unworthy, and egotistical to boot!

When the mind is stuck, it can turn anything into irrationality. Clearly I was not ready at that time to claim my intrinsic worth; I needed a few more years of experience of lack, limitation, and deprivation before I became receptive enough to shift out of my miserable stance about myself. But eventually, I was able to look back on this exchange and laugh about how irrational my beliefs were at the time – how I had exclusive rights to the only special 'bad' stamp on the planet;

me and several billion other humans who are convinced that they have the one and only 'bad' stamp.

Integrating the Knowledge of Your Intrinsic Worth is a Process

I ended up shifting into the knowledge of my intrinsic worthiness very gradually, over an extended period of years. First, I decided I was worthy of experiencing more love than I was currently receiving, which was almost zilch at the time, so that meant I felt worthy of receiving just a little bit of love and caring.

Well, I got what I asked for big time. The crumb of love I received in the form of a new relationship was so small that it was almost more painful than receiving none had been. But since I'd gotten what I asked for, I decided I could dare to ask for a little more. After struggling for several years attempting to convert the crumb of love into a whole loaf, unsuccessfully, I left that relationship, asked for more love, and immediately received more.

Unfortunately, while the level of love I experienced in my next few relationships was wonderful compared to what I'd had in the past, it came to me in the form of a 'no-strings' type of relationship. It was a big eye-opener for me to learn that I could, in fact, share in beautiful moments of Loving with another, but love alone was not enough to create and sustain a lasting relationship. Deep down, I was really yearning for a spiritual partnership, a true mate who would share my life and co-parent my children with me. The understanding dawned that while I now knew that I was worthy of plenty of love, I was still feeling lacking in commitment, respect, consistency, and several other key qualities that I suddenly decided I was worthy of having in my life.

At this point, I had the startling realization that feeling love, in and of itself, was not all that I wanted, and I began to feel worthy of asking for even more. As soon as I asked for more, again asking for my soul's guidance by declaring, "Show me the way. What is my next step?" I was immediately guided to attend USM, University of Santa Monica's Master's Program in Spiritual Psychology. Here, I was reminded again that healing is an inside job. There is a universal law that states 'as within, so without'. As long as I was looking for love to come from others outside of myself, I realized I would always be experiencing a lack of love. I needed to connect with my Loving Source from within and begin to feel the love that my own soul had for myself. In order to see love manifest on the outside in my relationships, I had to have it on the inside first. This time it clicked for me; I began to simply breathe into my Loving Source-energy, and I was immediately lit up and filled from within.

In addition to being reminded that it is an inside job, for the third time in my life, I heard the teachings of intrinsic worth spoken in a way that rang true for me. I learned, again, that I was intrinsically worthy. That meant that I had been born worthy, that I didn't need to earn my worth in any way. My worth was inherent, just like my blood, my teeth, and my bones. I had been born worthy, and nothing I thought, said or did in my life had ever had the power to take away my intrinsic worth as a being. Somehow, this time, the concept that worth is a given really got through to me on a deeper level, finally. As soon as I made the decision to embrace the idea that I was a fully worthy being, I was immediately reconnected with the feeling of wholeness and oneness I'd experienced during my spiritual field trip out into the cosmos at age eighteen.

What Has Been Your Story about Your Worth?

What has been your story in the past about your own worth? Have you ever felt unworthy, undeserving, or had a sense of low self-esteem? Take a moment to write down your old story about your worth.

You Are Equal with Every Other Being

Along with the issue of worthiness, many people who experience feeling a lack of worth also experience feelings of inequality, which are based on a huge irrationality that it is possible for some people to be better than others. This limiting belief causes so much pain and suffering. The truth is that we are all *equally* worthy at the being level, from our soul's perspective. We all have equal access to our source of Loving energy. This means we all have equal access to each quality that is available through our connection to Source; we all have equal access to infinite Loving, compassion, wisdom, knowledge, strength, authentic power, peace, joy, freedom, grace, beauty, and more. Not only do we have access to our Source, but we are also all equally important, unique, and valued as a being, no matter what.

If you have ever felt less-than or inferior to someone else in any way, I strongly encourage you to begin to let those old feelings go and come into a higher understanding of your own equality. The truth is that you are equal to every other being ever born. On the flip side, if you have ever felt better-than or superior to anyone else in any way, I strongly encourage you to begin to let those old feelings go and come into a higher understanding of your own equality. The truth is that you are equal to every other being ever born. There is no such separation into better-than or less-than from Source's perspective. We are all just radiant, divine energy-beings having a human learning experience here on planet Earth.

Think about the image of the sun as our source of Loving and all of the divine beings as individual rays of light. Do you think the sun is sitting there saying, "I really like this ray better than this other one. Yes, this ray is far superior…. And, this ray over here is useless, a really inferior ray…" Sounds so silly, right? Yet this is how we think in the fear-based, right/wrong paradigm; we engage in irrational, nonsensical dialogs inside ourselves all the time, comparing anything and everything as better-than or less-than. The truth is that the sun never even thinks to compare its own rays; the sun is simply radiating light and love equally, knowing that each and every ray is a beloved, divine expression of self.

Drop all Comparison and Claim Your Equality

If you have been comparing yourself in your life to anyone else and coming up short, right here, I encourage you to drop the comparisons and claim your equality with every other being. Everyone has their own special gifts. Not only are we different in regards to spiritual curriculum, skill level, natural talent, inclination, and natural abilities, we each have our own unique purpose or mission to fulfill here upon the planet. You are the only one to do whatever it is that you came here to do. As Oscar Wilde so succinctly stated, "Be yourself; everyone else is already taken." If you can stop wasting energy trying to be like someone else and focus your attention on just being the most radiant *you* that you can be, not only will you cease to cause yourself unnecessary suffering, your entire life will become more fulfilling and joy-filled.

Better-than and less-than are two sides of the same coin, so often, people who feel less-than on the inside will cultivate an effect of behaving better-than or feel or act superior to others as a way to feel better about themselves. There is no such thing as a superior person; superiority is an illusion that only exists within someone's own irrational, personality-based thinking. We are all equally valued, equally special, and equally important from Source's perspective. Everyone's contribution is of value to the greater good, no matter how big or how small. We are equal, and we are also uniquely different. We are all in a wide variety of places in terms of our own personal growth.

You can think about our differences like this: In the area of spiritual learning, there are different levels of ability and understanding in every given subject – just like our school system goes from Kindergarten-12, then college, then graduate school. We do not expect our 12th graders to make fun of or to pick on the Kindergarteners because it is pretty obvious that there is simply a vast difference in age and learning. There is an unspoken understanding that our 12th graders will be kind and supportive of our Kindergarteners – they will act as guides and role models. By the same token, we do not anticipate that these two widely differing individuals will have much in common or can relate as peers. A Kindergartener may be learning 1+1=2, and a 12th grader may be studying Algebra, Trigonometry, or Calculus. The 12th grader would not expect to talk math with the Kindergartener at the 12th grade level of understanding; if the 12th grader wanted to talk math with a Kindergartener, he would have to speak in terms that the Kindergartener could easily understand, such as 1+1. The 12th grader would not need to treat the Kindergartener disrespectfully or to hold an attitude of superiority over the younger child; the 12th grader would simply have the awareness that the Kindergartener was at a different level of learning due to age and experience.

To put this concept into practice in your own life, begin to see that everyone around you is in their own particular level of learning in every area of their life, and cultivate acceptance for them wherever they are. If you place your focused attention on this, you will easily be able to discern when someone is enrolled in a different level of spiritual learning than your own current level. The people in your family or at your place of work may be enrolled in entirely different courses than your own in the school of life. While you may be working on Spirituality 401, your co-worker may still be enrolled in Partying 101. In no way does this make you superior or better-than; it merely means that you are currently focused on a different area of learning. Holding this understanding, know that this means that you will be very unlikely to converse effectively about Spirituality 401 with this particular co-worker. If you wish to relate, you will need to take your interaction to the level of understanding of your co-worker, and maybe keep it to, "How was your weekend?"

Personally, I don't tend to spend time in superficial or polite small talk, so this means that I would simply smile at that co-worker and go about my business without even attempting to engage in conversation. As a result of my personal boundary, it is common in social or mainstream settings that I am sometimes judged as stand-offish or rude. I do not allow these judgments to affect my peace, because in truth, I am holding an attitude of inner equality with all beings, and I have the knowledge that anyone can achieve a higher level of consciousness if that is what they desire. At the same time, I also know that my time and my energies are top priority to me, and I get to decide how I want to use both in every given moment. My choices of how I spend my time and where I focus my energies have nothing to do with anyone's equality with me. We are all innately equal wherever we are in our learning.

As adults who are cultivating a new paradigm of Loving, filled with peace, joy, and compassion for all beings, it is imperative that we drop any and all feelings, attitudes, and behaviors of better-than or superiority toward others and come into the understanding that we are each operating from our own, individual level of knowledge in terms of our growth in any area. Certain people may be great basketball players.

Some may excel in the arts. Some may be computer geniuses. Others may be exceptional cooks, clerks, teachers, gardeners, or be good with children.

In the same way that people are focused on different things in their outer life, people will be focused on different things with their inner lives. Some people may have great awareness of their own innate spirituality, and others may still be unconscious of themselves as a soul in a body. Both levels of learning are equally as important in the grand scheme of things, and both people are still equal at the level of being. A person's level of skill, talent, awareness, or knowledge has absolutely nothing to do with their value as a being. No one is better or less than another as a person. Every being ever born is a beautiful, unique ray of consciousness, a divine emanation of Source, intrinsically worthy in every way, as special, valued, and equal at the being level as every other being ever born.

What Has Been Your Story About Your Equality?

Think about your own life. What has been your story throughout your life in regards to your equality? Have you ever felt less-than or inferior to someone else? Have you ever felt better-than or superior to someone else? Have you spent lots of time in comparisons? Be willing to be totally honest with yourself and take some time now to write down your experience of your own equality and uniqueness up until now.

You Are Whole in Every Way at the Level of Being

You are a whole being, at the level of Source. You are sourced from a whole, Loving Source. Your soul is a whole, Loving being, and at the human level, you are a whole being as well. Over and over again, on my spiritual journey, I have been shown the shape of a whole sphere. Large, heavenly bodies such as stars, moons, and planets come in spheres. Tiny, microscopic bodies that make up our molecules and cells come in spheres. All beings have a spherical energy field, regardless of the shape that the physical body takes.

Look at planet Earth; for example, she has a round, spherical shape, North and South poles, and a central core that runs energy between the poles. She is a whole, complete being, with all the resources she needs and full connection to all that is. Next, look at an apple: it, too, has North and South poles, in the form of a stem and a base, and a core that connects the apple energetically from top to bottom. The apple itself may not be perfectly round, yet its energy field creates a beautiful sphere of light all around it. The apple has all of the resources it needs to be an apple.

We, too, as human energy-beings, have a spherical energy field that surrounds our body in a field of light. We have a North pole in the form of our crown chakra, a point of entry for energy at the top of our head. We have a South pole in the form of our base chakra, or root chakra, in our perineum at the very base of our body. Our core runs from crown to base, connecting us energetically from top to bottom. We receive divine energy through our crown chakra, and we ground ourselves to the earth energetically through our base chakra. While our physical shape does not appear round, the master artist Leonardo Da Vinci's famous sketches of the man inside the circle show us that proportionately, humans are as wide as they are tall and can fit inside of a perfect circle when the limbs are fully stretched. On an energetic level, we are spherical beings. Our human energy field creates a ball of light around our physical form.

Now, picture a circle with your mind's eye. Follow the edge of the circle around the outside, see how there is no beginning and no end – no breaks in the circle at all. It is whole, complete. Then imagine that circle turning into a 3-dimensional sphere, see it again as having no beginning, no end, no breaks or holes in it; see the sphere as whole and complete. Every sphere created by the Loving is a whole, complete form. Every sphere contains all that it needs inside, whether it takes the form of an apple, a planet, or a human being.

If you happen to have been born with some type of physical or mental difference, such as hearing impairment, missing limbs, or Down's Syndrome, you may be thinking that wholeness doesn't apply to you, that there actually is a defect. You can trust that your soul has a reason for this; souls don't make mistakes when choosing birth circumstances. Actually, each of us chooses our own parents and situation before each incarnation. We pick the perfect set-up to ensure we have a maximum shot at reaching our soul's learning goals for this lifetime. The truth is that nobody is perfect in the literal sense of the word, yet each of us is divinely-perfect in the absolute sense. You can rest easy that you are made exactly the way that you were meant to be made and that you were born into the exact set of circumstances necessary for you to achieve whatever you came here to achieve in this lifetime.

Think about famous people who have had some sort of physical limitation – Helen Keller, for instance. She couldn't see, couldn't hear, and couldn't speak. Did that stop her from becoming a famous author? Is it possible that she came to the profound understandings that she was then able to share in her writings because of having to overcome so much challenge, and she wouldn't ever have faced such an extreme challenge had she been born with hearing, sight, and speech? What about those two all-time favorite blind musicians, Ray Charles and Stevie Wonder? Did you ever see the way they played that piano? Hearing is heightened when the sense of sight is removed, and vice versa. Would they have developed the same gift of music if they had been able to see? What about

Stephen Hawking, world-renowned theoretical physicist, and cosmologist who some say had the most brilliant mind on the planet? Would his mind have become so expansive if he had not spent years and years confined to a wheelchair, unable to do almost anything but think? There are paraplegics that paint with their toes and quadriplegics that paint with their mouths.

Understand that having a mental or physical challenge is actually purposeful on the part of your soul. There is a definite reason for the challenge. Your being is not defective in any way from Source's perspective; your being is whole. On the being level, a differently-abled person still has all of the inner resources they need to succeed fully in life and to fulfill their soul's purpose. And, on the energetic level, your being is totally whole and complete.

If you've ever heard of someone who has lost a limb claiming to still feel pain where the limb used to be (a phenomenon commonly referred to as 'phantom pain'), this is actually real and not imagined. Our bodies have several layers of energy. The missing limb is only missing at the physical level; there is still a mental-body limb, an emotional-body limb, and a spiritual-body limb. If there is trauma stored at any of the other levels of being, the person will still receive signals and messages of pain to heal the different energy bodies. Even if you were born missing a part or have had something cut off of or out of your physical body, you can trust that you are whole at the being level. The loss of a limb, a kidney, or a breast does not have the power to make you less-than in any way.

We are all intrinsically worthy of realizing our wholeness, of experiencing our wholeness on every level of being. Yet, most of us go through life, believing we are not enough. The irrational feeling of 'not good enough' or 'not _____ enough' is like imagining that somehow your sphere had a piece missing, that you were like an orange without a slice, somehow less than whole. On the level of the personality, having been raised in a critical, competitive, fear-based, right/wrong reality, most of us experience some form of lack; we believe we don't have enough, that we are somehow missing something. Know that on the soul level, you have it all. You contain all that you have ever needed, all that you will ever need or want. Like the seed that knows exactly how to grow into a beautiful rosebush, you are divinely-perfect in every way. You contain all of the information, all of the wisdom, all of the ingredients necessary to realize your full potential, to grow into the full expression of yourself as a unique, divine emanation of Source-energy.

Whether you have some sort of physical limitation that has caused you to feel less than whole in some way, or you simply felt less than whole based on your past beliefs and experiences, know that the feeling that you were somehow missing something or not enough was just that – a feeling. That feeling was based on a misinterpretation of reality that simply wasn't true.

We are not our bodies. We are not our emotions. We are not our minds. We have a multi-layered body that serves as a vessel for our being, and it is perfectly imperfect in order to serve us best to complete our soul's individual curriculum in this lifetime. On the being level, our souls are always whole, complete, and divinely-perfect in every way.

Claim Your Wholeness

You are whole. You are sourced from a Loving Source, which means your wholeness contains all the love you could ever need. You *are* the love, so, quite naturally, you are worthy of receiving that love. You deserve to feel, to know, to experience your Loving nature not just occasionally, not only sometimes, not just frequently - you deserve to experience love always. You are worthy of knowing yourself fully as a Loving being. You are worthy of feeling your own Loving nature in every given moment of your life. You are worthy of residing in the Loving paradigm. Claim your wholeness as an intrinsically worthy, Loving being.

Hearing the idea of intrinsic worth for the third time from two respected psychologists was what it took for me to finally allow for the possibility that I might indeed be already worthy. The moment I opened to that possibility, I was flooded with the memory of my out-of-body journey into the cosmos where I felt whole, joyfully alive, and at one with everything in the universe. Once I recalled the feeling of my own wholeness, the knowledge of my intrinsic worth was just a given. I felt whole. I felt the knowing that I had everything I'd ever needed inside of my wholeness, that I was indeed a self-contained unit, so to speak, containing everything that I needed or wanted to live a deeply fulfilling life. My feelings of lack were just that - feelings. They were not based on spiritual truth but were clearly irrational misunderstandings I'd believed true.

What Has Been Your Story About Your Wholeness?

Think about your own life. What has been your story about your wholeness? Have you always felt complete, or have you ever felt like you were not enough, like you were somehow missing something, defective, or lacking something? Take a moment now and write down your old story about your wholeness.

Are You Ready to Drop Your Old Story?

Are you ready to let go of the old, outdated story of your own lack of worth? How about the limited perception that you're not enough or less than somebody else? What about the irrational idea that you are undeserving of love because you're not good enough? If you feel even a drop of resistance towards changing these unhealthy beliefs, you might consider asking yourself the question, "How does it serve me to continue to believe that I am unworthy, less-than, or not enough?" Listen closely to yourself for your answer. You may feel these ideas keep you safe, keep you protected from hurt, or keep you feeling punished. Whatever your internal response is, I can totally guarantee that it is a fear-based response that is not supporting you to live the life of your dreams.

Let Go of Your Old Story

The truth is that buying into the old idea that you are an unworthy or defective being does not serve you in any way. Continuing to perpetuate the irrational beliefs that you are unworthy, less-than, or not enough simply keeps you small and prevents you from even coming close to realizing your dreams and potential as a powerful, radiant, divine being. Let your old story go, and claim your intrinsic worthiness as a divine child of the universe. If it feels too unreal to fully claim your own intrinsic worth all at once, you can start by simply allowing that it might be possible that you are already worthy, declaring that you are open to the possibility that it may be so.

Decide You Are Worthy

You do not need to have an out-of-body awakening experience or to hear the truth affirmed by respected psychologists to experience the knowledge of your intrinsic worth. All you need to do is to decide that you are already worthy. It is simply a choice to continue to believe the old story of your lack of worth or to believe a different story that allows for your own unique expression of divinity. Claim your intrinsic worth as a soul in a body, and you will immediately begin to feel better about yourself, to feel more whole, and to radiate joy.

For me, once I fully claimed my intrinsic worth, realizing that I was indeed worthy of being deeply loved, I felt my connection to my Loving Source as an immediate, palpable presence. I felt loved, felt surrounded by love, and I felt myself radiating love out into the world. In the same way that the sunray doesn't have to try to be the light, I didn't have to practice self-love; I simply needed to remember that I already *was* the love. When I finally declared myself worthy and Lovable, my own Loving essence was revealed.

As I was now literally being the love, I began to attract others into my life who had also claimed their worth as Loving beings. The incredible level of love that I experience is now mirrored back to me daily by my children, my intimate friendships, my students, sessions with clients, and my everyday interactions with people, animals, and nature.

You are a whole being. You are sourced from the Loving, made out of Loving. You have access to the Loving inside of you at every given moment. You have all of the internal resources to have and be everything you've ever dreamed, and beyond that. You are meant to shine! You are worthy and deserving of having it all, whatever it is that you desire from a Loving perspective. Like the seed that knows how to grow itself into the tree, you contain all of the inner resources to grow and thrive, to reach as high as you can toward the light. The question now becomes, "How high do I want to go?"

You are fully capable of realizing your highest potential, of shining your brightest light upon the planet. You are fully worthy of living the life your heart desires; you are worthy of having deep, intimate, Loving relationships, worthy of caring and connected friendships, worthy of fulfilling and meaningful work that inspires you, worthy of financial success, worthy of having plenty of time for your self-care, for exercise, fun, contemplation, and relaxation. You are worth having the life of your dreams, and you can begin to create that, right now, simply by claiming your intrinsic worth, your innate goodness as a Loving being, your equality with every other being, and your wholeness as a sphere of light on the being level.

Write a New Story about Your Worth

Right now, take some time to write a new story about your intrinsic worth, a new story about your equality with every other person ever born, a new story about your uniqueness, and a new story about your wholeness – that you have everything you have ever needed inside of yourself, are more than enough and have always been whole and complete in every way. Make your new story as supportive of your innate goodness as you can imagine. After you have written your new story, claim your intrinsic worth.

Remember, at the level of being, it is already so – your worth, equality, uniqueness, and wholeness are already a given – so all you are doing now is simply claiming that it is indeed so and moving into your real truth. Claim it. Own it. *Be* it.

If the ideas that you are already worthy, equal, uniquely special, and whole are news for you, many tears may flow as you claim your intrinsic worth. Rest assured that this is a natural and healthy part of letting go of old beliefs that no longer serve you. Just let them flow, allowing any old feelings to move up and out as you breathe and update your beliefs.

Exercise: Claiming your Intrinsic Worth

Begin by saying a protection prayer, setting conditions of love and light, and invoking spirit's presence.

Place your hands on your heart. Set an intention to access the highest vibration of Loving available. Breathe in the Loving and fill your body with Loving energies from head to toe. Then, set an intention to access the highest level of compassion. Breathe in compassion and fill your body with compassion from head to toe.

Repeat out loud any of the following that resonates, changing the vocabulary as needed to reflect your own beliefs:

"I forgive myself for buying into the irrational belief that I was ever unworthy." "My new updated belief is, I now know I am a divine child of God, intrinsically worthy in every way. My worth is a given."

"I forgive myself for buying into the irrational belief that I have to do something special in order to become worthy, that I have to earn my worth." "My new updated belief is, I now know I am already worthy just as I am. I was born worthy. I will remain worthy eternally. I am Source-energy in a body, and my soul is priceless. My worth is immeasurable."

"I forgive myself for buying into the irrational belief that if I behave in a certain way, my worth could be taken away." "My new updated belief is, I now know I am worthy no matter what. I was born worthy. I will remain worthy eternally. My worth is non-negotiable and an eternal given. My behavior and my worth are entirely different things."

"I forgive myself for buying into the irrational belief that because my _____ (mother, father, sibling, teacher, religion, etc.) said I was unworthy, that meant I was unworthy." "My new updated belief is, I now know I am a worthy child of God, just like every other being ever born. Intrinsic worth is a given, and my worth is separate from any opinions, judgments, or ideas that others may hold."

"I forgive myself for buying into the irrational belief that because I was born _____ (poor, black, female, deaf, differently-abled, gay, transgender, etc.) that means I am unworthy." "My new updated belief is, I now know I am worthy no matter what. I was born worthy. I will remain worthy eternally. My worth is non-negotiable and an eternal given. My birth circumstances and my worth are entirely different things. Every child ever born is a worthy child in the eyes of God/Source/the Loving."

"I forgive myself for buying into the irrational belief that because I was _____ (unwanted, abused, abandoned, adopted, neglected, ignored, mistreated, punished, shamed, blamed, pampered, indulged, etc.) as a child that means I am unworthy." "My new updated belief is, I now know I am worthy no matter how I was treated. I was born worthy. I will remain worthy eternally. My worth is non-negotiable and an eternal given. My treatment as a child and my worth are entirely different things."

"I forgive myself for buying into the irrational belief that some people are more worthy than or superior to me." "My new updated belief is, I now know all beings are equally worthy. I am equal in worth to every other being ever born. We are all sourced from the same Source, all part of a greater whole. We are all one, and therefore we are all equally worthy in every way. I now claim my full equality with every other being ever born."

"I forgive myself for buying into the irrational belief that some people are less worthy than or inferior to me." "My new updated belief is, I now know all beings are equally worthy. I am equal in worth to every other being ever born. We are all sourced from the same Source, all part of a greater whole. We are all one, and therefore we are all equally worthy in every way. I now claim my full equality with every other being ever born."

"I forgive myself for buying into the irrational belief that our difference in _____ (ability, skill, knowledge, net worth, etc.) has anything to do with our equality as intrinsically worthy beings." "My new updated belief is, I now know all beings are equally worthy, no matter what level of _____ (skill, talent, ability, net worth, etc.) a person has _____ level and equality as a being are two separate things, just like apples and oranges. I now claim my full equality with every other being ever born."

"I forgive myself for buying into the irrational belief that it makes sense to compare myself to anyone else in any way." "My new updated belief is that I now know that I am unique. I am the one and only me. I am the only one with my unique perspective, experiences, gifts, skills, knowledge, challenges, body, and consciousness. All I have to do is be myself. I now claim my uniqueness and individuality - I am a one-of-a-kind, rare, precious, unique expression of divine Loving."

"I forgive myself for buying into the irrational belief that I have ever been missing something, defective or not enough." "My new updated belief is, I now know that I am whole. I am sourced from within. I contain access to all of the inner resources I need to fully thrive, to reach my highest potential."

"I forgive myself for buying into the irrational belief that I need to live up to someone else's expectations to be worthy." "

My new updated belief is, I now know I am fully worthy now and forever, no matter what I've done or decide to do in the future. My worth is a given, and my worth is completely separate from other people's expectations. I now live my life for myself, knowing that other people's expectations are their own and truly have nothing to do with me."

"I forgive myself for buying into the irrational belief that I was ever unworthy of _____ (love, respect, caring, a committed partner, success, money, nice things, owning my own home, a degree, etc.)." "My new updated belief is, I now know I am worthy of having everything my heart desires. I am a beloved child of the universe, made manifest from my Source. It is my divine birthright to have all of the _____ I desire to have in my life. I am worth having it all."

Close your process by acknowledging yourself, expressing gratitude for spirit's assistance, and fully grounding your energy. Drink plenty of water.

CHAPTER THREE

Viewing Life from the Paradigm of the Loving

Are you ready to move from living a life of fear, judgment, or againstness into living fully in peace, joy, and Loving? If your answer is yes, then you are ready for a paradigm shift. A paradigm is simply the perspective from which something is viewed.

The perspective from which you view something colors your every experience. For instance, a parade viewed and experienced from the street-level perspective would look and feel very different from a parade viewed from the top of a tall building. At parade-ground level, things could be considered to be fantastic, indifferent, or awful, depending upon the spot from which a person is standing. It could feel good or bad. It could feel spacious or crowded. It could look beautiful or ugly. There is a constant cacophony of sound; horns and drums from the marching band, babies crying, people talking, announcements blaring from the loudspeakers, cheering from the crowd. At the ground level, from the middle of the crowd, perception becomes very narrow, limited to the immediate surroundings. The experience might be colored by annoyance with the person smoking nearby, overwhelm from the noise, or frustration towards a tall man with a big hat who keeps blocking the view. A person can only see what is passing right in front of them, and any problems or issues seem very large.

Now, imagine climbing five or ten stories up and looking out from a balcony at the same parade. Here, from this higher vantage point, everything is suddenly peaceful, and it all looks beautiful. A person can look down and see the bigger picture, aware of all of the floats that have passed and all that are yet to come. From this perspective, there are no annoyances, reasons to feel stressed, or feelings of overwhelm. The tall man with the hat is nowhere to be seen. There is a pervasive feeling of calm and serenity, regardless of whatever mishaps may be taking place down below. Those little issues seem smaller and simpler, nothing is blocking the view in any direction, and all is well from up here looking down.

From which perspective would you rather watch the parade? The ground-level view could be seen as viewing life from the fear-based perspective, and the balcony-level view could be likened to viewing it from the perspective of Loving. The perspective from which we view life affects every part of how we experience our reality. To change our life experience for the better, we have to change our perspective for the better.

We are intrinsically worthy, spiritual energy-beings having a human experience on planet Earth. Our divine nature is Loving, and at the deepest level of being, we all wish to reside in our natural state of Loving at all times. Making the paradigm shift from living a life of fear to living a life of joy, anchored in the Loving is our soul's mission in life. It is the process often referred to as self-realization or enlightenment. In order to make the shift, we must first come to understand the paradigm we are born into so that we may choose to live differently.

In our current Earth-plane four-dimensional human reality, we are all born into the paradigm that has been called the right/wrong reality. There are many other names for this level of reality, including the duality, the fear-based paradigm, and after the fall. If you picture a spiral that begins with a tight circle at the bottom and expands gradually up and out, you can get an idea of the movement that is currently taking place upon our planet. Our collective consciousness is shifting from a small, tight, narrow-minded position at the bottom of the spiral – this would be labeled 'fear-based right/wrong reality' – to a higher, more open, accepting, liberated perspective of Loving towards the top of the spiral.

From the parable in the Old Testament, once men and women resided in Eden, where they lived in complete alignment with God and followed the will of their souls. Adam and Eve represent innocent humankind; free, naked, and living in harmony with nature and all beings. As the story goes, they bought into the temptation to eat from the tree of knowledge of free will, and things went quickly downhill from there. Soon they felt terrible, guilty, and ashamed of themselves, needing to cover up their nakedness and slink away from the garden with heads hanging low.

The story of Adam and Eve is a much-simplified story of a paradigm shift that happened a long time ago over a gradual period to not just two people but to all of humankind. Since then, humans have been going through periods of tremendous darkness mixed with surges of growth and enlightenment, gradually becoming aware of themselves again as Loving beings.

The time has come now to let go of the fear-based reality once again and understand that – as Joni Mitchell wrote – "it's time to get ourselves back to the garden." It is time to shed the darkness, step into our light, to remember and reveal our innocence and truth as children of God, to live in alignment with the will of our souls, to say no to fear-based temptation despite our free-will choice, and to begin to co-create on Earth from a place of joy, freedom and Loving.

In order to make the shift to reside in the garden, to create peace upon our planet, to live in alignment with nature and our natural state of being as love in a human body – in order to reside entirely in the Loving paradigm – we must first examine where we are as beings who currently reside mainly in the right/wrong, fear-based reality.

In the right/wrong reality, all things are seen and judged as either good (right) or bad (wrong). It is our life's journey to remember we come from a different reality - that, in fact, on the being level, we reside in the Loving paradigm. So, we are here in these bodies to remember that we are at heart infinitely Loving beings, that there is no right or wrong from the soul's view.

Life is a School; We are All Here to Learn and Grow

From the perspective of Loving, life is a spiritual school; we are all here upon Earth to learn and grow as spiritual beings having a human experience. Everything that occurs is acceptable and in perfect order from our soul's perspective, and therefore Ok, no matter what is occurring. What this means, at the most basic level, is that whatever things we view as 'bad' – our issues, problems, and challenges – from the fear-based, right/wrong perspective are actually just fine. In fact, these things are more than fine; these issues are actually a necessary and most important part of our spiritual curriculum. When we can begin to view our challenges as learning opportunities for our own highest good, we begin to make the paradigm shift into a more Loving perspective.

To come into the knowledge that everything is Ok from the soul's perspective, we can begin to cultivate the quality of acceptance. True acceptance means that we fully accept and allow that everything that is occurring in our world is happening for a reason and is neither 'good' nor 'bad.' Acceptance means we do not need to judge what is occurring; instead, we can simply use it as an opportunity for more learning and to deepen our own understanding. It takes time and experience to come into a deep level of acceptance for everything that we see occurring, so be patient with yourself while you are moving into acceptance for all that is.

Gaining perspective of the Loving paradigm usually takes many years of lessons to achieve, and many souls do not accomplish this learning in their lifetime. However, in this time of accelerated change, if you feel ready to move out of fear into the Loving, it can happen very quickly once you make a conscious choice to do so. If you feel ready to shift into the Loving, acknowledge yourself for this. Spirit is celebrating with you right now.

Childhood in a Right/Wrong Reality

Since we are Loving beings born into the right/wrong paradigm, childhood can often be a period of tremendous suffering, especially for those who are more evolved spiritually or feel more connected to their Source. Children who are very open-hearted who experience abuse can receive this as a shock in many ways. Some just shut their heart down and build walls to defend themselves, and others develop codependencies to continue to feel loved. Many potential scenarios can take place for children engaged in right/wrong reality.

Let's take a look at some behavioral patterns that commonly result as children grow up in this fear-based paradigm.

If, while in the process of learning, a child takes an action that is deemed as 'bad' and is shamed, blamed, or punished, then that child usually becomes less likely to be willing to learn and grow out of fear of getting shamed, blamed, or punished again. Some children will attempt to behave in a 'good' manner, following as much as they can the perceived 'right' way to do things and looking outside of themselves for direction from parents, teachers, peers, and the media. The child's natural curiosity and creativity become stunted or atrophied from lack of use, as the child strives to conform to some predetermined model of whatever the parent's deem is 'right', 'good', or 'acceptable'. Inhibited from following the natural course of learning inspired by the will of his/her/their soul, that child will likely become a severe people-pleaser or perfectionist, unhappy, dissatisfied, and unfulfilled as an adult, leading to major issues such as anxiety, depression, alcoholism, drug addiction, anorexia/obesity, and more. The child that takes the 'good' route can stay very small and introverted as not to make waves out of fear. Or they may become an overachiever, doing everything they believe the parents will approve, trying their best to exceed their parents' expectations to make them proud.

Regardless of the level of outer, physical level success, the child that takes the 'good' route usually surrenders their own dreams and personal aspirations, ending up living their life to please someone else, causing inner feelings of deep resentment, lack of fulfillment, frustration, failure, or jealousy towards people who don't seem to care what others think. Sometimes, the child who takes the 'good' path becomes so wrapped up in doing everything 'right' or perfectly that they beat themselves up inside for every little thing they judge as 'wrong', causing themselves to feel miserable despite their skills, accomplishments, and outer-level success.

Another direction a child may take after getting shamed, blamed, or punished is to live up to the parents' and teachers' judgment that they are indeed 'bad'. It is as if they make a conscious or unconscious determination to prove that their parents are right – "You think I'm bad? I'll show you bad!" I have had many friends and clients who took this route, and they ended up rebelling completely, often running away from home, stealing, quitting school, or getting involved with drugs and alcohol in order to check out. The child who takes this path may turn out to be an underachiever as an adult, unconsciously living to spite the parents. Many people who have ended up in our prison systems took this route, either consciously or unconsciously deciding that they were 'bad', unworthy, lacking somehow, or otherwise disadvantaged from other 'good' people. Occasionally, this route inadvertently leads to personal freedom, as a person who is rebelling can sometimes spontaneously follow their dreams (especially if these are opposed by the parents, teachers, or society) and become highly successful. But more often, this child will end up feeling dissatisfied as an adult, settling in every way for living an unfulfilling life with tons of untapped talent and potential.

Then there are children who develop some kind of combination of the two, maybe acting 'good' in private in front of family, and acting 'bad' in public to appear cool in front of friends. Conversely, acting 'good' in public, trying to impress family, friends, and teachers, then acting rebelliously in private whenever they think they won't get caught. Growing up, I would see the Catholic high school girls walk demurely down the block from their school in the afternoon. The second they turned the corner out of sight of the nuns, they'd whip off their ponytail, toss off their sweater, roll down their socks, unbutton the top three buttons of their blouse, and begin applying red lipstick and mascara. A child who reacts in this way will grow to be an adult likely to be leading some sort of a double life, conforming to society's rules in some way, yet unable to find satisfaction unless having a totally different outlet where the rules can be broken. This adult may be secretly doing what they really want to do, yet will be filled with guilt for doing it.

As a child myself, I fell into this last category. I was desperate to please my mother and behaved like a 'good little girl' whenever my mother watched. When my mother wasn't around, I did whatever I wanted to do. Sometimes, my mother would appear unexpectedly, and I would get caught behaving 'badly'. I would be severely punished whenever this happened. The punishments did not deter me from behaving 'badly'; rather, the punishments taught me to become more creative about not getting caught in the first place and to be a better liar when and if I did get caught. While I felt tremendous guilt and shame almost constantly, my natural curiosity was so strong that I refused to become compliant.

Lastly, sometimes a child can become self-accepting at an early age and not be bothered by parents', teachers' and society's views of 'right' or 'wrong'. This child can be shamed, blamed, and punished, yet not identify himself as 'bad', but simply take it in stride as the parents' job. This child can do beautiful things and receive tons of praise for appearing 'good', yet not feel the need to surrender their own dreams just to please their parents. Children who are blessed to travel this route often follow the will of their soul much earlier than their peers and usually become well-adjusted and content as adults.

How did you relate toward an imposed right/wrong reality as a child? Were you ever punished for doing something someone else judged as wrong or bad? If so, did you resent your punishment or believe you deserved it? Did you try to conform to be like other people, or did you keep your own free will choice? Did you shut down or build walls around your heart to prevent feeling hurt? Whichever ways you reacted to the imposed right/wrong reality you experienced as a child, chances are great that there were times where you disagreed with the process or the outcome of things. Each of us has always been connected to the Loving, and many incidents from our childhoods would have felt out of alignment with us spiritually, in direct opposition to our true Loving nature.

Moving from Right/Wrong Reality into the Loving

Regardless of how you reacted to the fear-based, right/wrong reality you experienced as a child, the good news is that once you understand you have a choice, it is pretty easy to begin to make the paradigm shift to re-align with your own Loving essence. We are, first and foremost, spiritual beings whose very nature is Loving; therefore, existing in a right/wrong reality that causes us to think we are 'bad' actually provides us with a beautiful opportunity to rediscover our true divine Loving nature. How badly do we need to feel before we realize that we were never 'bad', that we were simply learning and growing? How scared or fearful do we need to feel before we understand that fear is an illusion? This is the journey, then, of spiritual evolution here on planet Earth – each and every human is given a lifetime's worth of experience to remember that they are actually a divine being, simply having a human experience of learning and growing.

So, when we have had enough of feeling bad or afraid, what do we do to get out of feeling that way once and for all? How do we begin to move into a life of joy and boundless freedom? How do we get to the place where we view our missteps as learning opportunities rather than as terrible mistakes that make us a bad, horrible person? For me, getting free of right/wrong reality required first really seeing it for what it was. For me, right/wrong reality was a whole set of beliefs that stemmed from fear. I grew up looking at the world through fear-colored glasses, and my whole belief system revolved around this fear-based, right/wrong system of reality that I had been born into in all of my precious innocence. To begin to move out of right/wrong, I had to see it as irrational, and I had to see the Love-based reality as my truth. Right/wrong reality is about judgment, is fear-based, is limiting, and is 100% irrational. The Loving paradigm is based on Universal Law, truth, and freedom and is the basis for all rational thought. Seeing this with clarity is what allowed me to begin to make a lasting shift.

Identifying the Irrationality of Right/Wrong Reality

If you really take a clear look at the right/wrong model of reality, you can see the irrationality it represents almost immediately. For instance, who gets to decide which things are right and which are wrong? The parents? The teachers? The government? The church? Social Media? What happens if these things do not line up? How do we know who is right and who is wrong?

Let's look at a few examples. Why is it not Ok and entirely disrespectful to burp at the table in England, yet in parts of Asia, the burp is the ultimate compliment to the host? Which culture is right? One culture says women are subservient to men, and another says all people are equal regardless of gender; which culture is right? One family says there is a Santa Claus, and the other celebrates Hanukkah; which family is right? One church says all people are inherently good, and another church says everyone is born in sin, and only if you follow these specific rules can one be saved. Which church is correct? You can begin to see that judging things strictly through a right/wrong filter of reality could cause quite a bit of difficulty amongst a large group of people with a multitude of different opinions on every matter.

It is hard enough just to figure out the rules in one individual family. Parents yell, "Don't hit!" or, "I'll teach you to be respectful" as they strike their own child. Is it Ok to hit people or not? Mom says alcohol is the Devil, don't ever drink, while dad chugs down a few six-packs every night in front of the television. Children are scolded, "Don't curse, or I'll wash your mouth out with soap!" Yet both mommy and daddy say those bad words sometimes, so why can't the child? How confusing it must be for children when the adults say one thing and model another. Not to mention the influence of television, movies, video games, and social media, where just about anything goes and is considered entertaining or cool. Is it Ok to kill, bully, or shame other people or not? Just about everything the children see online today involves some sort of againstness, including shooting, fighting, killing, or another form of judgment based very firmly on war mentality and social shaming – win/lose, right/wrong, good/bad, or better than/less than.

You can immediately see that it would be virtually impossible for a child to know automatically what was right and what was wrong, because right and wrong are totally arbitrary and ever-changing, based on the opinion of the parents, teachers, church, society, government, and social media. So, what happens is that, automatically, every child becomes 'bad' in some way, in someone's opinion – parents', teachers', the church's, society's, the government's, or social media's.

The right/wrong reality operates on a haphazard system of punishment and reward – punishment for being 'bad' or doing something 'wrong' and reward for being 'good' or doing something 'right'. Fear of punishment is used as a controlling device in right/wrong reality; many people operating in this paradigm are living in fear of getting caught as 'wrong' and have a compulsive need to be viewed as 'right' at all times. Some people become so immersed in being considered right, they spend their entire lives pointing out everyone else who they believe is wrong, spreading shame and blame about the planet in a never-ending attempt to prove their own goodness.

Other people have accepted the conclusion that they are bad, irredeemable, and unacceptable and are therefore surrendered to living a life of suffering, feeling that they must be deserving of perpetual punishment for all of their wrong-doing. Or, people accept that they are bad and unconsciously or even consciously decide to prove it, to really make their parents right, resulting in behaviors that are rebellious, angry, vindictive, harmful, or violent. The right/wrong paradigm creates an environment of fear, shame, anger, and despair. These energies are currently tangible upon the planet in almost every culture.

It is All Ok from the Loving Perspective

Since no one person on the planet seems to be in charge of deciding what is right and what is wrong, how *do* we know what is right and wrong? Or, is there even such a thing as 'right' and 'wrong'? My understanding is that, from the Loving Paradigm, there is no such thing as right or wrong; there is only what *is*. Everything that happens, no matter what, is Ok from the soul's perspective. Everything that occurs is simply an opportunity for growing, learning, and evolving. Earth is a school. Making mistakes is actually the way we learn and grow. When we fall down, we get back up again and learn to correct our balance.

Think of a child moving from baby to toddler. The child first crawls then gradually attempts to walk. The child may stand for a brief moment, wobble, then fall. Could you picture a new set of parents berating the child at this point? "Bad baby! Stupid baby. Worthless baby. You can't do anything right." No way! That would never happen, right? Parents universally accept that learning how to walk is a natural, normal process that is to be given the respect that it deserves.

Parents either neutrally allow the process of a child just learning to walk or express awe, delight, or amazement. "Come on, baby! You can do it… Yes! That's it! Oh, I see you just fell down… that's Ok, just try again. You can do it!" Guess what?! Spirit is watching us in every given moment, just like proud parents. Right now, even as you read these words, your soul and your guides are watching from the sidelines, clapping and cheering each and every time you learn something new, cheering you on, "Come on, baby, you can do it! Yes, that's it!"

We learn through a natural process of trial and error. Falling down, making mistakes, even falling down hard, is viewed as natural, normal, and Ok from the Loving perspective. Just like the child learning to walk, we are all simply learning and growing in every single moment of our lives. Our learning builds upon itself through a process of life experience. We take an action. We experience the consequences of our action. We learn something. We course-correct, refine, or redirect our next action. Learning is a natural, ongoing process for a divine energy-being having a human experience. We grow and evolve as souls as we learn. Every experience that we have is an evolutionary experience, from our soul's perspective.

When I'm teaching this principle in a class, someone invariably yells out, "But what about murder?!" or some other seemly atrocious example like rape, child molestation, or the Holocaust. The concept that everything that happens is Ok can be difficult to grasp at first because we have been so indoctrinated to believe in right and wrong that we hold strong judgments toward things we think are really, *really* wrong. If you find parts of your personality freaking out or grappling with this idea of infinite acceptance, be gentle with yourself and give yourself time to allow it to percolate.

From the perspective of the Loving, all things that occur, even rape and murder, are simply learning opportunities for our soul's growth and evolvement. Everything is alright from a spiritual perspective. Why? Everything that occurs is Ok and completely acceptable because Earth is a school, and it is set up as a space for souls to learn and grow in human form. All lessons are acceptable from the soul's perspective, and all lessons are viewed neutrally from the Loving paradigm. The very fact that something happens here on Earth is an indication that it is part of someone's growth and evolvement, no matter what it looks like. Anything that is possible is part of our collective curriculum. For some people, that is a horrifying idea. They hear this and think of mayhem and chaos upon the planet with no rules of right or wrong. If we were to believe that there is no such thing as right or wrong, how would people possibly know how to behave?

Humans Have an Internal Guidance System

Thankfully, this Earth-school system was set up to work beautifully; every person is specially equipped with their own internal guidance system, complete with inner guidance, discernment, and a feeling-barometer that lets them know when they are in what I call 'alignment'. What this means is that every human is fully capable of determining what actions or behaviors are in alignment with their own learning in every given moment. We have the ability to self-correct according to our own internal guidance system. This is fabulous news. Everyone is capable of monitoring their own learning.

But if this is really the case, what has stopped us from

using this internal guidance system in the past? Because, quite obviously, lots of people on the planet have acted out of alignment based on current events as well as the events from our recorded world history over the past few thousand years. That is simple. What has stopped us from utilizing our own course-corrective system is the feeling of disconnection from the Loving Source, the disconnection from our hearts, the disconnection from the knowledge of our intrinsic worth, the disconnection from our internal feeling-barometer, and the disconnection with our own inner guidance. In extreme cases, such as with a serial killer, studies always show that these individuals were vilely abused as children; these children received the kind of extreme fear-based modeling of complete lack of love, allowing them to feel totally unloved, uncared for, and unvalued. There is a clear, indisputable connection between a severe lack of loving treatment as a child and adult behavior that is seriously out of alignment with the Loving nature of all beings.

The solution to course-correcting the lack of alignment on the planet is not applying more judgments of 'wrong' and 'bad' toward the people who are acting out of alignment but in applying Loving to everyone who has ever felt a lack of it. We were all taught from an early age that we couldn't trust ourselves. Many of us were repeatedly told we were 'bad' and 'wrong' for our decisions, our words, our actions, and that only certain grownups knew what was right for us. So, as long as a person has been looking outside of themselves for directions, placing their trust out in others to tell them what to do, that person is not availing themselves of their own internal guidance system – their own inner guidance, their own discernment of truth, and their own internal feeling barometer. In order to become self-correcting learners, people need to reclaim their self-trust and begin to experience first-hand what is in alignment inside of themselves and what isn't.

To begin to look at this subject, what does it mean to be in 'alignment'? To me, the knowledge that I am in alignment means that I am 'lined up' inside with the will of my soul and, consequently, lined up with the will of God; in other words, my personality is connected to the Loving and my conscious self – the higher part of me that is awake and aware – is in charge, so I am taking my cues from my inner guidance, the part of me that is in communion with my soul, rather than allowing the parts of myself that still reside in the right/wrong reality to make my choices for me. I am thinking and acting in a way that serves my highest good, which means my thinking stems from a place of rational thought. I am thinking and acting in a way that supports me on the learning path of my own evolution. I am exactly where I need to be to learn what I need to learn next on my personal journey of transformation. Therefore, when I am acting in alignment, everything that is happening inside and out is in the flow with the Loving, connected, and flowing energetically with the Universe and everything around me.

When I am in alignment with the will of my soul, I am surrendered, trusting in and acting on the guidance of my higher self, listening only to that part of myself that is connected with my soul. When I am in full alignment, everything is happening with grace and ease. I feel calm, centered, at peace inside of myself. The experience of being in alignment doesn't mean there are no obstacles. When I am in alignment, and an obstacle appears, I simply move over or through the obstacle with ease, fully trusting that I can and will succeed. I learn with joy, free from pain and suffering.

Living in Alignment

Have you ever had that feeling before, where everything is flowing perfectly, and you feel so at peace inside? Being in alignment can be experienced as having a really great day, an exceptional hour, or even just a blissful moment or two. It can be felt in an intimate conversation where you either hear or are guided to say something that causes an 'ah-ha' moment. It can be experienced in a creative moment where a piece of art, music, poetry, or writing simply comes together. It can be sensed as a moment of power, such as a business deal, signing of contracts, or large purchase or transaction. It can be felt in quiet, peaceful moments, moments of stillness or silence where you simply know you are in the right place at the right time. It can be felt in simple moments where you may be driving down a street and having the light turn green at just the right instant. Whenever or wherever it happens, you will know that your life is going in the right direction.

Staying in Alignment Means Going with the Flow

When we are fully in alignment, our natural state will be experienced as one with the flow of nature and all things around us. We feel part of and connected to everyone and everything energetically, and our life operates in accord with our environment in every way, effortlessly. When we are going with the flow, we pull up to the store as a parking spot appears.

You likely know the feeling if you think about it. You may be gracefully moving through a crowded market and having a new lane open the moment you go to check out. These are simple examples of what I would call being in the flow. Being in alignment means that if something happens, that could potentially block the flow, you just flow over or around the obstacle in a way that doesn't affect your peace. For instance, you could be pulling up to the store and see that empty parking space. Then, just as you are beginning to turn in to park in that spot that you are certain is yours, another car could come from the other direction and whip into the spot first. If your peace is upset in any way by this happening, then you will now feel out of alignment. However, you could choose to just flow over this unanticipated obstacle with ease, stay perfectly calm and centered inside, and simply continue to go with the flow. Then you would peacefully find another parking space elsewhere and remain in alignment inside of yourself.

Whichever way we react, becoming upset or staying at peace, either is Ok from the soul's perspective. There is no right or wrong way to respond in any given situation. What is important here is that we can learn to identify those moments when we do get out of alignment, recognizing when we become triggered so that we can learn to get quickly back into alignment. Why? Because being in alignment simply feels better. In fact, it feels indescribable to be able to stay in alignment for long periods. Being in full alignment with the will of my soul gives me the deepest sense of contentment and well-being that I have ever experienced. It is a feeling that is deeper than what most people call happiness. There is strength to the feeling that goes well beyond the bounds of happiness into unfathomable peace. From that place, I have access to all of the qualities of Loving, including joy, compassion, grace, ease, trust, beauty, gratitude, and dozens more. When I am acting in alignment, I feel totally connected with Source and fulfilled within myself. This feeling of connection and fulfillment is what most clients who seek me out have been searching for their entire lives. You may be asking, "How can I get there?" The first step is learning how to use your internal barometer as a guide to let you know when you've gone off-course. Your internal barometer is the tool that will allow you to tell if you are in or out of alignment inside of yourself at any given moment.

Your Internal Barometer is Different from Inner Guidance

Many people confuse inner guidance with their internal barometer; to me, these are two different tools that help make up what I call my internal guidance system. Let's look at the difference.

I define my inner guidance in several ways, and I encourage everyone to determine how they define their own guidance. Some people call it conscience, some call it intuition, some call it instinct, some call it right-knowing, some call it gut feeling, and some call it signs from the Universe. To me, these are all wonderful tools that I can use to guide myself to act in alignment with my truth, but the actual 'barometer' of how I'm doing will always be my feeling-level response in any given situation. So, I call the tools that can guide me, such as instinct, intuition, or direct knowing, my inner guidance, and the compass that tells me where I am at any given movement, either in or out of alignment, my internal barometer. Together, along with my natural sense of discernment, they form a three-part package that I call the internal guidance system.

Your Internal Guidance System

Let me explain this more clearly. If my conscience tells me not to say a certain thing, and I trust it and don't say what I was thinking, I may feel peaceful inside about my decision to keep my mouth shut. My feeling of peace inside is my barometer that I acted in alignment with myself. I feel centered and on-course. If I were to judge this feeling, I would say it felt 'good' in a centered, neutral way. It is a feeling of being right on, and it feels both steady and peaceful. The neutral, peaceful feeling inside me is a measure, or a barometer, of how on-course I stayed by trusting my discernment to listen to my inner guidance, which told me to keep my mouth shut.

On the other hand, if I get an intuition to get off the freeway several exits before my destination, and I second-guess my intuition and decide to ignore my guidance and stay on the freeway, a few minutes later when the traffic comes to a grinding halt due to an accident, my reactive expletives, feelings of frustration, kicking myself for not listening to myself, etc. are my barometer telling me I went off-course from my natural flow. If I were to judge my feelings after ignoring my intuition, I would say I felt irritated or 'bad' inside. The bad feeling inside tells me something is off-course. So, my intuition was guiding me to act in alignment, and my feeling-response was an indication or a barometer of how I did with actually following my guidance and staying on course.

Very simply put, my inner guidance is the device that gives the instructions from my soul, and my internal barometer is the feeling-gauge that tells how I did with listening to and following the instructions.

When I trust in, listen to, and fully comply with my inner guidance, I act on-course, in complete alignment with the will of my soul. This is what it means to be acting in accordance with the will of God. I am acting in my divine flow, in the highest good of all concerned. When I am in alignment, I feel peaceful, centered, balanced, flowing, and free. I am fully trusting in the process and following all of my guidance, whatever I may call it - intuition, instinct, conscience, knowing, gut-instinct - whatever. Being in the flow feels wonderful. I know without a shadow of a doubt that I am fully on-course, moving forward in the best direction for my life, for my growth, for my expansion. I am on track with my life in the best possible way. I feel a pervasive feeling of contentment and know that all is well and everything is in divine-perfect order.

When I go against my inner guidance, I immediately get a tight feeling in my abdomen. I don't necessarily have to judge it as 'bad', meaning that I did something wrong; however, on an evaluative level, the feeling definitely doesn't feel so comfortable, and I really don't want to stay in that feeling for very long. When I go off-course, and my feeling-barometer lets me know I'm out of alignment, I will do anything that is necessary to get back on course. Once you have the tools to do so, you will too. Why? Because our nature is Loving, and more than anything else, all spiritual beings wish to feel the joy and peace that comes from being in alignment with the Loving. It is our true nature as well as our birthright.

Why is understanding that you have an internal guidance system made up of your inner guidance, your discernment, and an internal feeling-barometer important? There are many, many teachings out there that focus on following your intuition, but not many that assist people with the process of dealing with life when they don't. Understanding that there are several tools at your disposal to assist you with your growth can be invaluable. Some people think that these tools are only available for a gifted few. The truth is that everyone has all of the tools necessary to achieve self-actualization; we just need to know how to use these tools and then begin to apply them in our own life.

Learning to Listen to Your Inner Guidance is a Process

The fact of the matter is that learning how to hear, acknowledge, trust, and listen to your inner guidance is a process, not a one-time event. My experience has been that everyone has unique inner guidance, depending upon various different factors. Inner guidance can take many forms. People who are just 'waking up' to their own spirituality may need to take some time to learn to hear their own inner guidance. Some people experience it as a soft voice – a still, small voice. Some people get impressions without any words. Certain people have access to Direct Knowing and act as a conscious channel for their own souls. Some people hear their guides, angels, or a specific master teacher directly in clear, strong voices. Others just get brief messages, single words, pictures, or impressions. Still others see symbols, colors, or auras that give them information. All people have varying degrees of access to psychic gifts, which are not necessarily an indication of a person's level of growth.

Some people are very instinctual and have strong visceral feelings, sometimes called 'gut feelings' that they learn to interpret. Some people learn to ask for signs from their guidance and receive messages through nature, weather, traffic signs, numbers, and more. People who become aware of the level of spiritual guidance that is available often learn to use outer tools for accessing inner guidance such as kinesiology, astrology, tarot cards, angel cards, pendulums, tea leaves, rune stones, I-ching, and others. As with any tool, the tool itself cannot determine the outcome; rather, it is the user's skill that will determine the successful use of a particular tool. Again, there is no right or wrong way to access inner guidance. Many people use a combination of tools. Inner guidance is as unique as people are unique.

What does your inner guidance look, feel, or sound like? Do you feel comfortable accessing your guidance? If this is new for you, know that you can begin to cultivate a deeper connection with your inner guidance at any time. At the most basic level, your inner guidance is how you communicate with your higher self, which is the part of you that is directly linked to your soul's will. If your soul is very evolved, you may first receive communication with your spirit guides, whose role it is to serve you on your human journey of evolution and to act as an interpreter for the will of your soul. At some point, you will gradually be able to receive communication directly from your own soul. This can take time to evolve. Whether you are connecting with your spirit guides or your own soul is not so important; what is important is that you are making the connection with your inner guidance to begin to come into greater alignment with the will of your soul.

How you decide to strengthen and develop this connection is ultimately up to you. I would encourage you to begin by simply stating an intention to communicate with your soul at a deeper level and to be able to receive guidance in a clear, direct manner that is easy to interpret. If you do not initially receive your guidance with ease, ask for a higher level of clarity. Keep asking for more clarity until you can easily and effortlessly connect with Source-energy, receiving direct and clear guidance whenever you desire.

The Tool of Discernment

In addition to your inner guidance, you also have a beautiful tool called discernment. You have the ability to discern or to tell if something is true for you or not. Your tool of discernment, when you use it, will immediately let you know if something is in alignment or out of alignment with the will of your soul – whether you should take it as truth or non-truth in any given situation.

Only You Can Know Your Own Truth

What is most important here is to really acknowledge that your truth resides within. What does that mean? Your truth resides within *you*. You are the source – the only source – of knowledge of your own truth. Why is that? Well, because we were placed in a dimension that has free will. In a free will learning environment, every being must use their own discernment to determine what is true for them. So, if I hear someone else say something that I totally agree with, that person is stating a truth that is in alignment with my own inner knowing. How do I know if I am in agreement with something someone else says? Because, if someone else's truth is also my own, I will have a feeling of resonance; what they say will actually 'ring true' for me.

Sometimes my ring of truth is quiet, just an inner feeling of confirmation. Sometimes my truth rings loudly and resoundingly inside of me as an emphatic 'Yes!' of agreement. And sometimes, especially if I am having a healing moment, or if someone I'm working with has a deeply healing experience, my truth will ring with chills or goosebumps – the energy will flood down my neck and spine until every hair on my arms and body is standing straight up. On a feeling level, when I hear my internal 'Yes' ring true for me, I feel dead-center inside, as if I am hitting an internal gong or bull's eye that is right on target. It is neutral in feeling and simply matter-of-fact that it is so, even as it comes in varying degrees of strength. The certainty that it is indeed true brings with it a very calm, centered feeling – a feeling of peace.

What Does Your Ring of Truth Feel or Sound Like Inside?

Have you ever instantly discerned your truth before? What does your ring of truth sound or feel like inside? Make a note of this internal response so that you will always be aware of the times when something is true for you or not. Whatever the form of confirmation, we all have the ability to know when we hear our own truth. Some people haven't learned to trust themselves yet, so they may need support with learning to listen and acknowledge when something rings true for them. If you do not yet know what your truth feels like inside, spend some time asking for your guides' or your soul's assistance to learn to hear, sense, or feel what is true for you. The bottom line is that no one outside of you has the ability to tell you what is true for you. You are the one, the *only* one who can discern your own truth.

Once you claim this, it will get very easy to discern when you hear something that is not your truth. It will not resonate, no matter how someone may say it or no matter how you frame it; it just doesn't 'ring' true inside of you as accurate. If what you are hearing is out of alignment for you, if you tune into yourself closely, you will either hear the word or feel the energy of 'no' and simply know without a doubt that this is not for you. On a feeling level, it will feel anywhere from neutral to tight, uncomfortable or slightly off-balance. When this happens, all you have to do is acknowledge this on the inside and use your discernment as to how to proceed. I was taught to let go of any clear 'no' completely, to simply acknowledge inside of myself, "This is apparently for someone else; I can let this information/advice go on by."

Truth is Relative to Where You Are in Consciousness

In letting go of a 'no', learn to resist the temptation or need to explain yourself, to tell anyone else your reasons why, or to put someone else down for sharing something that is not true for you. Let go of the idea or need to make someone else wrong because there is no such thing as wrong from the Loving perspective. We are all in different places on the learning line of life; something that was true for you many years ago may not be true for you today – that doesn't mean you were bad or wrong years ago; it simply means that you have evolved into a higher level of truth. When I receive advice or information that does not resonate with me, I respond with, "Thank you for sharing." If someone is pushing or insistent that I take their advice, I respond, "Thank you. I really appreciate your caring. I will take that into consideration." And I end that topic of conversation. With practice, it becomes easy to acknowledge your own truth without needing to argue or convince another person you are right, and they are wrong. From the soul's perspective, there is no such thing as right or wrong, and differences are all Ok in the field of learning. Remember, our truth is relative to wherever you presently are on your own path, depending upon where you currently stand on the upward spiral of conscious expansion.

And, conversely, just because something does not ring true for you right now does not at all mean that it will never be true. You may hear something that sounds wild, something bizarre that seems unimaginable. Be open to the possibility that someone else may be working at a higher level of truth than you, and you may be as yet unaware of an expanded level of truth in any given subject. That is Ok. If this happens, you will get neither a clear ring of truth nor a clear 'no'. Sometimes there is just a feeling of doubt or a feeling of flatness. It can feel like a big darkness, as if you are moving into the unknown, and it may even bring up a feeling of fear.

There are times where we are given information that comes at a higher level of truth than we are ready to hear or to accept. It cannot yet resonate as true inside us because we are not yet at that level to match it. If you have ever seen anyone making the motion of the airplane flying over the head when someone cannot comprehend something, the gesture is an apt description of what is occurring energetically, although perhaps not a kind one. Change is scary at the personality level, so sometimes, the personality just shuts the information out as if it never happened. This is usually the case when someone's vibration is significantly lower than the vibration of the information, which is why it appears to go over that person's head. When we are able to hear something but are not quite able to understand or assimilate it, it usually means that it is something that will be important in our future understanding. So if you hear information that you are in doubt about, I encourage you to simply imagine placing it on a shelf in the back of your mind, with the intention that you will look at it later. If you learn how to do this, you will be amazed at how you will eventually grow into higher levels of truth with ease. A realization will occur, and you will say, "I already knew that on some level." Or, "I remember hearing that; *now* I get it."

There are many great examples of this happening. The story of how Galileo taught the Copernican System to prove that the sun didn't revolve around the Earth is an excellent example. He was imprisoned for the last twenty years of his life for this blasphemous untruth, which later turned out to be true for everyone as they reached the growth level to understand this information as true. Soon, everyone looked at the sunrise differently, and many of them were probably thinking, 'I knew that the Earth was turning all along'.

As each new level of truth approaches, there is a natural urge to deny it, even argue or fight against it, because change is scary for the personality. If you can accept that we are always evolving into higher and higher levels of truth, it will be easier for you to allow your mind to accept new information in your own divine timing and with ease.

When you hear something that is unknown, you may feel neutrality, uncertainty, blankness, anxiety, or even a degree of panic. You can simply acknowledge the feeling of fear if it presents itself, put the information on the shelf in the back of your mind, and forget about it, coming back to the present moment, trusting that whatever that was about will be revealed to you when you need to understand it. If you can begin to trust in your own inner knowing, you will be able to become one with your own source of truth, allowing you to come into alignment with the will of your soul very quickly.

So, whenever you think, hear, or read anything – and I sincerely do mean anything and everything that passes your mind – if the information is to be evaluated, you will have one of three reactions inside from your place of discernment: a knowing of 'yes', 'no', or uncertainty/blankness. In conjunction with your discernment, you will have a level of emotional feeling that can be used as your inner barometer. The two together can make for an obvious answer inside of you. A strong 'yes' will feel both neutral on a feeling-level and powerful. A strong 'no' will feel repulsive or off-center.

If you think about saying yes to a clear 'no', you will feel an immediate negative reaction inside that lets you know that idea is way off-course. A great example of this was a young client who wanted to pursue art as a career choice. His parents wanted him to go to law school. I asked him to picture letting go of the art dream (his internal yes) and enrolling in the law program (his internal no). The feeling-level response he experienced inside just picturing moving forward into a clear 'no' was so strong he literally felt repulsed. This little exercise gave him the strength he needed to let his parents know that he'd be making his own choices from here on out.

The reverse is true as well; if you picture saying 'no' to deny a clear 'yes', you will have a feeling-level response of negativity inside that lets you know that this will take you off-course. One client had gotten a clear 'yes' answer to her dream to move, but she was hesitating out of some old, codependent habits that were saying she needed to live in her home town to care for her extended family. When she imagined denying her clear 'yes' and pictured herself sticking around a place that no longer held any energy for her in order to please others, she felt instantly depressed and even despondent. This indicated how she would eventually feel if she failed to act on her discernment to make the move. She immediately cleaned up her affairs, informed the family, and made her move.

The most important thing to understand about your discernment is that it is yours alone – you are the one and only one who can interpret your internal response to what you hear to determine what is currently true for you or not. If you trust in your own inner knowing, wonderful! You will quickly be able to use your discernment to greater degrees in all areas of your life. If you have not yet developed self-trust, I highly encourage you to begin – right now – to cultivate trust in your own ability to discern your truth. Remember, absolute truth only resides at the level of God. In order to cultivate a higher level of truth inside yourself, the only way to do that is to strengthen your own internal connection with your divine Source.

Everyone Has the Ability to Learn to Receive the Word of God

There has been some misunderstanding on the planet regarding spiritual truth, prophecy, revelation, and who can, in fact, receive the direct word of God or Source. Understand that anyone and everyone has the innate ability to channel spirit at the highest degree of truth that they can currently access; the ability is lying unused and dormant in most people, some people are beginning to develop their ability, and a small handful of the population already has the ability to varying degrees of accuracy. We are, after all, all divine beings simply having a learning experience in human form, and we are always plugged into our Source of consciousness.

When we are tapping into our inner guidance, what we are essentially doing is listening to the higher part of ourselves that is directly connected to our Source at the level of our soul. There are various methods of communication, and some people can tune in to receive direct guidance in the form of words, as opposed to receiving feelings, signs, symbols, or other forms of communication. What is important to understand is that tuning in to divine guidance in the form of words is like tuning to a specific radio channel and that, depending upon how clear the channel is, the information may come through with a great deal of static on the line.

The ability to communicate with spirit in the form of words has absolutely nothing to do with a person's level of clarity or spiritual evolution. Someone who has cleared their baggage, completed their lessons, and is living in alignment with the will of their soul may have the ability to act as a pure, clear channel for a high level of spiritual truth to come forth. Sometimes people who are less clear may receive partial messages or are only able to interpret the information to the degree that their personality can understand and handle. We all view everything through the filter of our own perception – like the saying about seeing the world through rose-colored glasses; if someone has sunglasses on, everything they see is going to look a little bit darker. The same thing is true of hearing a higher level of spiritual truth – a person will hear everything through the filter of their own level of perception of the truth unless they have been specifically taught how to separate out their personality from the spiritual information that comes through them. This is a crucial point, because often people will make the assumption that because a person receives direct communication from their spirit guides, Archangels, their own soul, or some unknown disembodied entity that automatically means they are a true prophet, a master teacher, and that their word *is* the absolute true word of God.

Again, a person's ability to receive direct, verbal communication from spirit has *nothing* to do with their level of clarity, growth, rationality, or spiritual evolution. I speak from personal experience here to anyone who believes a person cannot receive a higher truth until they have achieved a certain level of growth; that idea is a total misinterpretation of reality. How do I know? People can open to channel words directly from spirit before they are personally evolved because I opened to channel myself when I was only 18 and was still thinking, feeling, and behaving like a total fear-filled, irrational mess. Therefore, much of what I initially channeled was filled with my own irrationality. It was as if there was an unseen hand controlling my inner radio dial; the station kept jumping around between various different levels, ranging from Archangels to the recently dead. Thankfully, a wonderful spiritual teacher taught me how to tune my radio dial into the highest frequencies, as well as how to create a cone of silence that would allow my personality to stay out of the way whenever I channeled. So, in my early twenties, I was able to learn to receive a very high level of truth without distorting it. But, because I knew I was still residing mainly in fear and irrationality, I decided not to channel publicly or write books until I was more integrated, just to be on the safe side. What I have seen in my life's experience is that not all people handle their ability prudently. Many people, as soon as they begin to receive communication from spirit in words, will start writing, blogging, teaching, working the psychic hotlines, starting churches, and shouting their epiphanies from the rooftops.

The problem with someone telling people that they are receiving the direct word of God before they have completed their spiritual curriculum is this: a person who does not yet have clarity will not be able to either discern what level the information they are receiving is coming from or accurately discern whether their interpretation of what comes through them is clear higher truth or colored by their own limited perception. Even if the information is coming from the purest, highest spiritual source, if the person receiving the information is still operating under any irrational, fear-based beliefs, they will automatically interpret whatever comes through in a way that makes sense to them, to fit in with their current beliefs and current understanding. What this means is that, depending on the level of information coming through and the level of clarity of the channel, maybe most of the words will be higher truth, maybe one out of five words might be true, or maybe only one in twenty.

People are desperately seeking connection with their souls. They are dying to hear the real truth and the actual word of God, so they are very susceptible to hearing a partial truth or a half-truth – from a minister, a guru, a psychic, a spiritual leader, or whomever – and thinking it is all 100% spiritual truth. This is where the teaching to beware of false prophets comes in handy. It is important to learn to know your own ring of truth and to practice using your discernment no matter who is telling you that something is true. What is vital to understand is that much religious dogma is based on information that is irrational and coming from what Source would consider 'false prophets', or people who are not yet able to accurately interpret the highest level of information it is possible for humanity to receive.

Because students of the masters were operating under their own level of fear-based, right/wrong reality, they may have made certain interpretations of the teachings in-the-moment. Then, these teachings were rewritten by others, sometimes hundreds of years later, edited down, rewritten to suit the religious practices of the times, or revised again to please the current government officials. Then these writings were translated into other languages by different people who also had their own interpretations of the material, so you can see how it might be possible for the ancient spiritual information upon the planet which we have access to today to have been misinterpreted at some point along the way.

Even though the original information from Source-energy may have flowed through a pure, clear channel, many master teachers did not record their own teachings; rather, their students and disciples did most of the recording. This is why some spiritual writings are riddled with fear, punishment, vengeance, and strong judgments of right and wrong when the true essence of the teachings is filled with neutrality, compassion, and acceptance. This means that it is very important that we use our own discernment when reading spiritual texts and begin to come to our own interpretation of any spiritual teachings we may be following or studying, rather than blindly following someone else's (perhaps misguided) interpretation.

If you are uncertain whether any spiritual information is true or not, you can check in with your feeling-barometer to gauge your truth. If the information is true for you, you will feel peaceful inside and have a sense of trust and alignment with the information. True rationality always feels good, neutral, supportive, and empowering. If the information is not in alignment with your truth, you will feel off-centered – scared, yucky, anxious, or uncomfortable in some way. Irrationality feels bad, unsupportive, and disempowering. Remember, just because someone heads up a religious organization does not mean they automatically speak the true word of God. Trust your discernment as God resides within you, and know that you are the only one who can know your own truth.

Absolute Truth Only Resides at the Level of God/ the Loving

We are all in our own unique place in consciousness in this Earth-plane school of learning. Truth is relative to where a person resides consciously, so what is true for one person may not be true for another. Absolute Truth resides at the highest level of consciousness, in the oneness with God/Loving. My understanding is that this level of being is not even comprehensible to us at our current level of evolution. So, not a single one of us is there yet, and we are all working toward that state in every moment of our growth and evolution.

Part of our curriculum as a soul in a body having a human experience is about learning how to choose to align ourselves with what is true for us right now, aligning with that which is in alignment with the will of our soul, and in doing so, aligning with the will of God, Nature, and our Universe. Hold what is true for you at this moment without clinging to it in any way, allowing for a higher truth to come forward at any time in the future, knowing that truth is relative to consciousness and that your consciousness will continue to grow and expand as you evolve spiritually. This learning is an ongoing process, so be gentle with yourself as you learn to discern your truth and listen to and act upon your inner guidance.

Learning to Access and Trust Your Discernment Takes Time

Learning to access your ring of truth and to hear and trust your inner guidance takes time, so go easy on yourself as you develop the tools of your own internal guidance system – your discernment, your inner guidance, and your feeling-barometer. We are, after all, only human. Human learning happens best through a normal, natural process of trial and error. There is no instruction booklet for personal evolution; therefore, everyone's learning will be different according to each person's individual needs. As a result, it may take one person a year to learn to discern their truth, to begin to trust and act on their own inner guidance, and it may take another person a lifetime. Many people will pass through life without ever discovering their own source of truth or acknowledging their inner guidance. Personally, I have been aware of my own internal guidance system for over 35 years, and there are *still* occasional times where I don't trust my discernment to follow my inner guidance, for whatever reason. When this happens, it is brought to my attention immediately by my feeling-level response; my internal barometer instantly lets me know that I've gone out of alignment. There is a whole range of negative feeling-responses inside of me, from a small feeling of tightness in my stomach to big feelings of "Ew, yuck."

When You Go Off-Course, be Gentle with Yourself

When this happens for me – specifically, when I receive guidance and do not pay attention or heed it – and I go off-course, I immediately flood myself with compassion for not listening to my guidance, allow myself to fully feel my feelings, acknowledging them for showing me I went off-track. After the compassion sinks in, I look for the learning opportunity. What made me act off-course? What is there to clear, heal, or update? Then I work my process around whatever is present for me, give thanks and blessings to the whole occurrence for the learning opportunity, and I am once again back to center, peace, and alignment. By the time you finish this book, you'll have the tools to be able to do this, too. In the meantime, be gentle with yourself when you find yourself in major learning mode.

When you go off-course from your guidance, it is vital to understand that you didn't do anything wrong. It is not bad or wrong to veer off-course; it is simply an indication that there is something more to learn or clear in that direction. Just like the baby is not a 'bad' baby for falling down, you, as a spiritual being, are not 'bad' for having an issue or an obstacle present itself in your life. Mistakes are not 'bad'; they are simply an indication that there is more information to be revealed to you in that particular area. Think about it: if you did everything perfectly and were fully able to live in constant alignment with the will of your soul, why would you even be here? Life on Earth is an opportunity for major spiritual growth and evolution. The whole reason for being here is to go through some challenges to get from one level to the next. And so, when you go off-course at any time, be gentle with yourself.

You could think of it as a video game: life on Earth is simply like one level to complete in the great cosmic game of becoming one. Would you consider it bad or wrong to re-do something while playing a video game for the first time? Of course not! You'd simply allow yourself to learn and improve. My son loves video games, and I've watched while he has learned how to navigate certain levels. He remembers where every potential pitfall is lurking, which path will net him the most extra points, where the treasure is hidden, and how high to jump to land on the platform without falling into the hot lava boiling below. He doesn't beat himself up when he lands in the lava; he simply restarts that level and does it again until he nails it and moves on.

Of course, in my analogy, you aren't using a hand-held controller; you are actually *living* the game of life. It would be totally irrational to think that you would know the exact course and be able to do everything correctly before you'd ever even traveled the path. Just like a giant obstacle course, it may take a few tries to get over some of those walls. You might spill out on the speedway. Or how about those slippery barrels to get across that river? I've never seen anyone learn to run on a wet barrel without flying off a few times first. Life is like that. In order to master any one part of it, you have to be willing to get a little messy. You can either curse and beat yourself up when you fall down, or you can laugh with the pure joy of it, knowing that you are simply learning more each and every time you land on your butt. You have free will choice over how to feel in every moment. You can choose either misery or joy. To the degree that you can begin to accept your learning as neither good nor bad, just Ok, you can learn in a state of curiosity and delight. I encourage you to accept that all learning is Ok, no matter what, and then you can simply have fun while you play the game.

Healing is a Process, Not an Event

While moving through life in alignment with the flow, acting in accord with the will of our soul, and residing in the peace of the Loving is the ultimate goal for a person on the path to enlightenment, it is important that you view moving into this state as an ever-unfolding process. If you are constantly getting down on yourself each time you get out of alignment, it becomes that much more challenging to experience the feeling of actually *being* in alignment. Understand that the periods of being in alignment will increase as you clear away whatever beliefs, patterns of behavior, or judgments you've taken on that have caused you to act out of alignment in the first place. To the degree that you can accept and embrace your own process as a journey of growth, you will be able to choose joy over suffering along your path. For me, knowing that peace was available if I just kept moving forward gave me the incentive to keep going no matter what. The first step to moving into joy within myself was to stop viewing my own process of getting off-course as 'bad'.

No One Can Bypass Their Own Curriculum

There is simply no way to bypass your own curriculum of growth and healing. You can pretend to be done with it, fake being done with it, ignore it, and do your best to avoid it, but until you have actually done the learning and healing you came here to do, your 'stuff' will continue to surface until you deal with it fully. What this means is that even though you may be choosing joy and acting in full alignment with the will of your soul, you will still get triggered up and get thrown off-course each time something from your past surfaces to be healed. There is no way to know when something will get stirred up inside of you, and that is why I highly recommend that you begin to embrace and accept the process; spiritual learning is not always convenient. An issue can surface at the darndest of times. Healing and resolving an issue is often uncomfortable. If you are judging yourself for having an issue brought to your attention for your growth, then you are adding unnecessary judgment to your issue, which simply gives you more judgment to clear.

Getting out of the Pattern of Learning Through Suffering

What I have found over and over again in my work with clients is that most people judge their process. When they go off-course and do not follow their inner guidance or trust in their discernment, they judge themselves as 'bad'. This takes them further away from the Loving they desire because not only do they have to deal with whatever took them off-course, they now have to deal with the self-judgment they are inflicting upon themselves for going off-course. This is what I call learning through suffering. When I judge my own learning, I cause myself tremendous pain and suffering. When I am able to see that it is Ok for me to be learning, that making mistakes is normal, that my learning isn't either 'good' or 'bad', but simply my spiritual curriculum, I am able to learn with grace, ease, joy, and lots of laughter.

For me, labeling my feeling-response as simply a 'barometer' for where I am at any given moment has allowed me the freedom of honoring my own process. It helps to see myself as separate from my feeling-barometer – I am a soul in a body, simply having a human experience of learning and growing. I have feelings to let me know how I'm doing on the learning path, and I exist apart from my feelings. My feelings are simply energy (e-motion: energy in motion), and I can acknowledge them and emote them responsibly. This is a way of detaching from personality-based identification, and allows me to hold the constant knowing of the 'I AM' presence, that I am truly a soul in a body, having a human experience. My feelings are telling me something, they are simply a gauge; I am completely separate from how I feel.

If you feel ready to move out of the right/wrong paradigm into the freedom and acceptance of the Loving paradigm, I encourage you to begin to update your beliefs to reflect your highest level of acceptance of the learning process, knowing that Earth is a school and that we all come here to get through our own unique spiritual curriculum. You are a soul in a body, learning and growing in every given moment. You are sourced with Loving from within and have all of the internal resources necessary, including a wise and beautiful internal guidance system urging you to reach your fullest potential. You can trust yourself to be able to discern your own truth, trust in your ability to learn what is in alignment and what is not, and trust in your capability of learning how to course-correct when you find yourself acting out of alignment with your own soul's will. By accepting yourself completely as you learn, you have the power to heal and grow through joy and laughter. Freedom is your birthright. Now's the time to claim your freedom. You are so worth it.

Exercise: Moving from Right/Wrong into the Loving

Begin by saying a protection prayer, setting conditions of love and light, and invoking spirit's presence.

Place your hands on your heart. Set an intention to access the highest vibration of Loving available. Breathe in the

Loving and fill your body with Loving energies from head to toe. Then, set an intention to access the highest level of compassion. Breathe in compassion and fill your body with compassion from head to toe.

Repeat out loud any of the following that resonates, changing the verbiage as needed to reflect your own beliefs:

"I forgive myself for buying into the irrational belief that there is such a thing as 'right' or 'wrong' from Source's perspective." "My new updated belief is, I now know 'right' or 'wrong' only exist in the fear-based paradigm, and that everything is viewed as simply an opportunity for learning from Source's perspective. Everything that occurs here on planet Earth, no matter what, is Ok from my soul's point of view. I now view everything as learning, accepting that everyone has their own individual curriculum to complete and that all learning is acceptable."

"I forgive myself for buying into the irrational belief that there is a right or a wrong way to do anything." "My new updated belief is, I now know there is an infinite number of ways to do something, and all ways are acceptable from my soul's perspective. I now know that just because I like to do something a certain way doesn't mean that everyone else needs to agree to do it my way. Conversely, just because someone else likes to do something a certain way, it doesn't make me 'wrong' or 'bad' if I don't do it their way. It is Ok for people to do things differently."

"I forgive myself for buying into the irrational belief that I've ever done anything 'wrong' or 'bad'." "My new updated belief is, I now know everything I have ever done has been Ok from my soul's perspective. I have always done the best that I could as I was learning and growing. I trust the knowing that if I could have done anything better at the time, I would have. I trust that I have gained powerful knowledge from my experiences, and that I am a stronger, wiser person for having done what I've done."

"I forgive myself for buying into the irrational belief that I need to continue to feel bad, guilty, or ashamed for something I did in the past." "My new updated belief is, I now know guilt and shame can only result from viewing something as 'bad' or 'wrong'; since there is no such thing as 'bad' or 'wrong', I can simply let go of all feelings of guilt and shame, knowing that I've never done anything wrong. I have always just been learning, and I now allow myself to learn from a place of infinite acceptance."

"I forgive myself for buying into the irrational belief that I need to be punished for the things I've done." "My new updated belief is, I now know I've always been deserving of Loving kindness and respect, in every given moment. Everything I've ever done has been Ok, and all people can be treated kindly as they go through their lessons. Just as I would not punish a baby for learning to walk, I let go of all self-punishment as I'm learning and growing. I treat myself with caring from now on."

"I forgive myself for buying into the irrational belief that it is not Ok for me to make mistakes." "My new updated belief is, I now know mistakes are a normal and natural part of the learning process. It is Ok and fine to make mistakes because we learn through a natural process of trial and error. We retain our learning, and our knowledge builds over a period of time as we gain more and more experience. I can now laugh when I make a mistake and learn through joy."

"I forgive myself for buying into the irrational belief that I need to be viewed as 'good' or 'acceptable' by others in order for me to accept myself." "My new updated belief is, I now know I am innately good; I am a divine soul in a body having a human experience, and I now accept myself fully. I am my own source of acceptance. I now accept myself, no matter what."

"I forgive myself for buying into the irrational belief that if I let go of believing in 'right' or 'wrong,' I won't know what to do." "My new updated belief is, I now know I have an internal guidance system that lets me know which way to go and whether I'm heading on-course or off-course. I trust that I am connected to Source and that I am continually guided to move in the direction of complete alignment with the will of my soul."

"I forgive myself for buying into the irrational belief that I cannot hear or trust in my own inner guidance." "My new updated belief is, I now know learning to hear and trust my inner guidance is a process. It is Ok for me to be learning and growing, and I can simply ask my guidance for more clarity if I feel I don't have enough direction."

"I forgive myself for buying into the irrational belief that I cannot trust my own discernment." "My new updated belief is, I now know I absolutely know my own ring of truth when I hear it. I have excellent discernment that lets me know 'yes' or 'no' inside of myself. All I have to do to connect with my own inner knowing is to ask that place inside of myself that knows my truth."

"I forgive myself for buying into the irrational belief that all things are either true or false and that what is true for me is true for everyone." "My new updated belief is, I now know my truth is relative to where I am in the learning process. Some things that used to feel true for me are no longer my truth in the now, and I am always evolving into higher and higher levels of truth as I grow and expand. And this goes for everyone else, too."

End your process by acknowledging yourself, expressing gratitude for spirit's assistance, and fully grounding your energy. Drink plenty of water.

CHAPTER FOUR
We Each Have Free Will Choice

To experience the vastness of who we truly are, we have been given the gift of free will choice. Planet Earth has been set up as a free will learning environment for humans to experience the opportunity of learning the difference between living out of alignment and living in alignment with the will of their souls. The purpose of the human experience is to remember that we really are loving beings; we are a soul in a body, and we are all one at the level of the Loving. On the soul level, we are already living in alignment with the Loving, connected to, and part of a greater Source. We know at the soul level we are one with all that is. When the soul chooses to incarnate in human form, it opens itself up to learning this truth at a deeper level in a denser, harsher environment. Upon entering the fear-based realm, the soul often takes a back seat while the personality drives the body vehicle. Free will choice allows the personality to drive off the road, drive into the mud pit, or even drive off the edge of a cliff if that's what the personality chooses to do.

If we imagine that the soul's path is driving perfectly straight down the center of the road, the personality will be learning through a process of trial and error how to steer the vehicle in alignment with the will of the soul, which is in turn living in alignment with Loving or living in alignment with God's will. At the beginning of the awakening process, we will often drive off-course, maybe run over the curb, smash into a mailbox or two, or even hit a pedestrian before learning how to stay on the road. The process of learning how to use free will to get into greater alignment with Loving is one of the biggest challenges of this thing called life. If living in alignment with the Loving on planet Earth were a given, there would be no great learning opportunity. Therefore, free will choice is a gift of learning how to come into and stay in alignment with the will of your soul.

Free Will is a Tool to be Mastered

Free will can be likened to a tool or an instrument to be taken up, learned, and finally mastered. Just as learning an instrument takes time and repeated practice to master, learning to use free will in alignment with the will of our soul takes time and practice. And, even after we have reached a very high level of mastery, it is always possible to miss a note. That is part of the beauty of free will choice; it is possible in any given moment to choose to act in an infinite number of ways.

Because we were all born into a fear-based, right/wrong level of reality, most of us felt disempowered as children. We were indoctrinated to believe we had no choice in the matter, whatever issue was at hand. We were raised to believe we had to do as we were told, speak a certain way, act a certain way, look a certain way, and do a certain thing with our lives. The truth is that even as children, we had free will choice. We have always had the freedom to choose our own response at any given moment.

From our soul's perspective, there is no right or wrong choice to make about anything; there are simply opportunities for growth and learning. As part of our curriculum, our soul has certain lessons that it intends for us to complete during each incarnation here on Earth. If, for instance, the lesson is one of power, the individual may choose to be born into a set of life circumstances that create a feeling of powerlessness for that child. The stage will be set for the child to move through certain obstacles or events that will provide the child with an opportunity to move from believing they are powerless into claiming their full authentic power. Lessons are set up in such a way that the person is given repeated opportunities to learn the course material. Perhaps the student needs to hear the material two or three times before they get it. Perhaps the student needs to hear it a dozen, twenty, or even a hundred times, shouted from megaphones or blared out of giant speakers before they get it. Since they have free will choice, they can choose to do the work to complete the lesson swiftly or choose to avoid, ignore, distract, hide, negate, or otherwise deny personal responsibility for that lesson.

One thing we do not have a choice about is experiencing our given curriculum. Our lessons are pre-set at the soul level, and the only way to stop the lessons from repeatedly showing up in our life is to complete the course work and graduate. We absolutely have free will choice about how to respond to our given lessons. While our soul does not judge our response, our own internal guidance system will be letting us know in every given moment whether or not we are on-course or off-course because our soul is absolutely pushing for us to get it.

Destiny vs. Free Will Choice

Our soul has goals to achieve in this lifetime. Destiny can be likened to a spot on the map of our life marked 'soul's destination'. Parts of our life will be 'mapped out', so to speak, with certain opportunities that will present themselves to us to move us closer to our ultimate goal. These spots that are mapped out are often referred to as fate. A moment that was fated to be can often be felt tangibly as a moment of great power. Even in such a moment, a person always has free will to go with the flow and seize the moment, or to turn the other way and simply ignore the opportunity for growth.

Some people are very connected with the will of their soul and jump at each predestined opportunity, quickly moving through their given curriculum and into doing the higher work of their soul. Other people take more time, sometimes needing the same or a similar opportunity to come around several times until they finally take it and move on to the next phase in their journey. By the same token, a person could exercise their free will choice to allow each predestined moment of major opportunity to pass them by, and live their whole life never even coming close to realizing their true potential.

This is a very simplified explanation of how destiny works - there are all sorts of exceptions - yet for the purpose of this teaching, the point I am making here is that a person can miss reaching their own soul's goals completely. Maybe a person sinks into a depression. Rather than taking the opportunity to get out of whatever situation is causing so much suffering, they surrender over to the personality's feelings of despair and commit suicide. Or, maybe the personality has such a strong will that a person simply ignores their soul's urging and lives life with blinders on, staying in fear, blame, and againstness to the point of creating physical level disease, then simply succumbs to the lack of ease rather than addressing the root cause. This happens and is neither 'good' nor 'bad' from the soul's perspective but simply a matter of free will choice in action. People need to know that while they can delay their own learning, there really is no getting around it in the long term. The soul that misses its predetermined goals will have to come back and do it again in another lifetime with another body-vehicle. That is the power and the freedom of the gift of free will choice.

People who believe that every little thing is already predestined and fated to be are at risk of sitting back on their butts like couch potatoes simply waiting for their ship to come dock on their couch. People who believe this might repeatedly miss their own boat. Spirit meets us at our point of action, so if we want anything more to happen in our lives, we must get out there and take some sort of action or movement towards our desire in order to bring on the opportune moment to complete a lesson and move into a higher level of learning.

Have you ever experienced a powerful moment of choice and opportunity in your life that felt like a predestined moment? How did you react to the opportunity? Personally, I was extremely reluctant to begin to follow my predestined path. I resisted many opportunities to up-level time and again. It just seemed too impossible, too big, and too scary. The longer I resisted, the more off-course I went, the more I struggled, the harder and more challenging my life became. My soul had to drag my personality kicking and screaming onto my path; I literally resisted until I was worn down to the bone. I finally surrendered only because I was so sick and tired of struggling. Once I got on-course in my own life, it became easier for me to take the opportunities to move forward as guided. I found that I was always supported by spirit to follow the will of my soul, so I eventually dropped the fear and began eagerly leaping at new opportunities to up-level again and again.

Coming into Alignment with Your Destiny Can Take Time

Sometimes people get very down-hearted, stressed, or upset when they cannot seem to excel or succeed at something. If this sounds familiar, take heart. Is it possible you are not *meant* to do that particular thing at this time? From my own personal experience, I learned that while there were many different things I could potentially do well, each and every time I tried to do something that would derail me from my soul's predestined path, I would experience a sense of failure or falling on my face. Before I came to terms with my true path, I wanted to be a dancer or an artist, not a transformational teacher. Yet any time I tried to make a go of earning a decent living as a dancer or an artist, I would create serious obstacles to my ultimate success. This does not mean that I am a horrible dancer or artist, although I did interpret it that way initially. It simply means that while I have some talent and a definite love of art and dance, my soul has a different agenda for me in this lifetime. It was my fear-based personality that thought I should be a dancer or artist, and I was struggling, pushing, and fighting to go in a direction that was not in alignment with the will of my soul.

What I have discovered is that if I keep my focus on my soul's purpose, I am absolutely allowed to indulge in moments of artistic creativity to fill my soul with joy. But, I was not able to make a go of being a professional artist or dancer because that would have prevented me from arriving at my soul's destination for me in this lifetime, which is about writing these words, teaching the tools of conscious healing, and assisting others with their own personal transformation. Once I understood that we are all equal and that we're all here to express our own uniqueness in different ways, I stopped comparing myself as less-than other artists and other dancers. I can now express myself in these ways to the degree I choose to, and I feel great about myself regardless of whether or not I am sharing these talents, knowing that my skill level at something is not a measure of my intrinsic worth or my equality with every other being.

Wherever you are on your path, know that coming into direct alignment with your destiny can take time. It is a process of trial and error. One way you can make it a little easier on yourself is to let go of getting invested in the outcome when you embark in a new direction. Be willing to try new things, and if the path is clearly closed to you – if you meet up with tremendous resistance – it is simply an indication that that may not be the on-course direction for you to go at this time.

For instance, when I attempted to start making money doing art, it seemed like there were five-hundred-foot walls in front of me at every turn. My path was blocked again and again; every way I turned, I met with enormous resistance. After beating myself up and banging my head against several of the walls for a while, I finally let go of my personal investment in the successful outcome of the venture and said something like, "Oh well, it is obviously not meant to happen. I gave it my best. It is Ok to move on to something else." After that, I learned that you don't even need to waste any time beating yourself up or struggling – you can simply take the information as an indicator of 'off-course' and move on.

When I finally followed my guidance to open my own healing practice, it seemed completely the opposite experience compared to my previous endeavors. People wanted to see me, were excited to schedule a session and wanted to attend my classes… it just flowed. Each and every part of setting up my business simply poured out of me with ease, even though I had some fear-thoughts come up as I moved through each part. After struggling over not having a business card for over fifteen years, the moment I was ready to write the words 'spiritual healing and counseling' on the card, it took me twenty minutes to draw up a logo and order my cards from the printer. A lovely, affordable office appeared within days. My daughter volunteered to build me a website. Before I could even take it all in, I was in business.

Because I got on track with my purpose, my career has flowed ever since. When you are moving in the direction of your soul's purpose, everything will fall into place; the path will open up before you, gates will be lifted, drawbridges will be magically lowered, the dragon at the door will smile in greeting… This is the difference between 'willing' something to happen with your personality and surrendering your will over to the will of your soul. Following the will of your soul feels effortless – there is no pushing, forcing, struggling, or 'trying' energy necessary at all. When you get on-course with your soul's destiny, everything simply unfolds in a natural, divinely-perfect manner with grace and ease. Remember, the universe supports you to do the work of your soul.

After I had come into alignment with my own soul's path, I began to observe other people's journeys. I saw some people who were avoiding their spiritual paths as I had done. I saw quite a few people who had started on their paths, learned just a little bit, and then became stuck, thinking they had arrived at their destination when they had barely begun to scratch the surface. I saw handfuls of people who had fully embraced their paths and were willing to do whatever it took to reach their soul's ultimate destination. And, I saw many, many people who were so entrenched in the outer-level of reality that they would never even begin to admit they had a soul's path… Reflect on the people in your life. You, too, will be able to see people you know who are denying their destiny, afraid of their destiny, moving into their destiny, or already in alignment with their destiny.

When a soul chooses to incarnate in human form, it is giving itself over, in part, to the vessel in which it chooses to reside. Each human vessel contains its own unique personality, which often seems to have a mind of its own. I have seen that the fear-based personality will often make choices that do not allow the soul to fulfill its own destiny. How can this possibly happen, you might ask. It is simply the way that free will is set up; we have the freedom to choose our actions at any given moment. If the personality has a good grip on the wheel, it could decide to take the vehicle way off-course. When this happens, some learning will occur. Still, the soul must incarnate again and give another personality the shot at reaching its destiny before that particular lesson has the potential to be completed.

What this means is that our soul will be urging us to listen to our inner guidance, to go in a certain direction, to follow a certain path, to reach our spiritual goal, and do whatever we are here to do. On the level of the human personality, we have the free will choice to either listen or to ignore our soul's urging. We also have the free will choice to move very slowly or to move rapidly through our lessons and towards our soul's mission in life. What I have found to be true for myself, time and time again is that major pain and suffering result if I willingly and blatantly choose to resist or ignore my soul's guidance toward my spiritual goals.

Consequences of Choices are Equal to Level of Awareness

There is a physical principle that states that for every action, there is an equal, opposite reaction. What this means is that there is always a balance of energies being created in every given moment. In the area of my own free will, to the degree that I willingly and knowingly choose to go against the will of my soul and act out 'willfully' from a place of fear, I will create consequences or lessons that are equal to my level of awareness. This is very much like how our human law works; people are tried and sentenced based upon their own level of willing participation in the incident, whatever the case may be. There are levels of penalties, levels of consequences a person must face, that are judged to be equal to the level of the person's conscious involvement in the situation.

For instance, there are several degrees of murder. A person could expect to get a tougher lesson or sentence if they willfully, purposefully planned to kill another human being – this would be considered 1st-degree murder or premeditated killing. On the other hand, a person who commits murder in self-defense in the spur of the moment is likely to face a lesser sentence or lower level of consequence because they didn't consciously plan to kill anyone – this might be considered 2nd or 3rd-degree murder. A person who was a driver of a car involved in a fatal car accident would likely receive an even lighter sentence or consequence, as there was no ill will involved toward the other party at all – this might be called involuntary manslaughter. A driver who was illegally driving under the influence of drugs or alcohol could expect to receive a tougher sentence or higher level of a consequence than a driver who was sober because the inebriated driver was knowingly putting other peoples' lives at risk by driving while under the influence of a substance known to impair reflexes. So, our spiritual lessons and consequences work in a similar way. Some people call this karma; every action has a consequence, and the consequence is always equal to our level of conscious awareness in relation to each action we take.

I believe that is where the saying 'ignorance is bliss' comes from. Have you ever known anyone who is acting out unconsciously with total disregard for others, the environment, or their own soul's presence? They seem to suffer no consequences from their actions, and if there are some consequences, they seem very small and easily forgotten. This is because until a person has 'woken up', they will only have the capacity to handle a certain low level of awareness. Rest assured that this doesn't mean that they will not have to learn from their actions. When a person has been acting out unconsciously, the lessons are piling up behind them out of sight, just waiting for when the person is awake enough to handle the heavy load of curriculum. We each, always, have to take the consequences of our actions at some point, whether it is in-the-moment or at some later day far, far down the line. This would be the teaching of 'you reap what you sow'. For those who are awake and aware, their tree will bear fruit almost instantly. For others who are still sleeping and unaware of the consequences of their behavior, it may take many years or possibly lifetimes for the fruits of their lessons to appear.

Since you are awake, I encourage you to move into the highest level of personal integrity that you can at this time, as this will immediately begin to alleviate your suffering. The more awareness you attain, the higher the level of integrity you must demonstrate with every step you take, and every choice you make. Suppose you are willfully ignoring your own soul's urging and refusing to follow your inner guidance. In that case, you will be creating an equal level of consequences that may come in the form of pain or suffering or obstacles that cause you a challenge or great difficulty to overcome.

Are you experiencing any significant pain or suffering in your life? If so, this could be a pretty clear indication that you are choosing not to follow the will of your own soul in some way. I encourage you to be willing to take a deep and fearless look at the choices you've been making. Are you listening to your soul's urgings, or are you in resistance to moving forward in your own life? Be honest with yourself. If you have been ignoring your own soul's path up until now, chances are pretty good that you aren't feeling fulfilled or satisfied with your life. The good news is that it is never too late to begin to follow your own soul's guidance.

If you have been following your soul's urgings, are you on track in your life currently? Are you truly fulfilling your soul's purpose? For some of you, you may not yet even know what that is. One way to find out if you are currently on track with your soul's purpose is to ask: Are you working through your issues regularly, working through your spiritual curriculum? Are you stretching yourself to continue to grow and expand? Are you fully utilizing your gifts and talents? Are you satisfied in every area of your life? If your answer to these questions is 'no', you may need to do something different to get yourself on-course with your soul's mission.

You may be right on track and just not know it. It is possible that you are engaged in a learning process and are moving toward fulfilling your soul's purpose. Depending upon your age and level of self-awareness, getting to your life's purpose on the soul level will take varying amounts of time. If you are acting on-course with your destiny, even though you may be experiencing pain and suffering as you move through your curriculum, you will have feeling-level indicators that you are indeed on-course. There will be great joy and celebration accessible between moments of suffering, and life will be getting better and better all of the time. You will have your discernment giving you a clear 'yes' that lets you know you are right on track.

Going too Far Off-Course can Lead to Atrophy

If you have the knowing that you are not dealing with your issues and completing your spiritual curriculum, aren't stretching yourself in any way, aren't utilizing your gifts, feel no real joy, no clear 'yes, I'm on track', and no deep satisfaction in your life, all of that would be an indicator that somehow you may have gotten off-course with your soul's goals for you in this lifetime. People are similar to houseplants; we are either growing or dying.

Do you feel like you are growing or dying? Even if you feel like you are dying, I encourage you to take heart. Houseplants perk right back up when given water and light. Love is your water, and inspiration is your light. If you can connect with your source of Loving and simply begin to follow your inspiration and soul's urgings to grow, you will soon find yourself thriving like the healthiest of plants. Your soul wants you to grow spiritually more than any other thing in this life. Your inner growth is more important than where you live, what you do, how much money you earn, whether or not you have an intimate relationship, what kind of car you drive, or whether or not you even have a car or anything else in the material realm. In fact, your personal growth is the *only* thing that matters from your soul's perspective.

Fulfillment is an Inside Job

Many people worldwide are experiencing a deep knowing that there is more to this life than simply outer-level, physical, or material goals. Yet most of us were raised to believe that our happiness was based on attaining a specific set of outer circumstances – completing a certain degree, having money in the bank, finding a spouse, keeping a dependable job, owning property, or whatever outer symbol of success was deemed popular at the time. The reality is that a person could have all of those material things and still be terribly dissatisfied with their life. Another person could have none of those things and be completely content on the spiritual level, as long as they follow their soul's deepest urgings. Access to joy and personal fulfillment is inside us, flowing from our Source, and has nothing to do with external reality. Real, lasting joy and satisfaction only come when a person aligns themselves with the will of their soul and begins to follow the path toward their soul's ultimate destination.

Do you have access to pure joy? Do you feel fully content and satisfied in every moment regardless of what is going on in your outer world? Or, do you base your happiness on what is going on in your outer life or how much 'stuff' you currently have?

Because money can't buy love or cause a person to fulfill their own spiritual destiny upon the planet, some spiritual teachings have advocated denouncing or abstaining from all things material. Maybe it might be easier to achieve alignment with the will of our soul and, in turn, the will of God if we simply didn't involve ourselves in the trappings of the material world. The idea is that if we'd just give up dealing with wealth, property, sex, and relationships – take a vow of poverty and abstinence – we'd be that much closer to God. If we could somehow limit our own free will choice, it would be likelier for us to choose to act in alignment.

Understand that this is an ancient idea that came about during a time in which people had very weak wills, there was more fear and lack upon the planet, and alignment with the will of the soul was much more difficult to achieve. If you know that abstaining is part of your soul's path, go for it. Conversely, if you have been confused or struggling with that particular teaching, I encourage you to simply let it go and begin to follow your joy. We are at a place of human evolution in which our wills are now strong enough to participate fully in life on every level while still achieving all of our soul's goals. Not only can we achieve complete alignment while being fully engaged in life, but it is also imperative that as many of us model that as possible. How else are the masses who are currently enmeshed in the physical level of reality going to wake up and move out of the right/wrong paradigm into living in alignment with the Loving?

Denying all of the physical things in life can cause a person to miss out on all of the invaluable growth and learning opportunities that the physical aspects of life have to offer. It is accurate that there is a very small percentage of the population whose soul's purpose is to do nothing except hold in a higher state of being – to hold the vision of peace and energies of higher consciousness – in order to make them available so that the largest percentage of humanity can make the paradigm shift. These are the monks and masters who sit in silent meditation on mountaintops at various points strategically located around the globe. However, the majority of souls are needed to participate in the full physicality of the planet. We are, after all, a soul in physical form. Our purpose is to be fully integrated with the will of our soul– this means in complete alignment with God, Humankind, and Nature – while still in physical form. This entails embracing our physical world rather than denying it and bringing each aspect of our physical reality into spiritual alignment. To move forward as a collective into the Loving, our job, literally, is to create heaven on Earth. We have the ability to achieve mastery at the game of life, and this means we can master each and every part of it, including and not limited to experiencing prosperity, intimate relationships, sex, delicious food, material possessions, or any other area at the highest level, in harmony and balance with all things. We can have a full outer-level reality of physical engagement in the material world – as a true expression of divine form in action – while having our will align completely with the will of our soul on every level of being.

Source-energy Wants Us to Have Everything Our Heart Desires

The beautiful and fabulous truth is that Source-energy wants us to have everything in this life that our heart desires. Our soul wants us to experience life fully, to live in full color in every moment. We are co-creators with Source, and the Earth-plane is a canvas upon which we are here to paint. Spirit rejoices for us to create freely, to live in joy, prosperity, and success, as long as it is in the highest good of the planet and all concerned. When we act in our own highest good, it is automatically connected to all that is and therefore naturally in alignment with the highest good of all concerned. Understand that your heart's desires and soul's desires will be very different from old, personality-based, or fear-based desires that many are still seeking. Only the unconscious personality is interested in the destruction of nature and our planet; only fear is a motivation for war, the widespread use of chemicals, mass consumption, manipulating nature, and poisoning our bodies and planet. If we, as a collective, want to heal our planet and avoid early termination as a species, we need to get involved, take personal responsibility, become love and rational thinking in action. Now is the time to choose. Feel free to choose to follow your bliss. When you follow your bliss, this usually leads directly onto the path that is in right-alignment with the will of your soul.

What do you most love to do? What brings you the deepest feeling of satisfaction in your life? What brings you the most joy? If you are using and following your internal guidance system, it will be leading you toward doing more and more of that thing that lights you up, whatever that may be, in your life. When you are following your path towards your own destiny, you will feel a deep sense of personal satisfaction, an internal knowing of heading in the direction that is in your own highest good.

Wherever you are upon your own, unique path, knowing that you have free will choice along the way can be both empowering and scary at the personality level. Some people seem to be able to ignore their soul's will without a single qualm, and others agonize over each and every choice they have to make. How we relate to ourselves internally says a lot about where we are on our own learning path. Once we have claimed our source of Loving, internalized the knowledge of our own intrinsic worth, and come to see the irrationality of viewing things from the rigid fear-based perspective of right/wrong reality, we can begin to use the tool of our own free will choice to assist us in moving into greater alignment with the will of our soul.

How Free Will Choice Works

Here's how free will choice works: You make a choice. There are natural consequences that occur as an outcome of your choice. You will like, feel neutral, or won't like the outcome, so your internal barometer will register certain feelings towards your results, which you can then evaluate as information. Based on your experience, you will learn something. You now have more knowledge to help yourself make your next choice.

From the place of free will, there is an infinite number of choices to make at any given moment. There are no right or wrong choices, only whichever choice we make and its natural outcome. No matter which way we choose in any situation, learning will result. The game is set up to guide us toward the completion of our soul's lessons so that we may fulfill our soul's destiny. When we act out of alignment with our soul's will, we will register a feeling-level response that can range from mildly unpleasant to excruciatingly painful to let us know we've gone off-course. When we choose to act in alignment with the will of our soul, life will feel peaceful and joy-filled on the inside, and we'll feel good about our choices.

Temptation: A Natural Part of Free Will Choice

But what fun would the game be without a little extra challenge? Our Earth-plane reality has been set up so that our free will choice will also come with urgings that are in direct opposition to the urgings of the will of our soul. This personality-based urging is what is known as temptation. Temptation is often illustrated as a little devil perched upon a person's shoulder, while the voice of the soul is the angel on the other. While this image can be humorous, it is locked in good/bad, right/wrong reality. What is really taking place for us as humans is neither good nor bad, and our choices are not always so clear-cut.

Instead of picturing temptation as a little devil, I like to imagine temptation as a tray holding very rich, enticing foods that aren't really that good for me. This tray will be passed right under my nose by an invisible server during the party of life. The foods on the tray may look very appealing. They may even smell delicious. But deep down, I always have the knowledge that if I eat from that tray, I'm not going to feel very good. Those foods will give me anything from a stomach ache to a major bout of food poisoning, depending upon what the choices are and how much I eat. I absolutely know that I will feel much better about myself and stay much healthier if I can simply resist the urge to reach for what is on the tray.

How do I know those foods aren't good for me? Naturally, I've tried them before! That is usually the way we humans learn – from personal experience. Once I tasted the foods from the tray of temptation, I had the experiential knowing that they made me sick. However, sometimes by the time I became aware of how a particular food made me feel, I was well and fully hooked on it. The challenge for me then was to learn to care enough about my own health and well-being that I was able to gather the strength to pull away from the lure of the unhealthy food.

Temptation can be viewed simply as a test to pass. If we ignore the will of our soul and go with the impulse to give in to the tempting, personality-based choice, we will experience some sort of pain or suffering as a direct result – this is our feeling-barometer's way of letting us know we are off-course. We absolutely will have the same platter of temptation pass by for another test, sometimes dozens or hundreds of times. It is as if the server of that particular tray learns of our craving and comes by more often asking, "Would you like another taste of this one?" The server is simply eager to please and will not stop passing that tray in front of our nose until we make it clear that we no longer want any part of what is on it. Only when we are very firm will the server of that particular tray leave us alone. When we clearly say no to temptation and make a choice to act in alignment with the will of our soul, that test will be successfully passed and we will move on to the next lesson, which will likely bring on a new server with a different tray of enticing, slightly less unhealthy choices.

When a person is just beginning to awaken to themselves as a soul in a body, learning and growing, discerning the difference between temptation and our soul's will can be a tricky thing. Some tips to consider: temptation will usually bring only short-term relief to whatever issue is at hand and will derail a person from heading in the direction they really want to go. Temptation will almost always be urging a person to settle for something less than what they really want. Temptation will guide a person to postpone or avoid taking action toward fulfilling their deepest goals and dreams, bringing on more pain and suffering. Temptation will be sly, slick, and cunning, often sounding totally reasonable and practical. Temptation will always be fear-based, even if no actual fear-energy seems to be present.

Let's look at some typical examples of the temptations that many people face. A person who is quitting an addiction may be faced daily with hearing in their own mind, "You know you want that drink/cigarette/drug right now." A person who is committed to getting into better shape may hear, "Go ahead, eat it! It will taste great, and you'll feel much better. Come on, what harm is one doughnut going to do?" The woman recovering from abusive relationships may hear, "So he's a little insensitive. You can't expect perfection, and would you rather end up alone?" The person who is ready for a new career may get a less-than-ideal job offer and hear, "So what if it's not what you really want. You'll never get a better offer than this. You could be secure for life…" and so on. The person addicted to sex will be faced with more sex, the person addicted to gambling with more chances to roll the dice, the debtor the opportunity to go deeper into debt, the workaholic with more opportunities for work, the codependent with more people to help, the sugar addict with a box full of chocolates, and so on – all for the purpose of reminding us that it needs to be under our own free will power that we overcome any obstacle and pass the tests of our given curriculum.

Understand that our subconscious mind will be freaking out at the up-leveling we are ready to take and will do everything in its power to keep us small, safe, and comfortable at whatever frequency our current level of energy or comfort zone resides. We must make a choice to change in order for our lives to begin to change for the better.

The Gift of Free Will Choice is a Gift that Keeps on Giving

Not only do we need to make one choice to change, but we also need to decide over and over and over again to keep choosing to make that same choice because we have free will choice in *every* given moment. As an example, what happens for someone typically looks something like this: a person who has the behavior of overeating may decide one day to change their unhealthy eating patterns. They may say, "I am going to change; from now on, I am only having one serving of food instead of two or three." That night at dinner, they will say 'no' to seconds. They may successfully say no to seconds for a week or two. Until one night, there will be a special holiday dinner or a favorite meal. The platter of temptation will come on a little stronger and say, "Are you *sure* you don't want another helping? It's your favorite… Come on, it's going to taste *so* good. Just this once…" This is the personality's way of attempting to pull the person back into the old, fear-based comfort zone, and the soul's way of testing someone's resolve.

If a person has not yet claimed the power of their free will choice, they may give in to the temptation to let go of their goal, falling back into the old pattern of overeating. They will end up feeling bad about themself, saying self-defeating things like, "I have no will-power. That didn't work. I never keep my promises. I can't help it." The person will then need to choose again to change to be stronger than temptation and the subconscious mind's urge to self-sabotage, or they will spiral downhill again. Then they will continue the unhealthy pattern of overeating until they either die or get so tired of themselves that they gather the strength to attempt to change the pattern once again somewhere down the line.

Free will choice can be likened to the laundry or dirty dishes – they are both never-ending! I recall how bewildered I felt when I first had dominion over my own environment as a teenager in my first apartment. How did those new dirty dishes appear on the counter when I had just washed them? And the laundry just continued to grow, seemingly no matter how many times I did another load. It was mystifying. I thought these things were *done*, finished in a final kind of way, and yet I quickly discovered that they were part of an ongoing process that needed my constant and repeated attention. At first, I tried to ration my attention by saying to myself, "I will clean and do laundry once a week – every Sunday." My apartment was a disaster zone by Wednesday; by Thursday, there were no clean dishes, and on Friday, I had no clean clothes to wear. Very quickly, I came to see that a tiny little bit of attention, frequently applied to the dishes or laundry, was actually much easier to maintain than doing mountains of work once a week. I also discovered that I liked living in a clean, neat apartment better than a messy one. By choosing to do the dishes and the laundry regularly and resisting the temptation to let them slide, I learned the process of personal upkeep.

Using the tool of free will choice to resist the temptation to settle takes constant, ongoing attention, and upkeep. Just like deciding to do the dishes or laundry only once a week takes more work and effort than deciding to do the dishes once a day or after each meal, so does deciding to do just about anything infrequently require more effort than doing it habitually. Let's look at a few examples. Take an easy one – tooth brushing. Brushing and flossing your teeth several times a day makes the upkeep of teeth-cleaning much easier. People who only brush occasionally have to go through torture at the dentist's office to get all of the buildup scraped off of their teeth.

How about exercising? Many of you can likely relate to this next example. A few years ago, I felt somewhat out of shape and became determined to do something differently to improve my physical level of fitness. I would go to a yoga class or go for a long walk, and I would be panting within the first 15 minutes of exertion. It felt hard because I hadn't done it in such a long time. The next day, I'd be sore all over and make dozens of excuses to myself about why I couldn't exercise. Giving in to the temptation to skip my new workout plan was easy. The next day, I'd miss it again, telling myself I'd make up for it tomorrow. Suddenly, two weeks would fly by, and I'd realize I hadn't kept my commitment to exercise regularly. I'd renew my resolve, go to yoga the next day, start panting and get sore again, and repeat the whole cycle all over again. Because I didn't stick it out long enough to build any stamina, each time I exercised felt as hard as the last. I had to repeat this pattern for several months before I could find the strength to decide to ignore the temptation to skip and really get committed to building my level of physical fitness. Once I got more committed to a regular routine, it became easier to make a choice each time to actually do the exercise.

Think about it; the word 'pattern' implies something that repeats itself over and over again – the pattern of wallpaper, the pattern on the tile border, the pattern of numbers… So, to create a new behavior pattern, we first must be willing to repeat the new behavior a few times in a row before a regular pattern can become established. This requires saying 'no' to the temptation to continue to repeat the old pattern and a level of commitment and resolve towards cultivating the new one. You can do it. Trust me, your will is stronger than you may think.

The tricky thing about temptation is that if you give into it just once, allowing it to sabotage your intention to change, it will be on to you and get even stronger the next day and the next. Sometimes people just give in because they feel worn down by it. Understand this: you are not your tempting thoughts! You are not the parts of your personality that are still residing in fear and wish to hold you back or keep you small. You are a separate being, and temptation actually holds no power over your free will choice. You are absolutely strong enough to say 'no' to temptation, to say 'no' to fear every time. You have the full power of free will choice to choose what you want and know what is in your own highest good at every moment!

Have you ever given in to the voice of temptation? I hope you were honest with yourself and said 'heck yes' because I've never met anyone who hasn't. In fact, I've never met anyone who hasn't hundreds of times. If you are human, you will experience the temptation to settle for less than what you really want. You will be enticed to stay small, safe, secure, and comfortable out of fear when, in fact, your soul is urging you to play it big, bold, loud, and expansive.

Temptation isn't Bad; it's Simply Part of the Free Will Package

From the soul's perspective, a temptation is not a bad thing. Temptation is part of the tool package that goes along with having the gift of free will choice. See, here's the thing: without temptation, the human experience would be too easy. If we just made a decision to change and simply chose one time and a major change occurred, we wouldn't really have to expend any effort. Everything worth having comes with a price attached, and the price of change costs whatever it takes for us, personally, to stick to our resolve. Temptation is a neutral party, simply acting as a sign-post along the way. Maybe it can be likened to having the server ring up your tab at the end of that day's party; if you surrendered your will over to your personality by giving in to the temptation to settle, you have to then pay the price because it will cost you extra effort to renew your own resolve. If you say 'no' to temptation, there is no tab to pay, and you simply pass that sign-post that says 'I'm sticking to my resolve to change this pattern'.

You will notice with any old pattern that the platter of temptation will come by several or even many times after you have said no before it will drop off entirely. This is simply your soul's way of checking in to see if you are really over it, whatever 'it' may be. Once you say 'no' clearly, usually three or four times in a row, you will experience a strengthening inside that comes with the knowing that you cannot be tempted by that particular thing anymore. Sometimes, if we are clearing a chronic or long-term pattern, such as drinking alcohol or using a drug, we may be faced with many different scenarios that ask us, "What about now?" or, "How about under these circumstances?" When this happens, I'm often reminded of the Dr. Seuss book, Green Eggs and Ham – "Would you, could you, in a house, with a mouse? In a boat, with a goat? On a train or in the rain?" No matter how ridiculously strong the temptation may appear, it is simply a matter of saying 'no' for long enough to allow the pattern to shift. As long as a person clearly refuses the temptation to settle for going back to the old behavior, the temptation will gradually fall away.

My Story of Letting Go of the Temptation to Settle

For years I gave into temptation in my relationships, settling for uncaring, disconnected, dysfunctional, unhealthy, emotionally abusive, and sometimes even deceitful relationships where I'd find myself thinking limiting things like, "This is the best I can do," "He needs me," "No one else would want to be with me," and my all-time favorite, the classic, "I made a *vow*, and I will keep it no matter what." Once I let go of the limiting beliefs and committed to following the will of my soul, I was guided to say no to anything less than everything my heart desired in my partnership. This was a radically different approach to relationship for me, as in my past, I'd simply gone with whichever man first asked me out. As a result of that clever strategy, I had two divorces under my belt and was determined to do it differently the third time around.

To prepare myself for a healthy, committed, deeply spiritual relationship, I took a year off of dating and spent the time figuring out what I really wanted in a relationship. I made a list of all of the qualities I wanted in my partner, then I embodied each one fully. When I felt ready, I asked for spirit's assistance and read my list out loud to the Universe. Within days I was asked out on my first date. The man was lovely, yet I immediately knew that I would be settling for less than what I really wanted if I said yes when he asked to see me again. I was able to say no, and even stuck with it when the man expressed his objections. The following week, I met another man, and he presented an even bigger temptation than the last. He was a musician, a writer, spiritually aware... he had so many qualities that I admired and wanted in a partner, including kindness, warmth, humor, excellent communication skills, self-reflection, desire to grow, and more. He was attractive to me in almost every way, and he seemed very interested in seeing me again. The only conflict I could see was that he had shared that he had an intensely demanding career that created periods of significant stress in his life, and part of my vision was to have plenty of time together with my partner free of stress. I really felt ready to live in peace at that point in my life, and my soul urged me not to settle in any way. Saying no to seeing that man again was one of the tipping points in my life.

The third time the platter of temptation came by with another man that didn't match my vision, it was much easier for me to say no immediately. Spirit got the message that I was not going to settle, and I met my next partner, Marc, two weeks later, exactly thirty days from when I'd asked for spirit's assistance with finding myself a committed spiritual partner. Marc fully embodied every quality I had been seeking, and I had a resounding 'Yes! He's the one' ring throughout my consciousness the moment our eyes met. And he was the right one for me for the next ten years. Having had a conscious relationship with this man was one of the most rewarding parts of my entire life experience thus far. I am so grateful that I did not give in to the temptation to settle for less than what I really wanted in my love relationship.

To Change a Pattern, Just Say No to Temptation

Once a person understands how temptation works, it becomes easier and easier to simply laugh and say 'no' to temptation when it arises. Know that if you decide to change any particular pattern of behavior, whatever it may be, you will be called upon internally to restate that decision, to support that decision over and over again as you permanently change that pattern for the better. You can do it!

How do you know you are done changing an old pattern? When the temptation to sink back into the old pattern no longer presents itself regularly, you can rejoice and know that you are firmly anchored in your new, healthier pattern of behavior.

Temptation Never Goes Away; it Just Becomes More Subtle

Understand that no matter how enlightened you become, no matter how evolved on the learning journey, no matter how aligned you become with the will of your soul, temptation will always be a part of your free will choice package. However, it will certainly pass by less frequently. As you say no to the more obvious temptations, the platter of temptation will simply become more and more refined, more subtle to discern.

Let me give you an example of the level of temptation which I have faced in my own life. I've been blessed to make my own work hours as a healing facilitator, yet I have struggled with finding the right balance between how many hours to work and which times to schedule. My soul was urging me to write a book. But when I focused solely on writing during the day, I would suddenly have clients calling me for late evening appointments, say from 8:00pm-11:00pm. If I gave in to the temptation to do a client session that late, I would be buzzing from all the Loving energies until at least 1:00am. If I didn't get enough sleep, I would sleep in late the next day and miss out on most of my morning writing time. If I forced myself to wake up at my normal time, I'd feel tired and cranky from lack of sleep and be unproductive. I felt better physically when I got a solid night's sleep, so I knew it was in my own highest good to see my clients earlier and be done with work by evening so that I could begin to wind down to fall asleep at a reasonable time. Knowing getting to bed early was in my best interest, I set the intention to up-level my self-care so that I was getting plenty of sleep nightly and creating a new pattern of regular early rising. As soon as I set the intention to uplevel, the Universe began testing my resolve, "Would you, could you?" over and over again.

At first, I resolved the temptation to see late clients pretty easily by letting go of renting an external office space. Without an office, I could only see clients in person in my home, so it was a simple matter of letting clients know that evening times were no longer available as my family was home. But then tricky temptation came around with several clients who lived in other states…. I did my out-of-town sessions over the phone, so the fact that my family was home at night didn't necessarily mean I couldn't speak over the phone. I gave in to temptation a few times, did a few late phone sessions, paid the server's price by feeling very tired and cranky the next day, and had to firm up my resolve to say 'no' next time.

I said no a few times, rescheduling those phone clients to daytime hours, so then the platter became even more tempting, "What about in this case? Would you, could you?" I now had several clients with young children saying, "The *only* time that will possibly work for me is after the children are asleep. Please can we do 8:00pm? I won't be able to schedule with you otherwise." When this occurred, the lingering dredges of my people-pleasing part of my personality whispered, "You have to say yes! It is your job to assist them," while the voice of my soul simply reminded me that the only way I would be able to create the life and schedule of my dreams was if I refused to settle in any way for less than what I truly desired.

I will admit that I gave into temptation to have late sessions for several years before I finally had the ongoing willpower to say no to working with clients after 6:00pm. I simply continued to forgive myself, knowing that I am a work-in-progress, just like everyone; we are each doing the best we can in every given moment, and we will always have some level of temptation testing us no matter where we are on our journey. What I know from experience is that each time I am really ready for a better quality of life, I will refuse to settle in any way for less than what I truly desire, and that is when I'll take another up-leveling once and for all. I can do it, and so can you.

Temptation Includes the Occasional Pop Quiz

Have you ever been chopping vegetables and had the random thought flit by, "I could cut off my finger if I wanted to," or maybe be walking by a cliff and think, "I could just jump right off that edge," or even, "I could push so-and-so right over that edge"? Some people get all freaked out by these types of random thoughts, worried that they are going nuts or something. Not to worry. This is just another example of free will choice in action. Sometimes our soul presents us with pretty drastic options, like a pop quiz just to check in to see how we're doing. Are we on track, clear about the direction we're going right now? If so, we simply say, "No, thanks," and just let that thought go. I highly encourage laughing at this type of thought – laughter dissipates the energy instantly. At other times, if a fear-based thought that seems totally random pops into our mind, we may simply be picking up on other people's negativity or fear-energy. Remember, we are all one at the level of consciousness, so we will often unknowingly tune in to someone else's fear-based thoughts. If you hear a thought that doesn't feel like your own, just let it pass with no attachment. These kinds of thoughts don't have the power to upset your peace. Remember, you are *not* your thoughts.

People who actually entertain the idea of saying "Yes, Ok, I'll do that" to the random, bizarre-type of tempting thoughts that occasionally flow through their minds will definitely receive more of these types of thoughts. This would be spirit's way of saying, "Really? Are you sure you'd really do that if given a choice? Ok, how about *this*?" And, sadly, sometimes people with very weak will actually do listen and act upon some of these types of derailing thoughts. The next time you hear the story of the mother who drove her kids off the bridge or whatever shockingly bizarre scenario, just send compassion to all of the souls involved, and give thanks that you've achieved your own level of strength with the usage of the tool of free will.

You Always Have the Power to Choose Your Highest Good

Wherever you are currently in your life in regards to temptation and free will choice, it is vital to claim your own power to choose your own response in any given circumstance. The truth is you always have the power to choose to act in your own highest good. To do this, you may need to let go of old beliefs that have empowered a source outside of yourself. For instance, many religions teach that temptation comes from the devil or is evil. The idea that there may be some negative force outside of yourself that is stronger than you are is a cop-out. Using 'the devil made me do it' as an excuse is a way to deflect personal responsibility and serves no one to entertain.

In addition, since most of us have given in to temptation a few times (Ok, a few hundred or a few thousand times), the ideas that we are sinners, are 'bad', and are going to hell are all ideas that do not serve us to continue to hold if we desire to change and grow. If we believe we have already been consigned to hell for our sins, why would we need to strive to do better? Conversely, if we believe that all we need do is give our power over to some religious figure or certain organization, and we are guaranteed a spot in heaven, we will be giving in to the temptation to settle all over the place and simply expecting that everything is magically going to change because we are on the 'saved' list.

This used to drive me crazy as a child. I was raised Catholic, and I could not comprehend the way my own parent could listen to the priest on a Sunday, spend the entire week doing everything the priest said not to do, and then take communion again the following Sunday, knowing all was forgiven, simply to do it all over again another week. There was a completely irrational idea being perpetrated that people didn't have to be held accountable for their own actions as long as they believed they were saved and went to church.

Since growing older, I have heard of dozens of churches where people are told they are 'saved' just by getting baptized into the church and signing on the dotted line as a member. I've heard of spiritual figure-heads who claim that they can clear their followers' karma for them as if the student doesn't have to lift a finger to complete their own spiritual curriculum. I have heard certain religions claim that if you just do x, y & z, your soul will be forever saved. I have listened to religious figure-heads claiming that certain people or even whole groups of people will be eternally damned for not doing x, y & z. Let me clearly state that from the Loving perspective, all of that is what I would call fear-based, irrational dogma and has no place in real spiritual transformation. The truth is that each of us needs to be personally accountable for our choices, clearing our own baggage, and completing our own lessons in order to move into alignment with the will of God.

Definition of Sin from the Loving Perspective

From our Source's perspective, mistakes, mishaps, missteps, and falls are all a natural and necessary part of the growth process. Let's get real; if we were already able to do everything perfectly on the first try, what would be the purpose of Earth School? We are here to learn and grow, and learning takes place through an experiential process that includes learning by observing others as well as learning by doing. The doing of anything new usually includes a great deal of trial and error. Learning is not neat and tidy; learning involves tripping, falling, spilling things, making messes, and cleaning them up. My understanding is that the word 'sin' as used in the Bible came from the Greek language and was an archery term that meant landing 'off the mark'. So, in the process of learning, we may begin by aiming in the wrong direction entirely. We may land well off-the-mark on our first few tries, maybe even dozens or hundreds of attempts. However, our soul will be urging us on, whispering directions to us in the form of our intuition, gut feelings, or instincts. Each time we take aim and take another action if we are persistent and willing to follow our soul's instructions, we will get closer and closer to hitting our soul's intended goal or mark.

Landing off-the-mark is never a bad thing, from the spiritual perspective; it is simply an opportunity for growth and learning. I think there have been certain behaviors or attitudes that have been labeled as 'sins' in certain spiritual teachings in order to assist human-kind with becoming more aware and getting back into alignment with the will of our souls. Certain behaviors are going to take us further off-course than others and will cause us more internal pain and suffering as a result. Things like adultery, stealing, lying, murdering, cheating, acting out in vengeance, greed, gluttony, jealousy, coveting, and so on are human experiences that are typically filled with lots of pain for the learner if they give in to the temptation to choose these options. This doesn't mean that a person won't need to go through them to learn and grow. Remember, I only learned that the platter of tempting foods made me ill *after* I ate from it repeatedly.

Sometimes, no matter what excellent advice a person hears cautioning them against a certain behavior, a person just needs to do the painful behavior themselves in order to get it and grow. So, regardless of whether or not these behaviors appear on a list of commandments or deadly sins, if any of these behaviors are part of a soul's curriculum to overcome, then it only follows that the soul will have to have some sort of experience in those areas in order to overcome whatever obstacles are presented to pass that lesson. And, so, to 'sin' or land off-the-mark is neither 'good' nor 'bad' from the soul's perspective; it is simply accepted as a natural and normal part of the human experience.

This by no means implies that everyone should run out and lie, cheat, murder, rape, steal, or commit adultery on purpose just because it is all Ok from the soul's point of view.

That would be very silly, since the further off-the-mark we land, the more internal pain and suffering we experience as a result. When these types of lessons occur before we are consciously aware enough to stop ourselves, they are usually important course-work in our spiritual curriculum. If you have ever had personal experience with any of these types of painful lessons, you will have learned a tremendous amount of invaluable information. Everything that occurred for you will have assisted you in your awakening process, bringing you to a higher level of awareness, acceptance, compassion, and so on.

And, if you have engaged in any of the so-called 'deadly sins' or broken any of the ten commandments in the past, if you haven't already done so, I would strongly encourage you to spend some time sending compassionate self-forgiveness to your younger self via your memories. You can hold the knowing that if you could have done it any better at the time, you would have. You did the best you could at that time, given your level of awareness. Flood yourself with compassion, making it all Ok until there are no longer any parts of yourself that are stuck in shame and suffering.

Doing things we know will create tremendous suffering unconsciously from a perspective that is still lacking in that particular awareness is one thing; willfully choosing to engage in any of these things consciously is another. Since our soul is always aiming for the bulls-eye of Loving, it would not be in our own highest good to purposefully choose to head in a direction that will knowingly create more pain and suffering for all involved. And yet, sometimes in a person's life, that is precisely what we choose to do – purposefully, willfully, and knowingly head in the opposite direction of our soul's urgings. When this happens, we end up in hell.

Hell is a State of Mind and is Completely Optional

From my own personal experience, I have learned that hell is of a person's own making. I was in my own state of hell a few different times in my life, and I have to say that the best advice I ever heard was something I read on a T-shirt I bought for my former partner, Marc, that said, "If you find yourself in Hell, keep going." ~ Winston Churchill. This is excellent advice and, in fact, the only real solution. Hell is an experience of feeling a complete separation from Source, which includes feelings of tremendous suffering, pain, self-judgment, doubt, fear, and despair. It feels as if you have been placed into total darkness, cut off from God/Loving, your own soul, and the source of all light. It feels totally hopeless, as if you have been abandoned and cast out into a dark pit to rot, alone. Finding yourself in hell is neither good nor bad from the spiritual perspective; it is just one particular place or state along the path of your journey. Understand that there is no condemning or judgmental God that has put you in this place. It is only your own behavior and your own self-judgment that has gotten you there.

Earlier, I talked about the consequences of our behavior as being equal to the level of conscious awareness involved when choosing to go against the knowing of our internal guidance system. To get to the true depths of hell, I discovered that I had to *knowingly* and *willfully* go against my inner guidance, my own feeling-barometer, and my own discernment of the truth of what was in alignment for me at that time. When I willfully decided to ignore what I knew to be my on-course direction and instead chose to jump off-course in a direction that was definitely, clearly, and even blatantly going against my highest good, this is when the consequences I experienced as a result of my choice became the toughest; I found myself burning in a hell of my own making.

Landing in Hell is not Wrong or Bad, It is Simply Experience

Landing in hell somewhere along your life's journey is neither right nor wrong, nor good or bad. It is simply one experience in the full spectrum of free will choice. You could liken it to having your ball end up in the swamp during a game of golf; while you are screaming, cursing, and loathing yourself for your poor aim, your soul is just neutrally observing with detachment on the outcome and feels only compassion towards you whether you wallow in your apparent failure for hours or get over it and move on.

Or, a state of hell may be like finding yourself in a particularly challenging level of a video game where there is a level of difficulty which you've never previously encountered; you may be wondering, "Am I going to be able to survive this?" Your video character may need to crash and burn a few times, maybe even die and start all over again from level one. That is Ok in the video game, and it is Ok in life, too. And, while you may feel like it will kill you, once you are conscious, you do not need to die in a state of hell. You just need to start climbing up out of the dark pit into the light.

Know that no matter what sort of hell you've gotten yourself into, you *will* be able to get through it and get back on track again. If you are currently experiencing an internal state of hell, do not despair! Yes, you can survive and overcome this if you begin to choose what's in your highest good.

A State of Hell is Only Temporary

A state of hell is never permanent. Like in our current penal system, you can get a lighter sentence and early release for good behavior. The faster you can forgive yourself and begin to be gentle with yourself, the faster you will be released from your internal state of hell. Conversely, if you get so down on yourself that you simply keep perpetuating punishment with your self-judgment and negative self-talk, you could very well stay imprisoned for life. Understand that this is a *choice*. If this were to happen, and you willingly chose to perpetuate your self-inflicted punishment and stay in a state of hell, your soul would have to work toward freedom in another lifetime.

All paths lead to God, although some may take a while longer than others. If you find yourself in a hell of your own making, I say choose joy over suffering by doing these two things right now: choose internal freedom, which means stop inflicting the self-punishment by being kind and gentle toward yourself, and say 'no' to temptation by choosing a healthier behavior. By doing so, you will be choosing to align yourself with your own soul's will, which will direct you straight out of hell and accelerate you on your personal path to self-actualization.

Heaven is a State of Mind and is Completely Optional

Just as we can get ourselves out of a state of hell if we don't wish to reside there anymore, we also have the freedom to choose to reside in a state of heaven at any time. Getting into hell is much easier, as it is readily available in the fear-based, right/wrong paradigm. Giving in to temptation requires no strength of will, and once we give in a few times, it becomes easier and easier to continue down the slippery slope into the hell of our own separation from Source. Choosing to reside in a state of heaven requires a much stronger will. It requires making the free will choice to make the paradigm shift from living in fear into living in the Loving on absolutely every level of being – which, by the way, includes living in full alignment with God, humans, and Nature.

The state known as heaven on Earth will be available to anyone who chooses joy and freedom over misery and suffering and embraces unity for all forms of life. We will create that state as a collective as soon as enough individuals make a choice to uplevel into the Christ Consciousness. Getting there requires dropping all againstness towards anyone or anything. A while ago, I heard a heartwarming story of a group of Christians with signs at a Gay Pride parade that read, "We are so sorry for having judged you in the past," "Jesus Loves All," "Judge Not," and more along those lines. The people from that church are absolutely heading in the right direction. Heaven is a state of perfect peace, with infinite acceptance of All That Is, which includes living in harmony with nature. Don't worry about how that part will come about. Your first priority is to get yourself aligned with the will of your soul.

Most importantly for you to understand right now, the state of heaven includes residing in a state of *innocence*; in order to experience heaven on Earth, we first need to let go of all shame, blame, guilt, and self-judgment, coming back to the innocence of the child, knowing that each of us is simply learning and growing as a soul in a body.

If you're familiar with Christianity, you may have heard this quote from the Bible, which refers to the second coming of Christ: "To those who eagerly wait for Him He will appear a second time, apart from sin, for salvation" (Hebrews 9:28 NKJV) Notice how this time Christ is appearing on the planet 'apart from sin'. My translation and experiential knowing: Christ Consciousness is a state of innocence. To reside there, we must up-level from the fear-based consciousness into the higher level of Christ Consciousness, also referred to as the Christos.

The Difference between Religion and Spirituality

On the ever-rising spiral of consciousness, religion, or practices based on fear, intimidation, exclusivity, againstness, and rigid right/wrong thinking reside at the base of the spiral of consciousness. The more fear-based the beliefs, the smaller and more narrow the view; subsequently, the lower the vibration the people residing there will experience. Religious or spiritual practices that are based on love, compassion, equality, unity, peace, and freedom are residing higher up the spiral. The more inclusive, Loving, and free the beliefs, the higher up the spiral, and the higher the vibration people residing here will experience.

It is important to understand that all religion is simply a form or a method for becoming more connected to our Source. All religions have stemmed from beliefs or practices that have been based on a group experience around teachings from a person who has reached a higher level of consciousness than the average person of that time period. The religion is attempting to create a path or a tried and true way of getting to that same higher level of consciousness. This is where all dogma originates because the people inadvertently make assumptions that become religious decrees that say, "You *have* to do it this way or you will not _____ (for example; be saved, reach Heaven, become enlightened, get to Valhalla, reach nirvana, etc.)."

True spirituality is innate. We are all innately spiritual beings, whether we believe we are or not, whether we know we are or not, whether we care about spirituality or not. We are each a soul, we are each a unique divine emanation of Source/Loving, and we are all one at the level of consciousness. To the degree that we become aware of our own loving essence, we will begin to experience our own innate, indwelling spirit at higher and higher levels of truth. Deepening in our spiritual connection with our higher self and Source is an inside job and can be done either with or without religious beliefs. From a spiritual perspective, neither is better.

My personal feelings on the matter are if you practice a religion or are a part of a religious community that brings you love, compassion, joy, innocence, and peace, by all means use it to support your connection to Source. If your current religion brings you down, puts others down, engages in harsh right/wrong judgment, or promotes fear, guilt, shame, blame, or againstness of any kind, I highly encourage you to find a more caring sanctuary. Understand that whatever form you follow or practices you perform, these are just ways to lead you towards experiencing your own divine essence of Loving. Spirituality is about your essence, experiencing yourself as a divine emanation of Source-energy at the level of your own being. This can only be experienced from within.

We Are All Children of God

From Source's perspective, we are all children of God. Jesus was called 'the Christ' because of his level of mastery. The Christos, or Christ Consciousness, refers to a state of consciousness that can be realized while in human form. It is a state that includes residing fully in the Loving, complete with the embodiment of the qualities of infinite compassion, acceptance, innocence, joy, unity, and grace. There has been record of many enlightened masters reaching this state of being throughout history; Jesus just happens to be one of the most popular among them. Jesus simply claimed his 'I AM' presence, saying "I AM the way. I AM the light." And so forth.

The part that masses of people have missed is that Jesus repeatedly instructed, "Do as I do." If we follow that teaching explicitly, and actually do as he did, we would then repeat his words exactly, saying ourselves, "I AM the way. I AM the light." Just by saying those words, we open up to the Christ Consciousness that is just waiting to be lit from within. Jesus also was recorded to have said, "Ye are Gods, men. This, too and more shall ye do." Jesus never meant or expected to become deified; in fact, anyone who worships Jesus is going against his spiritual teaching by placing a false idol before

God, because the only true form of connection to Source is through one's own soul.

If you are familiar with the stories in the Bible, over and over again there are stories of people throwing themselves at Jesus' feet in subjection. Each and every time, over and over, he tells them to get up, to stand tall. The same thing happens in the stories where the angel appears. The disciple reports falling to his knees, and the angel admonishes him to get up. Why? Because we are all *equal* in the eyes of God. We are not less-than in any way and therefore do not need to grovel. If you have been placing Jesus or any other master above you in any way, I encourage you to take down that pedestal. Try saying something like, "Jesus is my big brother. I now know I can grow up to be just like him and can do everything he did." After all, this is specifically what he has been asking of you in all of his teachings.

If this is a radically new concept for you, be gentle with yourself. Know that you are currently undergoing construction to rebuild your new vessel at a higher level of consciousness. Allow yourself to take some time to assimilate this information. Whenever things get stirred up during construction, be patient; it may take a little while for the dust to settle, yet the new framework you are building is so beautiful it is definitely worth the time and effort you are investing.

The idea that Jesus is not the only son of God is a radical paradigm shift for many people. New Thought churches have been gradually bringing this shift to the western world for several decades now. This is not, however, a new concept upon the planet. This spiritual truth has always been available and understood by a percentage of people, including people from several other major world religions, including Judaism and Hinduism. If this idea feels blasphemous to you, inconceivable to you, outrageous to you, I encourage you to be patient and stay open to the possibility.

Understand that resistance to a new idea is normal. There is always a huge push back whenever a big change reaches a population. If it feels more comfortable for you, simply shelve this new idea in the back of your mind and let it go. If you feel upset in any way, I would encourage you to work your process around whatever feelings, thoughts, or beliefs have surfaced for you. Nothing has the power to upset your peace, unless you give it your power.

It is Ok to Reach Out to Our Sisters and Brothers for Assistance

It is absolutely Ok to ask for various servants of God/the Loving to assist us on our journey if we wish, such as our guides or the ascended masters like Jesus, Mary, St. Germaine, or any other enlightened being. This can be particularly helpful if you haven't yet reached the level of communication with your own soul where you are openly channeling in words. And, if you are open to channel, it is an invaluable resource to be able to communicate directly with those who have reached a higher level of mastery in any given area. When I was in college, I used to channel Pythagoras to help me with my math and chemistry. What was fabulous about connecting with a higher source of knowledge was that rather than just getting the answers, I received a full download of understanding that allowed me to comprehend the subject in a much deeper way. Needless to say, I aced every class when I called for assistance.

It is also Ok to call upon the archangels, such as Archangel Michael or Archangel Gabriel, for special needs. Specific archangels cover certain areas; there is an angel for every subject, from birthing to dying, healing to manifesting. As long as we understand that there is only one actual Source, one God, one consciousness, and that we are an intrinsic part of our Source, we can ask for and receive as much support from our spiritual family as our heart desires.

The danger in worshipping any source outside of our own connection to God or Source comes when we view ourselves as 'less than'. If, for example, we view Jesus the Christ as up on a pedestal or above us in any way, it sets it up in our consciousness that we are separate from him. *He* is the son of God and we are not. This greatly prohibits our own chances of self-realization, which requires becoming one with the 'I AM' presence within.

The Loving 'I AM' Presence Exists in All Beings

Viewed in this light, you are a divine soul in a body, and Jesus was another beautiful soul, a brother who had access to and was a channel of higher truth, just like Moses, Abraham, Mohammed, or the Buddha, just to name a few. In our current day, we could liken him to the 14th Dalai Lama, Pema Chödrön, Thich Nhat Hanh, Ram Dass, Eckhart Tolle, Byron Katie, or any other highly evolved person. If you want that level of clarity, go for it. Claim your 'I AM' presence. You have the capacity to become just as evolved as any of the enlightened masters; freedom is your birthright.

A few years ago, I heard a funny story about a man who runs a fear-based and highly-dysfunctional polygamist compound. The community was apparently erecting a 30-foot statue of this man, their leader and prophet, who claims to be the incarnation of the second coming of Christ. He has been heard to claim, "You can stop looking. I am the Christ, returned." What is so tickling about that story to me is that while he is clearly operating from his personality and out of alignment with the Loving, he is actually partially correct and on the right track with claiming his 'I AM' presence; he just missed the part of the download that says we are *all* the second coming of the Christ, but only if we are, in fact and deed, willing to do what it takes to become Christed.

This is a common misstep that many people who are deeply entrenched in fear make when they receive the 'I AM' download. Learning that they are really Source-energy in a body can be quite a heady thing to someone who is still seeking fear-based power from the personality level. They hear this and go a little bonkers, like 'Wow! I am GOD!' They often end up on the streets mumbling to themselves because nobody will listen, in the psych wards under heavy medication with well-meaning psychologists trying to convince them that what they are hearing isn't real, or their personality immediately kicks in with the temptation to lord their newfound power over all of their powerless, wretched, little minions... Have you ever known or heard about anyone who has gone this last route?

There is a reason I covered 'worth' and 'equality' in chapter two. Integration of the personality with the higher self is crucial to holding this understanding and then taking it to the cellular level and being it. You'll want to start by moving out of the fear-based, right/wrong thinking and get firmly anchored in the Loving before claiming your 'I AM' presence from a place of stability and integrity. You do not need to rush this. I encourage people to work their process around whatever issues are most present first, and the 'I AM' knowledge will seep in gradually until it is eventually fully integrated. Know that the internal feeling that accompanies claiming your 'I AM' presence at the highest level is filled with innocence, peace, joy, unity, oneness, and gratitude – indeed, it is actually a humbling experience. It is an internal knowing that we are all completely ordinary and unfathomably extraordinary at the same time. It is a knowing that we have been entrusted by our soul to actually really *be* the highest expression of the divine, while we are in physical, human form, which can seem like a pretty daunting job at first glance.

I can recall my own initial resistance to this knowing, which lasted for many years. I had so much difficulty taking responsibility for myself as a soul in a body, that I clung to the identity of myself as an unworthy, lowly worm with all my might. It would be easier, I thought, to be the pathetic worm. It would be so much easier to just stay human and leave the God-thing to Jesus – he does such a great job of it, after all. If I admitted I was, in fact, also God in a body, I would have to *do* something about it. I would have to think differently, speak differently, act differently… I didn't think I was up to the challenge, so I pretended not to hear my soul's voice telling me to step up and get cracking. If I could just sleep a little longer, maybe someone else would wake up and be God in a body, and I could pretend I overslept and didn't hear my alarm.

Here's what I eventually realized: I AM God in a body whether I take responsibility for myself or not. I AM God in a body even if I choose to pretend I'm not awake and continue to give into countless, fear-based temptations. I AM God in a body even if I decide to perpetuate all of my unhealthy patterns for the rest of my life.

And, I finally realized, the planetary shift in consciousness is going to take place with or without my support. That part is a given; the planet *is* taking an evolutionary leap. If I decide to play possum, it's my free will choice. Those who are awake and willing to step up to take responsibility, willing to drop their fear and *be* the Loving, will move forward without me, and I will have to eventually deal with the consequences of my choice to pretend to have overslept.

After doing my absolute best to resist my calling, I finally surrendered and admitted my own divinity, and humbly asked for divine assistance to show me what to do next. Practically the minute I asked for spirit's support, I was completely guided as to how to move forward. It took that one, clear, simple choice to get me out of the hell of my own making. The moment I decided that I was ready to align myself with my soul's will, which is also the will of God, I surrendered myself to my divinity, my higher power, and the light flooded in. I was instantly out of the dark pit of despair and moving upward, lit from within.

While I was no longer residing in hell, thankfully, moving past my previous comfort zone took commitment, persistence, determination, repeated decisions to stick, and a strength I didn't even know I had to get myself out of my old, familiar, fear-based patterns of behavior. The light within myself stayed bright, guiding me, supporting me, and providing unending encouragement for me to keep going, no matter what, until I was finally free of the darkness and living in light. And, if I could do it, so can you.

You are a Divine Child of God

You are a divine child of God whether you want to be or not, whether you are willing to wake up or not. You are a divine soul in a body... streaming your own precious, priceless ray of consciousness... having a wild, adventurous, human experience of living on a four-dimensional planet that is currently moving into another dimension. The planet is going to go for it with or without your permission, your consent, your buy-in, or even your physical presence. The question I pose to you is this: Do you want to go along for the ride, to be an integral part of creating the peace of heaven on Earth?

Becoming the Body of Christ

The thing is, attaining a personal state of heaven isn't as easy as simply claiming you are the Christ; each and every person actually has to *become* Christed by moving from the fear-based paradigm into the Loving paradigm, and then clearing anything and everything that stands in their way of the clarity of the level of the Christos. As Gandhi said, "We must *be* the change we want to see in our world". It is an inside job, and only you can do it for yourself.

The stories in the Bible of the second coming describe Christ as coming in on clouds, light and wind. Here are just a few of the many passages that refer to the second coming of the Christ:

"…who maketh the clouds his chariots; who walketh upon the wings of the wind" (Psalm 104:3)

"And then shall appear the sign of the Son of man in heaven: and then shall all the tribes of the earth mourn, and they shall see the Son of man coming in the clouds of heaven with power and great glory" (Matthew 24:30).

"And he shall send his angels with a great sound of a trumpet, and they shall gather together his elect from the four winds, from one end of heaven to the other" (Matthew 24:31)

"Behold, he cometh with clouds; and every eye shall see him" (Revelation 1:7).

"Wherefore if they shall say unto you, Behold, he is in the desert; go not forth: behold, he is in the secret chambers; believe it not. For as the lightning cometh out of the east and shineth even unto the west; so shall also the coming of the Son of man be" (Matthew 24:26-27).

Multiple times throughout the Bible the second coming of Christ is described in terms of wind and clouds, encompassing all directions. Also repeatedly in the Bible, there is warning about not buying into false prophets – in other words, not listening to one person who claims to be the one and only reincarnation of Jesus the Christ. Understand that what was being foreshadowed as the second coming is a collective, energetic experience of a paradigm shift upon the planet that has the capacity to affect as many people who are open to receiving it as possible.

Guess what? The concept of a collective consciousness couldn't be described in terms of energy or a state of inner beingness, because those ideas were not yet part of the group consciousness at that time. The truth of the teaching is in its essence: clouds of white light will touch the planet, and simultaneously across the globe, the Christ Consciousness will become available to one and all.

The 'clouds', as they are referred to in the Bible – which are the energies of Loving consciousness – have actually been rolling in gradually, over a long period of time. There was a dramatic energetic up-leveling in the sixties, which empowered the equal rights movement and women's liberation. There have been many up-levelings over the following six decades, including the most recent wave on December 21st, 2020. The Christ Consciousness is fully present and available upon the planet – it is now simply a matter of receiving, assimilating, integrating, and embodying this higher frequency of energy.

Each of you reading this right now is a part of the Body of Christ, making the Christ Consciousness, also known as the Christos, which is the highest level of the Loving paradigm to which we have access, available to everyone upon the planet. When a certain number of people have received the full download and have done the clearing and updating necessary to embody the truth of the Loving paradigm, the energies of the Christ Consciousness will become instantly available to the masses. When this occurs, humanity will take a step up into the next level as a collective.

It is just like the hundredth monkey theory: As the story by Ken Keyes Jr. goes, a group of monkeys on an island were eating sandy sweet potatoes. When several younger monkeys showed their mothers how to rinse their potatoes off in the ocean, the monkeys excitedly began teaching each other this new trick on one side of the island. When the hundredth monkey was shown how to wash the sand off of the sweet potato, instantly, the collective consciousness of the monkeys shifted. All over the island, simultaneously, all of the monkeys began washing off their potato before eating it. Once this new way was assimilated by the monkeys on that island, the knowledge was transferred to monkeys on other islands, on the mainland, and in other countries.

Now, the gist of the theory is that when a certain percentage of a population makes a shift in consciousness, evolution takes place for the entire species. We currently have nearly eight billion people on the planet, so it is likely going to take a few more than a hundred people to make the paradigm shift as an entire species. All you have to do is do your part to move yourself into the Loving consciousness. Other people will have to make the choice whether or not to move into the Loving themselves.

Once the planetary shift takes place, people who are stuck in fear and resistant to the Loving will need to incarnate again to continue their lessons at the four-dimensional level, while the rest of humanity will begin learning from a higher state of truth. How do we claim and integrate the Christ Consciousness so that we can reside in the Loving fully? We learn and apply the tool of self-forgiveness, which is the main ingredient of self-actualization.

Forgiveness is Available to Everyone, Always

The truth, from the spiritual perspective, is that everyone is worthy of compassion, which is the main ingredient of forgiveness. The energy of forgiveness is made up of love and compassion. Forgiveness is our birthright. It is already given. We are born loved and we'll die loved from Source's perspective, no matter what occurs here for us on the Earth-plane of life. There is no such thing as an irredeemable person, or a permanently lost soul. Believing that would certainly be giving over a tremendous amount of power to some negative force. If we believe we are sourced from a Loving Source, we can see that all rays come from the Source and are connected to the Source; it is not possible to 'break off' a ray of light from its compassionate source of Loving. The sun and the sunlight are all one complete entity. We are all connected to our source of love and light, even though we may at times feel like we are disconnected.

The Light is Always Brighter than the Dark

Let's look at this issue of good vs. evil in terms of light and dark. If you picture standing in a dark room, and you don't want to be in the dark any more, what is the solution? …Exactly… turn on the light. The minute you add light, the darkness simply dissipates. How cool is that? The darkness, in and of itself, doesn't really exist as separate from the light, but in fact is just an absence of light. Now, if you were standing in the dark and just lit a little candle, you'd still have a lot of dark corners. If you lit the 400 watt light bulb, your room would be free of darkness, and you may still have some shadows or darkness in the closet. If you open the door and walk out into the noon-day sunshine, even the shadows cease to exist. Any way you go, you can trust that your experience of the darkness is not 'bad' or 'good', it simply is what it is. In the same way, your experience of internal darkness is neither 'bad' nor 'good'; it just is what it is – a temporary feeling of darkness or disconnection from your source of light and Loving. It is only a feeling, not really true, because on the being level you are always connected to your Source.

If you have ever entertained the idea that there is some powerful, dark force that is out to get you, I strongly encourage you to drop that fear-based idea and simply choose to turn on your own inner light. Darkness has no power over light, because darkness ceases to exist in the presence of light. Fear-based energy is transmuted by the energy of trust in the Loving. Put your trust in your own internal light, choose to align yourself with the will of your own soul and light yourself up from within.

People who believe in evil, in the devil, in the possibility of an eternal damnation, or any other gloom and doom scenario are simply giving energy and power away to that which they most fear. Believing in fear simply feeds the fear. The minute you go into a state of fear, you dim your own light and become very small and dark yourself. Since like attracts like, from this place you will begin to gravitate towards more and more fear, until you are jumping at shadows and flinching at every sound. Fear begets more fear. Why would you want to add to the sum total of fear and darkness upon the planet? If you have bought into these fear-based ideas, take your power back! I encourage you to put all of your belief, all 100% of it, into the Loving/God. Why entertain any doubt? It is absolute truth at the level of Loving that we are all one. The only issue anywhere ever is simply the illusion of separateness from the Loving. How does it serve you, anyone else, our planet or the greater universe to perpetuate the idea that something or someone can have complete separation from All That Is? The truth is that it doesn't serve you at all to entertain this idea, and only adds energy to the illusion that something is separated.

The idea of eternal damnation is completely contradictory to all of the spiritual teachings of Loving, compassion, acceptance, forgiveness, and most especially free will choice. Someone who believes they are eternally damned may decide to perpetuate that illusion for a long, long time. And yet, at any given moment, all they would need to do to get undamned would be to take one breath of the infinite compassion that has been surrounding them all along. One good 'I forgive myself' is all it takes, and the life-sentence in solitary confinement is instantly lifted. It is an inside job to decide to be damned or undamned at any time. No one else gets to decide. No one else has the *power* to decide.

The idea that darkness can have any power over the light is nonsense and self-defeating, and yet this is an idea that is fully promoted by those who wish for the masses to remain locked into the fear-based illusion of reality. Those who use fear-based energy know that the only way they have any feeling of power is to attempt to smother the light by continually producing more and more fear within any given group to the point that individual lights are very dim and weak. Fear is used as a method of controlling a population, and of course it would be wonderful for those who wish to keep the status quo if the people would continue to buy into irrationality and keep feeding the fear. Does this mean you should comply and continue to buy into a fear-based, control-based life? Heck no! Freedom is your birthright. Your soul is urging you to drop your fears and irrational beliefs and step fully into the light of the Loving.

The Power of Free Will Choice

This is where the full power of your free will choice comes in. As beings with free will, every moment becomes a deciding moment. Everything that occurs gives you the opportunity to exercise your free will choice. In any given moment, you have the power to say no to fear, even if you've been giving it your power for your entire life so far. You have the full power to say no to temptation – whatever your current temptation is right now in your life. You have the power to decide to believe differently, to think differently. Freedom from fear is a *choice*. Freedom from settling is a *choice*. Joy is a *choice*. We really do have the power to choose, and in any given moment, we can choose misery, or we can choose joy. What qualities you experience in your own life are totally up to you.

You Are the Driver of Your Own Body Vehicle

You are the one and only driver of your physical, mental, emotional, spiritual body vehicle. If, at any point in time, you find yourself driving in a direction you do not wish to go, you can always decide to turn around. One day, I was sitting at an outdoor cafe near a busy intersection in a Los Angeles suburb. Right in front of my eyes, a huge eighteen-wheeler truck came barreling through the intersection, applied the brakes, and swung a death-defying U-turn in the face of four lanes of on-coming traffic about a half a block away. I felt shocked, stunned and finally awed at the fearless maneuver. This happened as I was considering the beauty and the power of free will choice – the idea that in any given moment we have the power to choose our own direction. This truck driver passed the street that would have led to the freeway. As soon as the driver crossed the intersection and noticed he was heading in the wrong direction, going off-course, he immediately applied the brakes and pulled a U-turn, headed back to the intersection and turning toward his goal of the freeway entrance. I will admit that I initially had dozens of fear-based thoughts flash across my mind as I watched him – ideas like 'that's illegal!', 'that's irresponsible', 'he can't do that', 'he'll never make it', 'he might tip over', 'he could crash', 'what if he doesn't make it in time and the cars don't stop' and then I watched as he made the turn effortlessly, with speed and panache, without tipping, without crashing, without getting hit and without even getting stopped by a cop and getting a hefty moving violation. In fact, he made it look so effortless it seemed like child's play. It was a pretty awesome U-turn. I don't condone reckless driving, yet what a great metaphor for free will choice.

Make a U-Turn if You Find Yourself Headed Off-Course

Our internal U-turns can be just as radical and awe-inspiring. You have the free will choice to make a U-turn at any time, for any reason if you decide that you are headed off-course. It doesn't matter what anyone else thinks about your U-turn. Others may think your U-turn is illegal, impractical, irresponsible, unethical, immoral, unacceptable, dangerous or whatever. Guess what? You are the driver of your own body vehicle. You are the one and *only* one who gets to decide if you are heading in the direction that is in alignment with the will of your soul. Feel free to make a radical U-turn if you find yourself headed off-course at any time – no matter what anybody else thinks. It is, after all, your life.

This means: be willing to cancel the wedding if you realize it is out of alignment for you to marry – even if the dress is made, flowers are ordered, and guests are waiting in the chapel. Be willing to go back to highschool or college, even if you decided years ago you'd never complete your degree, if that is what your soul is urging you to do now. Be willing to quit that ho-hum job as guided, even if everyone says you'd be nuts to leave it. Be willing to end a relationship or get a divorce if you are living out of alignment, even if you decided years ago to stay married forever. Be willing to say 'no' to something if your intuition or feeling-barometer tells you 'off-course', even if an expert says you should say 'yes'. Be willing to decide to change your major in what would have been your final year of college. Be willing to make an unpopular choice, to break the laws of politeness, to flip the bird to conformity, to drop the family expectations and to say 'no' to fear. Most of all, be willing to change your mind about something. Otherwise you may risk feeling lifeless, stuck in a rut because you don't think it's 'Ok' to change your mind about whatever course you decided upon decades ago when you were totally unconscious. When it comes to following the will of your soul, I highly recommend shouting 'yes' at the top of your lungs and deciding to follow your course – whatever that may be – even if it means making a drastic turn, even a radically drastic, death-defying U-turn toward freedom.

Freedom is Always a Choice

There is a huge amount of power in the knowledge that you are not your own thoughts. Our thoughts will often only give us what appears to be a very narrow spectrum of choices. Sometimes it may seem like there are only two choices in a given situation. In the love-based reality, there are numerous choices. At any given moment, you can simply say 'no' to your own limited thinking, and in that moment, a door will open to infinite possibility. You can also ask for your guides or your soul's assistance to show you the way. You will then need to use your discernment to decide which choice is most closely aligned with the will of your soul. This is where checking in with your feeling-barometer comes in very handy; if you imagine taking the road of temptation, you will feel bad or uncomfortable inside. If you imagine following your inner guidance and taking the path that is in alignment with the will of your soul – the path toward freedom, the path toward the embodiment of the Christos and the creation of heaven on Earth – you will feel anywhere from neutrally steady to totally wonderful. When you act in your own highest good, you can absolutely trust that whatever happens as a result is in the highest good of all concerned.

I encourage you, right now, if you have not already done

so, to claim the full power of your free will choice, begin making self-honoring choices that bring you into closer alignment with the will of your soul, and let your love-light shine.

Exercise: Claiming Your Free Will Choice

Begin by saying a protection prayer, setting conditions of love and light, and invoking spirit's presence.

Place your hands on your heart. Set an intention to access the highest vibration of Loving available. Breathe in the Loving and fill your body with Loving energies from head to toe. Then, set an intention to access the highest level of compassion. Breathe in compassion and fill your body with compassion from head to toe.

Repeat out loud any of the following that resonate, changing the verbiage as needed to reflect your own beliefs:

"I forgive myself for buying into the irrational belief that I have ever been powerless to choose." "My new updated belief is, I now know I have always had free will choice. I was born with the freedom to choose, I now have the freedom to choose, and I will always have the freedom to choose my own response in any given moment."

"I forgive myself for buying into the irrational belief that I had no choice or no say in my own life." "My new updated belief is, I now know I have always had a choice in my own life, even if someone else said that I didn't have a choice. I can trust that I did the best that I could at the time, given the circumstances, my beliefs, my modeling, my skills, etc. I now know that I have full free will choice in every given moment."

"I forgive myself for buying into the irrational belief that I had to listen to what someone else wanted/needed/expected me to do, rather than make my own choice in the matter." "My new updated belief is, I now know I now know that I am equal to every other being, and that I can make my own choices about my life in every given moment."

"I forgive myself for buying into the irrational belief that someone else knows better than me what the best choices are for my life." "My new updated belief is, I now know I am my own best expert in my own life. I know what is best for me in every given moment; in fact, I am the *only* one who knows what is best for my own self, because I am the one experiencing my own life and my own connection to Source."

"I forgive myself for buying into the irrational belief that I cannot trust myself to make my own choices." "My new updated belief is, I now know I can trust myself to make excellent choices. I have the knowing of my own ring of truth, and I trust my discernment to decide what is in my own highest good. I know that when I follow my inner truth and act in my own highest good, it is in the ultimate highest good of all concerned."

"I forgive myself for buying into the irrational belief that I ever need to follow someone else's orders/advice/opinions/suggestions again." "My new updated belief is, I now know from now on, I can take other people's advice as simply more information. I can say something like, 'Thanks for sharing. I'll take that into consideration.' I do not need to act on any information that does not resonate within me as my own truth. I now know that when I act in my own highest good, it is in the highest good of all concerned."

"I forgive myself for buying into the irrational belief that I need to feel afraid of things or that I need to live in fear in any way." "My new updated belief is, I now know I now know that buying into fear simply creates more fear. I now know that my light dissipates the dark, and I can hold in energies of Loving, peace, joy and trust in spirit when fear energies are present. By remaining in the light and the Loving, I actually transmute the fear into Loving, and become a catalyst for change upon the planet. I AM the love and the light; I now shine fully and freely in every moment."

"I forgive myself for buying into the irrational belief that I need to fear temptation." "My new updated belief is, I now know I now know that temptation is a neutral party, simply one limited choice available in the infinite array of choices that exist in every moment. I can simply say 'no' to temptation if I don't choose to settle for less-than again and then choose to act in my own highest good. If I do choose to say 'yes' to temptation, I can trust that there will be more learning there for me as a result of my choice. When I am fully ready to complete that lesson, I know and trust I have the power to say 'no' for good and I will immediately level up."

"I forgive myself for buying into the irrational belief that I need to fear sinning or hold the idea that sinning is 'bad' or 'wrong'." "My new updated belief is, I now know landing 'off the mark' is a normal and natural part of the human learning process. To the degree I can accept my own actions, I can simply apply love and compassion to my own suffering, and move on. I now know that everything I've ever done is Ok from my soul's perspective, and I now accept myself fully as I learn and grow."

"I forgive myself for buying into the irrational belief that I need to fear going to hell or eternal damnation." "My new updated belief is, I now know that hell is simply one choice of many. I now know that if I ever find myself in hell, I have the freedom to choose to move out of it and end my state of suffering at any time. I have the freedom to choose joy over suffering. If I can claim and integrate the knowing of my own and others' innocence in all things, I can choose to reside in a state of heaven."

"I forgive myself for buying into the irrational belief that everything written in a sacred text must be right or true, and if I don't believe something literally, I'll be committing blasphemy." "My new updated belief is, I now know my Loving Source is inside of me. I can trust in my own discernment and my own ring of truth to let me know what is in right alignment with me. My soul guides me from the inside. There is no book, no person, no religious leader that can interpret my own inner knowing of God/the Loving better than me. I now trust my own discernment, knowing that written words in the sacred texts were initially interpreted by humans who were residing in the fear-based, right/wrong reality. It is up to me to hear what is true for me and to let go of what is not."

"I forgive myself for buying into the irrational belief that a state of heaven is somehow going to miraculously 'happen' to me, or that I am saved just because I have _____ (for example: been baptized, joined a certain religion, become part of an order, tithed to my church, signed on the dotted line, been promised that by my pastor/guru/minister/teacher/leader, made a certain vow, followed the rules, etc.)." "My new updated belief is, I now know I now know that I am the one and only one who can save myself by aligning my will with the will of my soul and embodying the Loving consciousness. When I reach a state of innocence and clarity of the Christos, I can then be a part of creating peace, harmony and grace upon this planet. When I learn to live in alignment with All That Is, I will be part of the co-creation of the state of heaven on Earth."

"I forgive myself for buying into the irrational belief that once I make a decision, I need to stick with it for life." "My new updated belief is, I now know I now know that it is Ok to change my mind. When it comes to following the will of my soul, it is Ok for me to course-correct; to go a different way and to even make a complete U-turn, no matter what anybody else may think. I always have the free will choice to change my direction in life. I now choose to follow the will of my soul."

Close your process by acknowledging yourself, expressing gratitude to spirit, and fully grounding your energy. Drink plenty of water.

CHAPTER FIVE
Taking 100% Responsibility

From the Loving perspective, each and every being is a whole, complete entity and therefore 100% responsible for themself in every way. This is an empowering concept that necessitates letting go of blame and any other aspects of victim mentality.

Taking 100% Responsibility is the Key to Enlightenment

My first spiritual teacher once told me, "Taking 100% responsibility for one's self is the key to enlightenment. If you do only this one thing, just take full 100% responsibility for everything in your life, you could achieve enlightenment. No one can reach mastery without first taking full responsibility for themselves." This was many years ago, so I am certainly paraphrasing, yet that was the general gist of what he said.

At the time, I didn't even write it down, because my mind couldn't really wrap itself around this idea. "What, is he crazy?" I thought, "How could simply taking responsibility lead to enlightenment?" In my young mind, taking responsibility meant remembering to feed the cat or take out the garbage. Maybe it meant paying the phone bill and showing up for work on time. And, as I thought of the few images I had of enlightened masters, it seemed to me that none of them even *had* any responsibilities: The video I'd watched of the Maharaja showed him getting waited on hand and foot, the Buddha just sat under the tree for 40 days meditating, Gandhi had had an entire entourage taking care of everything, including the driving. And in the book series, The Masters of the Far East, the masters simply manifested their meals with the wave of a hand. What was he talking about - responsibility is the key to enlightenment? Certainly, I thought, there must be some confusion. Wasn't unconditional love more important? What about compassion? Wisdom? Acceptance? I could think of dozens of qualities I'd rate as more important than responsibility, and I let this idea go.

Luckily, my wise teacher had started off his course with some sage advice. At the beginning of the class, he'd said, "Take what rings true for you, let go of what doesn't resonate and put whatever you do not understand on the shelf in the back of your mind; one day it will be revealed to you." This proved to be very useful; since his words regarding personal responsibility did not make sense, I'd simply tossed them up on the shelf in the back of my mind.

Astonishingly, everything my teacher ever said to me that didn't make sense at the time has now crystallized into full knowing. Although I only worked with him for a few short years in my early twenties, his words made an enormous impact on my life. One of the big realizations I've had was that he had been right on about responsibility as the key. And I saw clearly how I'd been gradually integrating that idea, very slowly over a period of about thirty years.

My first conscious step toward taking responsibility in my

own life came in 1992 when I took personal responsibility for my own level of Loving by leaving an unhappy marriage and beginning to cultivate self-love. I recall making the decision inside of myself, "I claim that I am worthy of receiving love," and it was so. I remarried a few years later into a seemingly more outwardly caring and affectionate relationship, yet this second relationship was codependent and highly dysfunctional; there were still major mirrors of places where I was out of alignment in my life. While I had declared I was worthy of receiving love, I quickly realized that I hadn't said what level of love, how often, in what form, and that I was still receiving a lot of other unpleasant things in the bargain. Thankfully, I immediately realized I needed to get more specific.

In 1998, when it became crystal clear that my current partner was not on the same page or even interested in reading the same book, I left my second marriage, claiming full responsibility for my joy, happiness, truth, discernment, integrity, and more. I became much clearer, yet was still out of alignment in many areas of my life. Financial disaster followed me for the next five years, as well as ill health and several more codependent relationships.

In 2003, I did a full overhaul of my life, for the first time ever taking full 100% responsibility for my choices, my finances, my actions, my thoughts, my patterns, my beliefs, my feelings, my words, my energy field, my health, my diet, my car, my appearance, my living space, my clothing, my relationships, my teeth, my authenticity, my authentic power, my voice, my schooling or lack there-of, my job, and dozens of other things, including hundreds of fears and judgments.

Responsibility Means 'The Ability to Respond'

First and foremost, I redefined my meaning of the word 'responsibility'. Instead of meaning 'remembering to feed the kids/cat' and 'paying the bills on time', I came to see it as 'my ability to respond' in any given situation. Broken into two words, 'response' and 'ability', you can see how it really means 'the ability to respond'. Responsible becomes 'response able', or 'able to respond'. By clearly defining the meaning for the word, I was able to think of taking personal responsibility in a new way, and to clearly see that I was indeed capable of taking charge of my own life, of being 'response-able' – that I was able to respond in a way that's healthy and supportive of creating the life I wanted to live.

Taking 100% Responsibility Radically Changes Your Life

What I can say for certain is that taking 100% responsibility for your own self will change your life, radically and immediately. You will no longer feel like a powerless victim being swept to and fro by unseen, negative forces. You will have the power and the ability to transform your life in every area, in any way your heart desires.

When I finally took 100% responsibility for myself, I let go of the bitterness and resentment from years of blaming other people for my chronic problems, my stories of lack, my own dysfunctional patterns of behavior, and my old baggage. I took full power for the life I had created, and knew instantly that if there was any part of it I didn't like that it was up to me to change it. No one else was in charge of my life experience besides *me*. I took the key called '100% Responsibility', and I put it inside of myself and turned it, accessing the door to freedom within. It took several years for the dust to settle. I won't lie and say it was easy, because in reality it was like opening Pandora's box – all of the negativity I'd stuffed away inside the dark recesses of my consciousness flew up and out into the light the minute I turned that key. The incredible part was that so much light flooded in through the opening that I didn't even mind the mess! I could literally taste the freedom, and the light was pulling me upward. The only thing between me and the crystal clarity of that light was all of my obstacles of crap flying around. So, naturally, I had a tremendous desire to sort through it and clean it all up as quickly as humanly possible in order to get all the way into that beautiful light. The divine qualities in that light made themselves available to me with each bit of clearing that I accomplished. Every time I said no to temptation, cleared up a judgment, or updated an old belief, a higher level of love and light was instantly available to me.

Gradually, I accessed the divine qualities of joy, beauty, gratitude, compassion, strength, determination, perseverance, peace, authentic power, authenticity, integrity, trust, honoring, respect, caring, acceptance and many others. In 2008, I accessed grace, which was a profound up-leveling within my own consciousness.

As I took full, 100% responsibility for each area of my life, I rewrote my script, rewired my brain, releasing all of the old, irrational, fear-based beliefs that were not supporting me. I created new beliefs, based on Loving, and I rebuilt my life from the ground up. I created healthy relationships with friends and family where before there had been codependent ones; I created financial support where there had been only lack; I created health where there had been illness and weakness; I created joy where there had been suffering; I created deeply meaningful work that I loved to do where there had been stagnation and resentment; I created beauty where there had been dullness. Finally, I created a relationship with a truly Loving partner where there had been a lack of intimacy and dysfunctional relationship. In every way, I completely transformed my life, seizing the full power of claiming my true responsibility for my life. I claimed and then acted on the idea that I create my own life; I completely owned that I am 100%

responsible for everything I am experiencing in every given moment. The power in this one idea is unfathomable.

What do *you* want to create in your life? To quote one of my teachers, Dr. Mary Hulnick, "Once you get this concept, the only question becomes, 'How good can you stand it?'"

Let's take a look at what it really means to accept full, 100% responsibility. For me, this came area by area in my life, as I integrated the divine qualities available through the Loving. Each person heals and evolves in divine-perfect order; no two people's process is exactly alike. You may have already claimed full responsibility in one area of your life, and still be stuck in blame or victim-mentality in another. As an exemplifying process, I'll begin with the concepts most basic to living a life of joy and freedom from the perspective of the Loving paradigm.

To begin this journey of claiming full responsibility for your life, first, you must dispel the myth that anyone else besides yourself has ever been responsible, in any way, for creating any part of your life.

Exercise: Take 100% Responsibility for Creating Your Own Life

Begin by saying a protection prayer, setting conditions of love and light, and invoking spirit's presence.

Place your hands on your heart. Set an intention to access the highest vibration of Loving available. Breathe in the Loving and fill your body with Loving energies from head to toe. Then, set an intention to access the highest level of compassion. Breathe in compassion and fill your body with compassion from head to toe.

Say out loud:

"I forgive myself for buying into the irrational belief that anyone else has ever been responsible for my life, in any way." "My new updated belief is, I now know I am fully, 100%

responsible for every area of my life. I now take full responsibility for my life. I know that I co-create my life with my own soul, and that I create my own reality in every moment. I claim full responsibility for creating my life."

Read your beliefs re: 100% responsibility if you ever feel energy of blame toward anyone or anything in your life.

You Are Responsible for Your Thoughts, Feelings and Actions

One thing a person seeking peace or enlightenment must come to understand is that each of us is entirely 100% responsible for our own self in every way. We are each a separate energy-being, experientially, although we are all sourced from the same Source and all one at the most cosmic level. This means that in every given moment you are 100% responsible for your own thoughts, feelings, and actions.

Picture the sun, and then picture the rays of the sun. Each ray reaches out in its own direction, separate and uniquely different from the other rays. Each ray shines at a slightly different angle or degree. No two rays cross or get their power from another ray; each ray is only connected at the source. Each ray is independent, and each ray has equal access to its source.

Imagine now, that the sun is God, the source of boundless Loving, and that the rays are souls, each a unique, divine emanation of Source-energy, made in the image and likeness of God. Each being, therefore, operates independently from each other, even as they are all part of a greater whole. We are all connected through the Loving; we are all connected to the same Source, energized from the same Source, made out of the same Source. Yet each one of us exists independently as we shine our individual ray. None of the rays cross each other, so none have the power to cut another off from the Source. Likewise, none have the power to push, coerce, force, or make any other ray radiate its own expression differently. Each ray has the full power to shine by itself. Each ray has internal sovereignty to shine as it wishes. Each ray can only get real power from the Source, although each can shine on the surrounding rays, sharing its light and love.

Part of the gift of human experience is that we have been given free will choice. This means that each of us is fully capable of choosing how to act, and that each of us has the ability to respond to our own circumstances and choose our own reaction. Each one of us is 100% responsible for our own thoughts, feelings and actions. We are each responsible for creating our own lives. We are sovereign individuals at the level of being.

What is beautiful about this idea is that it gives us instant power to choose joy over suffering. Austrian Psychologist Viktor Frankl said, "…the last of human freedoms is the freedom to choose one's attitude in any given set of circumstances, to choose one's own way." This is a radical and empowering idea which is completely opposed to what most of us were led to believe.

Growing up in a family with five children, all very close in age, my siblings and I were convinced that everything that ever happened was someone or something else's fault. We grew up in a blaming environment, and learned to blame each other and everything else as well for our suffering. If someone in my family was late, it was because of someone else's stupidity, car trouble, the traffic, the road construction, or the storm. If someone got into trouble, it was invariably a mistake because it was really someone else's fault. If two of us were fighting and my mom caught us, it was, "He started it!" "No, she started it!" "No, really, *he* started it!" If there was no one else in the room, it must have been the cat who broke the lamp! Truly, the level of blame and accusation I engaged in growing up in my home bordered on the absurd.

The first time I ever took full responsibility for my lateness while waitressing was both empowering and very humbling. I said to my boss, "I am late. I take full responsibility. I didn't leave for work on time. I will try to plan better next time." I was terrified I would get fired, yet sick of coming up with lame excuses like horrific traffic accidents or the UPS truck blocking my driveway. My boss looked at me for a moment then said, "Ok."

That was it? I thought, just 'Ok'? Wow, this taking responsibility for my actions stuff was pretty good. I didn't get any of the scolding, criticism or shaming I was expecting. What I quickly came to realize was that what I got by taking responsibility for my actions was respect. People can tell when someone is making excuses, blaming others or blaming outside circumstances for their behavior. People can also tell when someone owns their behavior fully, and this is a very attractive quality.

Taking ownership of our actions is a clear way of saying we are awake, aware and willing to grow. In the old model of blame, we didn't have to change anything about what we were doing because we simply deflected the issue onto someone or something else – "It was so-and-so's fault." This allowed us to stay safe in our own minds, yet all that it really did was keep us small. When we take full responsibility for our own part in every moment, we become conscious co-creators of our own reality. We are admitting, to both ourselves and others, that we are aware of our own actions and responses, and that we are willing to accept the consequences of our choices in every given situation.

I went from saying to my partner, "You hurt my feelings!" in an angry and blaming way, to fully owning my own power to choose my feelings, saying things like, "I feel hurt right now, and I know it is my stuff. I need to go take a moment to be by myself so I don't say something unkind while I'm feeling this way." After doing this for a period of time, I was able to clear dozens, maybe even hundreds, of old, irrational ideas I'd had about relationships, expectations I had of how I thought other people 'should' behave, limiting ideas of other people having the power to cause me hurt, and so on. I eventually cleared so many triggers that I am now largely free from upset. As a direct result of my clearing, I now have peaceful, joy-filled interactions with my students, my family members, and my friends. By taking full responsibility for my own power to decide how to feel and react in any given moment, I have transformed my relationships. My relationships have gone from dysfunctional to healthy in every way.

One tremendous upleveling occurred when I stopped blaming my parents and my upbringing for my issues, and immediately began healing them, just by taking full ownership. To do this, I had to realize that my parents never did anything *to* me; they simply did what they did, and I chose to react, feel, think, and respond the way I did. By taking responsibility for my freedom to choose my response, I empowered myself to see that I *could* have chosen differently had I had the foresight. And, that it was Ok that I responded the way I did. I did the best I could at the time. It had happened the way it happened; I can accept that that is what my parents chose to do, and that is what I chose to do in response. In this way, I began to view every memory of my past with compassion for all of the suffering, knowing that each of us was simply doing the best we could, learning and growing in a fear-based right/wrong reality.

Where Are You Giving Away Your Power in Blame?

Where are you giving your power away in your life? Is there anyone or anything you are blaming for your own suffering? Are you blaming your past, your parents, or your siblings for your issues? Are you blaming life, bad luck, or fate for your own supposed misfortunes? Are you blaming your friend, relative, or spouse for your own bad feelings? Are you blaming your boss, your teachers, or your co-workers for your current salary? Eleanor Roosevelt said, "No one can make you feel inferior without your consent." This is absolutely true. To take that further, no one can cause you to feel bad in any way unless you agree. You have the free will choice to choose joy in every given moment, regardless of what anyone else may say or do. No one person or circumstance can cause you to act in a certain way, either. You have the freedom to choose your actions, and the ability to own your actions, whatever they may be.

Exercise: Taking 100% Responsibility for Your Thoughts, Feelings, and Actions

Begin by saying a protection prayer, setting conditions of love and light, and invoking spirit's presence.

Place your hands on your heart. Set an intention to access the highest vibration of Loving available. Breathe in the Loving and fill your body with Loving energies from head to toe. Then, set an intention to access the highest level of compassion. Breathe in compassion and fill your body with compassion from head to toe.

Say out loud:

"I forgive myself for buying into the irrational belief that anyone else has ever been responsible for my feelings." "My new updated belief is, I now know I have always been responsible for my own feelings. I have the freedom to choose how I feel, in any given moment. No one has ever had the power to make me feel a certain way. My feelings are my own responsibility. I claim that I am fully, 100% responsible for my own feelings. I am the only one who can choose how I feel."

"I forgive myself for buying into the irrational belief that anyone else has ever been responsible for what I think." "My new updated belief is, I now know I have always been responsible for what I think. My thoughts are mine and mine alone. I have the freedom to choose what I think, and I can change my thoughts at any time. I claim that I am fully, 100% responsible for what I choose to think. I create my own thoughts based on what I believe to be true. If I choose to change my thoughts, I have the power to change my beliefs which will allow me to think different thoughts."

"I forgive myself for buying into the irrational belief that anyone else has ever been responsible for my actions." "My new updated belief is, I now know I have always had the power to choose my own actions. I have always been fully responsible for the way I have acted at any time. I claim that I am fully, 100% responsible for my own actions at all times, no matter what. I have the full power to choose how I wish to behave in every given moment."

"I forgive myself for buying into the irrational belief that anyone or anything is to blame for how I think, feel or act." "My new updated belief is, I now know I am the only one who is responsible for what I think, how I feel and how I act. I now release all blame and againstness, and take charge of co-creating my own life."

Close your process by acknowledging yourself, expressing gratitude to spirit, and fully grounding your energy. Drink plenty of water.

Letting Go of Victim Mentality

There is no such thing as a victim from the Loving perspective. In the right/wrong, fear-based reality, since there is no knowledge of equality, everyone is always vying for power over one another. We humans play out roles of superior/inferior, perpetrator/victim, better than/less than, strong/weak, and more. From the paradigm of Loving, all beings are created equal. We all have equal access to our source of love, equal access to authentic power, wisdom and strength. Any idea that one person is better, stronger or more powerful than another is only an illusion. What most people think of as power is just a fear-based illusion of power and control. Real, authentic power comes from the source of Loving. All of the rays of the sun are infinitely beautiful, and each has equal access to its source of power. Each can pull as much light from the Source and shine as brightly as any another. Any idea that one person has power over another is a complete irrationality.

By taking responsibility for my own power, I was able to free myself completely from the illusion that I was ever a victim. Tapping into any time in the past where I felt like a victim, I took the knowledge of my equal power back in time to that memory. It is amazing how healing it is to declare that no one has ever had the power to hurt me. I had the power to choose to feel hurt and betrayed, and I also had the power to choose to feel love, compassion and detachment. Since there was no perpetrator and no victim from the eyes of Loving, I was never really a victim. I was simply playing out a role called 'victim' that had no basis in truth.

I may have felt like a victim in the past, and I can take responsibility for my choice to feel that way. I may have thought I was really a victim in the past, and I can take responsibility for my choice to think that way. I may have acted like a victim in the past, and I can take responsibility for my choice to act that way.

Let's take another look at that Fall of Mankind story from the Bible; interestingly enough, many people have taken this story literally and decided to blame Eve, or womankind, with the downfall of humankind. The truth from Source's perspective is that each and every person has free will, and there is no such thing as fault or blame. If it was, in fact, a woman named Eve who first plucked the apple of free will choice and decided to move out of alignment within herself, it was certainly not her responsibility if some guy named Adam chose to taste it as well. If Adam thought that Eve truly had the power to *make* him follow her, then clearly they were playing out roles of perpetrator/victim. Trust me here, Adam was never really a powerless victim; he always had access to his authentic power and the free will choice to choose to act in full alignment with the will of his soul. If he chose not to do so, he would need to take full responsibility for his choice to follow Eve. And visa versa; the story could just as easily have had Adam doing the plucking and enticing, with Eve giving in to temptation and following. In order to up-level as a collective consciousness, anyone holding in blame against Eve or womankind can let go of the irrationalities that women are more powerful than men, that men are weak-willed, that women have the ability to force men to do things that go against their will, that women are evil temptresses, that women need to be contained, suppressed or otherwise controlled, etc. Think about how much power men have been surrendering over to women by persisting with these types of ideas. As a woman myself, it might seem flattering on the personality level to think that millions or perhaps even billions of men believe that women are so powerful as to lead them astray or even destroy them, but the truth is that men are not poor, helpless victims; on the being level, we are all equally powerful as well as equally responsible for ourselves and our choices. This means that the reverse is true as well; women can stop giving their power away to men, and to understand that they have *always* been equal at the being level.

One of the big issues surrounding the women's liberation movement has been the level of anger that has been directed toward the male population as part of the fallout of women reclaiming their equal power. While anger is a normal and natural emotional response when facing something that is out of alignment with our truth, once we come back into alignment, it is imperative to transmute the anger into Loving and come into peace. It does womankind no good and actually creates more suffering when women stay in blame and againstness toward the men who have been simply playing the other side of their coin in the game of victim/perpetrator, inferior/superior, less-than/better-than, and so forth.

Unfortunately, in our mostly fear-based modeling, many women do not understand how to break the patterning of the perpetrator/victim mold, and instead of simply dropping into the neutrality and acceptance of the Loving, they are trying to gain the upper hand in the old paradigm by flipping to the other side of the coin. They are irrationally supporting ideas of fear-based power, and think they need to be stronger, smarter or 'better-than' men in some way in order to prove themselves and to feel powerful. Nothing could be further from the truth. We are all already equally powerful at the level of being. There is nothing to prove on either side, male or female. In truth, each and every one of us contains both male and female energies, regardless of our gender, and it is time we each took 100% responsibility for our own use of power.

The Fall of Mankind is just an old teaching story, after all, and if we focus on blame we are missing the actual point of the story, which was to let us know what had occurred in the past – we, the whole of humanity, fell out of alignment with the will of our souls and therefore with the will of God/the Loving – to bring us to this point in our human evolution and inspire us to take personal responsibility to get back to the garden. There is no such thing as blame from the spiritual perspective; there is simply what happened, everyone involved had 100% responsibility for their free will choice and we are where we are now as a collective consciousness.

Are You Ready to Let Go of Old Ideas of Victim Mentality?

Are you ready to let go of any old, painful and irrational ideas that you were ever a victim? Whether you gave your power over to your parents, your relationships, your teachers, the church, society, the government, social media or simply life circumstances matters not. Right here, right now, you have the free will choice to take responsibility for yourself and reclaim your authentic power.

If you haven't yet felt or experienced your own equal power, it isn't because you are lacking in any way; it simply means that you have not yet tapped in to your source of authentic power. You are connected to Source at the energetic level. All you have to do is own your power by acknowledging it and breathing it in. The knowledge that you are equally powerful as every other being on the planet is all that is needed to provide you with instant access to your own source of power. Right here, you can let go of any and all victim mentality you've been carrying, and come into your true inner strength. Self-empowerment is an inside job. Only you can empower yourself. I encourage you to go for it!

Exercise: Taking 100% Responsibility for Your Source of Authentic Power

Begin by saying a protection prayer, setting conditions of love and light, and invoking spirit's presence.

Place your hands on your heart. Set an intention to access the highest vibration of Loving available. Breathe in the Loving and fill your body with Loving energies from head to toe. Then, set an intention to access the highest level of compassion. Breathe in compassion and fill your body with compassion from head to toe.

Repeat out loud any of the following that resonate, changing the verbiage as needed to reflect your own beliefs:

"I forgive myself for buying into the irrational belief that I have ever been a victim." "My new updated belief is, I now know I have always had equal access to my source of authentic power. From now on, I view myself as equally powerful to every other being. I now claim full 100% responsibility for how I choose to view myself, knowing that I co-create my life. I claim my full authentic power."

"I forgive myself for any time I ever acted like a victim and gave my authentic power away to anyone else." "My new updated belief is, I now know I was simply doing the best I could at that time, with the tools I had, the beliefs I had; if I could have done it any better, I would have. I now know that I have always had equal power as every other being. I now take back any power I gave away and from now on, I view myself as equally powerful to every other being. I now claim full 100% responsibility for the use of my authentic power, and I choose to use it only in alignment with the will of my soul. I now use my power for Loving purposes."

"I forgive myself for buying into the irrational belief that anyone has the power to force me to surrender my authentic power or to make me do something that I know is not in my own highest good." "My new updated belief is, I now know I am equally as powerful as every other being, and my authentic power is my own. I always have free will choice in how to use my authentic power, and from now on I choose to use it only for my highest good. I trust that when I use my power in my own highest good, it is in the highest good of all concerned."

"I forgive myself for buying into the irrational belief that any man or woman has ever been more powerful than me." "My new updated belief is, I now know I now know that men and women have always been equally powerful. Both men and women are sourced from the same source of Loving energy, and both have equal access to authentic power."

"I forgive myself for buying into the irrational belief that I need to fear someone else's power." "My new updated belief is, I now know I now know that my power is equal in strength to anyone else's. I have full free will choice and I am empowered at all times to act in alignment with the will of my soul. No person has power over my freedom to choose my own response. I claim my full authentic power and trust in myself completely to choose what is in my own highest good."

"I forgive myself for buying into the irrational belief that anyone else's power needs to be controlled, contained or otherwise squelched in order to protect me from harm or temptation." "My new updated belief is, I now know I have all of the strength and authentic power I need to follow the will of my own soul, to trust in God's guidance, to say no to temptations and to act on my guidance in every given moment. I am a powerful and connected being, a soul in a body, simply having a human experience. From now on, I take full responsibility for my own use of power, and know that everyone else is responsible for themselves."

Close your process by acknowledging yourself, expressing gratitude to spirit, and fully grounding your energy. Drink plenty of water.

Taking Full Responsibility is Life-Changing

As you can see from the above examples, you can indeed take full responsibility for each and every area of your life.

I did this myself in absolutely every area including but not limited to my health, my self-care, my finances, my friendships, my familial relationships, my main love relationship, my patterns of behavior, my communication, my career, my home environment and so on. If I were to write about how I went about taking full responsibility for each of these areas, this book would be thousands of pages long. So, I've decided to limit it to just a few areas that I found monumentally life-changing. Know that once you grasp this idea and begin to apply it fully in each area of your life, your experience of life will begin to immediately and radically change before your very eyes. I encourage you to grab hold, claim your power & capability to transform your life by taking full responsibility. By doing so, you will begin to co-create the life of your dreams. Go for it! You are worth it.

CHAPTER SIX
Making the Paradigm Shift by Updating Your Belief System

Our belief system contains everything we believe, all ideas that we have gathered throughout our entire life and have filed away as 'fact' inside ourselves. Whether or not these ideas are rational or accurate is another story. Regardless of whether our ideas are based on fact or fiction, rationality or irrationality, our belief system is wired energetically throughout our whole body. Our individual cells contain a vibratory energy that equals our beliefs. When our beliefs are greatly fear-based, our energy consequently vibrates at a lower frequency. When our belief system is based in Loving, we are more open, expansive, and flowing, and our energy is vibrating at a higher level of consciousness.

To whatever degree we are viewing life from the fear-based, right/wrong perspective, we are residing in the lower, tighter, more restrictive base of the spiral of consciousness. To make a paradigm shift to a higher level of consciousness, we can choose to view life from a higher perspective. When we shift our perspective to a higher level, our belief system will begin to reflect more open, loving, expansive interpretations of reality, and we will start to move higher up the spiral where we then have a broader, more encompassing, more accepting view of life.

Making the paradigm shift is a process, not a one-time event. It takes time to rewire your whole belief system to align with your spiritual truth. The exercises in this book are just a guide. There is no right or wrong way to go about making a shift in consciousness. If you begin trusting your inner guidance, you will be shown the way that is right for you.

Each belief contained in your file begins in your brain as an original idea or a passing thought. Repeat experience then solidifies certain ideas into beliefs, which vibrate at a certain frequency of energy. The energy that makes up your beliefs is contained in every cell of your body. Your beliefs then go on to vibrate inside of your cells to create repeated thoughts, which in turn create your feelings, which lead to your response, which then produce a certain outcome or the results in your life. So, beliefs lead to thoughts, thoughts lead to feelings, feelings lead to actions, and all of it together equals your reality. B->T->F->A=R

The Equation of Inner Reality Creates Outer Reality

Your inner reality creates your outer reality. Therefore, in order to create different results in your life, you would first need to change your beliefs. Think of your life as a math equation. If your current belief system is vibrating at a one, your thoughts will be equal to your beliefs, your feelings will be equal to your thoughts and beliefs, your actions will be equal to your feelings, thoughts, and beliefs, and your results will be equal to all of the above: $1 \times 1 \times 1 \times 1 = 1$. On the other hand, if your beliefs are vibrating at a nine, your equation will read 9x1x1x1=9.

Most people wonder why they keep getting the same results over and over again, year after year. Typically, most people attempt to resolve their problems by changing their physical level results or their outer level reality. This would be like trying to change an equation's answer without first changing or addressing the existing problem. Have you or has someone you know ever broken up with someone, established a new relationship only to have the same issues that plagued the last relationship show up again in the new one? How about changing a job and having the same problems eventually appear at the new job? Running away to a new town only to have the same challenges come up as in the last?

Personally, I experienced two very similar marriages/divorces, and sometimes even forget which event happened during which relationship – same issue, different face! This is very common with people trying to change their outer level reality without first changing their inner. Their lessons simply repeat over and over, usually getting worse if not addressed. I eventually learned that if I wanted true change in my life, I needed to change my inner reality first.

When I first started taking responsibility for my life, I learned about the power of positive thinking. As a quick learner, I was soon practicing regular meditation, visualizing, and saying positive affirmations over and over again. These tools were frustrating to me at the time because, while I felt a little bit more optimistic, my outer results stayed about the same. My frustration caused me to grow very adamant about learning how to make lasting change. Eventually, I discovered the equation of manifestation – beliefs create thoughts, thoughts create feelings, feelings lead to actions, actions create our results. I realized that while I was distracting myself by thinking positive thoughts, saying affirmations, and distracting myself from my fears, my subconscious mind was still quietly running the old, negative thoughts anyway, just at a level below my conscious attention. The truth was that I didn't believe my positive affirmations; perhaps some small part of me believed, but there was a definite part of me that was saying something under my breath like, "This is bullshit. You don't really think this is going to work, do you? You are such a stupid idiot…" and so on. Once I clearly heard the part of myself that was negating all of my positive thinking, I realized that by running around saying affirmations all day, I was just trying to brush my issues under the rug rather than healing them. I knew, deep down, that there *had* to be a better way.

About this time in my life, I was in an unhappy marriage, feeling pretty depressed about my life, and feeling quite a bit of pressure from my soul to get on with my life's work, which I'd been altogether avoiding. A divine series of events transpired that offered me a huge opportunity to grow. I had a long bout of pneumonia, followed by a series of panic attacks in which I was convinced I could not breathe. Now, since I'd already had my near-death awakening experience at age eighteen and had opened to channel, I had an ongoing connection with my guides and masters, who assured me that I was not going to die. My guides had a great sense of humor; they'd joke that while I may *wish* I were dying, I wasn't going to get out of my contract so easily. I had work to do here, so I simply needed to get busy. Knowing that I needed to fulfill my spiritual commitment just caused me even more anxiety at the time, bringing on more frequent and severe panic attacks. My guides simply laughed and urged me to move forward. In desperation, I ended up contacting a relative who'd had some experience with anxiety; I received a referral to an organization that provided support for people who suffered from panic attacks.

Attending the meeting of this anxiety support group, I spent the next hour in a state of outrage over the amount of complete nonsense foisted upon the fear-filled participants. Tips like 'don't ever rearrange your furniture again' and 'give up driving forever' were delivered as if these were precious pearls of wisdom I'd be a fool not to swallow. The basic premise of the meeting went something like, "There is no cure for fear or anxiety, this will be a life-long issue, learn to cope with the panic, take meds, deal with it." None of that rang the slightest bit true for me.

What I can say about that meeting is that it was a life-changing experience for me because I became galvanized inside to prove differently. Every fiber of my being revolted at being told I'd have to live with *this* level of fear – or any level of fear, for that matter – for the rest of my life. After all, I'd already had a taste of the freedom available in the Loving paradigm, and I'd felt fearless. At the thought of never feeling that kind of freedom again, I felt a loud, clear, resounding 'NO WAY' screaming throughout my entire being, and I got up and left that meeting before it concluded. A lovely and distraught woman followed me out the door, urging me to stay to receive help for my terrible condition. I recall laughing nearly hysterically, saying something like, "If that is your idea of 'help', *no thank you*." While I felt bad about my reply later because I could have responded more kindly, I wasn't feeling particularly nice at that moment. More accurately, I felt irate. My feeling-barometer was screaming, '*Way* off-course!' Frankly, what they offered sounded like a life sentence in a tight, dark, squalid prison – I was not even remotely interested.

It was the late 1980s, way back in the day before the internet, when looking up 'how to heal panic attacks' was not an option. It appeared that I only had two choices: taking the mainstream medical route of getting a prescription for anti-anxiety medication or taking the alternative course of actually addressing my anxiety. This was a no-brainer for me since I was already fully aware that medicating my fear was not going to resolve it in the long term in any way.

Thus began my journey of practicing meditation, yoga, breathing techniques, positive affirmations, repeating mantras, and anything else I could find. While all of that was beautiful, supportive, and sometimes even produced short-term relief, the problem was that I wanted more than just a quick fix. I still had all of the same fears and anxiety swirling through my body when I wasn't actually meditating, positively affirming, or hanging out in a headstand. In reality, I was a young mother with two very active children, and I didn't have the calling to join an ashram. I needed to be available to be with my kids, engage in life, go to the grocery store, as well as move forward into doing the work of my soul. Having spontaneous, unplanned panic attacks for the rest of my life was simply not an acceptable option.

I went through a phase where I was totally pissed at the world, so angry with myself and all of my fears. Eventually, I decided I was done with my fear and that I would do whatever it took to make it go away. I began to say no to my thoughts, and they kept coming back. I got mad at my fear-thoughts, and they kept coming back. I berated, screamed at, and criticized my fear-thoughts, and they kept coming back. I begged and pleaded and bargained with my fear-thoughts, and they kept coming back. I did my best to avoid and distract myself from my fear-thoughts, and they simply kept coming back. At some point, I came into the knowing that I needed to respond differently to my fear to heal and resolve it for good.

What ended up happening? I was guided to accept my

fear. My guides instructed me to start listening to the fear rather than trying to get rid of, suppress, soothe, avoid, deny, or distract. I began to listen, not censoring my thoughts in any way. As I listened from a place of neutral acceptance, I became more aware of my fears, began to identify certain threads of thought, and eventually began to follow those threads of thought back to their origin. I would picture myself as a child, maybe a specific memory would come up, or sometimes I would feel myself at a certain age or period in my life. By simply listening to myself from a space of receptivity, I was guided directly to the root of my fear and shown how I'd gotten stuck in a fearful pattern of thinking based on the beliefs I bought into as a child. I began to flood myself with compassion and to wrap my younger self in love and kindness. Then, I was guided to clear my old, fear-based interpretations of reality and create new beliefs based on my current understanding of spiritual truth.

To the degree I was able to apply compassion inside myself, I could feel and sense my old belief lifting from my body. When the old belief lifted, the fear around it disappeared. Very quickly – within days of discovering this new tool – the panic attacks disappeared; soon, my anxiety was a thing of the past. It was the most amazing and profound feeling. I felt washed clean of the old, fear-based ideas and wrapped in love, joy, and support by my new ideas.

At times when I was not able to access compassion for myself inside of myself, I stayed stuck in my old belief, which caused repetitive fear-based thoughts to arise, which led to feeling awful inside. I could give a new belief lip-service mentally a hundred times, repeat positive affirmations until my face was blue, but the old belief would not lift until I was able to access the feeling of compassion and apply compassionate self-forgiveness on the inside for the suffering this belief had caused me. This is how I came to understand just how important the ingredient of compassion is to the process of updating my belief system. I learned that if I wanted freedom, I would need to persist until I felt the compassion toward myself attached to each and every memory of suffering.

Incredibly, as I applied compassion to myself regularly, the old fear-based beliefs permanently lifted, and new ones took hold. Each time I integrated a new belief, my fear-based thinking lessened, and my positive, supportive thinking came more naturally. Eventually, I updated all of my files and transformed my thinking, my subsequent feelings, and my subsequent actions, which led me to produce entirely new and different – healthy, joy-filled, loving, authentic, empowering – results in my life. I now live in joy and freedom, thanks to the healing power of compassion.

Taking Inventory of Your Belief System

Before you can begin the process of updating your own belief system, you first have to identify the irrationality that exists in your current belief system. Let's take a look at some commonly held beliefs. I invite you to go ahead and see if any of these are beliefs you hold currently or have held in the past to any degree. As you read each belief, give it a rating to show how it resonates in your consciousness. You can number it from 0-10 or give it a word rating- 'never', 'occasionally', 'sometimes', 'frequently' or 'always'. You could do a Y or N for yes or no, or use a checkmark. However you decide to do this is up to you; I encourage you to use some form of a rating system as this will give you more insight into your own current set of beliefs.

Exercise:
Ask Yourself, "Do I ever think…"

Life is a struggle _____

I have little control over my life _____

Other people are luckier than me _____

I have to work really hard to do it all _____

I'm not supported enough in life _____

There is a lot of pain and very little joy in life _____

There isn't enough for me to have what I want _____

Money is difficult to get _____

My problems would be solved if I had more money _____

Really rich people are snobs _____

I don't deserve to have nice things _____

Poor people are more spiritual than rich people _____

It is selfish for me to want more than I need _____

There isn't enough to go around, so we need to scrimp ____

Managing money is stressful _____

Work is hard and stressful _____

I cannot earn enough money doing what I love to do _____

I have to have a steady job to provide security _____

I cannot support myself; I need someone else's help _____

If I don't do it myself, it won't get done right _____

Things need to be done a certain way _____

I'm not a good enough _____

I need to be perfect at all times _____

It's better not to try than to screw it up _____

If I make a mistake, I'm a failure _____

If I make a mistake, I deserve to feel ashamed _____

It's my fault _____

I need people to like me in order to feel ok _____

If people don't talk to me, they must be mad at me _____

I have done something wrong and cannot be forgiven _____

It matters what other people think _____

Other people's needs are more important than mine _____

I need to do everything to make other people happy _____

If I do what I really want to do, I'd be selfish _____

I need to keep up appearances to appease someone else ____

My children's behavior is my personal responsibility _____

My children's needs should come before mine _____

I'm responsible for keeping my kids happy at all costs _____

I'm responsible if I hurt someone's feelings _____

Someone is to blame for hurting my feelings _____

Other people's opinions are more important than mine ____

I have to take care not to make someone angry _____

I cannot trust myself to do the right thing _____

I cannot make the right decision; I doubt myself _____

I screw everything up; I must be stupid _____

When someone is blaming me, I should feel guilty _____

I should have known better not to _____

If I can hang onto my anger long enough, I'll show them ____

People who are bad deserve to be punished _____

People should know right from wrong and act accordingly __

Because I know I'm not perfect, I am unworthy _____

I'm unworthy of having everything I desire _____

It would be selfish & greedy of me to have everything I desire _____

People who want things are ungrateful _____

Having everything I desire is impossible _____

I have to settle for having just some of the things I want ____

I don't deserve any better than this _____

There is no way I could have the life of my dreams _____

People need to stop dreaming and live in the real world ____

People need to be tough in order to get ahead _____

I need to be in control of my relationships to be safe _____

People should listen to me when I'm speaking _____

Nobody cares what I think anyway _____

My needs are not important _____

I need to raise my voice to be heard _____

It's not Ok to argue in front of the children _____

Having a relationship is difficult _____

I never get enough love or attention _____

If we don't have sex, I feel unloved or unwanted _____

Love is painful and challenging _____

I'll never have the kind of relationship I really want _____

True intimacy is scary; being vulnerable is unsafe _____

I'm not worthy of being loved unconditionally _____

I deserve to be treated poorly in relationships _____

I cannot love and respect myself after all I've done _____

I should have done _____ differently

There is no such thing as a happy couple _____

My happiness depends upon how others treat me _____

I only feel good when someone is showing me they care ____

I need someone to care about me to feel loved _____

What Did You Learn About Yourself?

Take a look at your responses. Every one of these ideas is fear-based and completely irrational. What did you learn about yourself? If your answer was 'never' or you gave a rating of zero to any particular idea, I would say that belief does not apply to you. If you said 'yes', 'sometimes', 'frequently' or 'always' to any of these ideas, I highly encourage you to update those beliefs to new ideas that will better support you. This list is just a starting point to give you an idea of what irrational beliefs look like and sound like in your own thought process. Irrationality stems from fear, is limiting, judgmental, restricting, and disempowering. Rationality is based in Loving, is expansive, accepting, open, and empowering.

Once you understand the difference between fear-based, irrational thought, and love-based, rational thought, you can quickly learn how to identify your own irrational thinking. From there, you can begin to identify your old, fear-based beliefs and transform your belief system. Let's take a look at some different types of irrational thinking.

Irrationalities Based on Negatives

The easiest irrationalities to spot in your own thought-process will be based on a negative such as 'can't', 'don't', 'not', 'shouldn't', and any other obvious negative. "I can't do it", "I don't know how", "I'm not good enough", and "I shouldn't even bother to try"' are just a few of the many, many negatives most of us tell ourselves every day. People who are afraid of making mistakes or failing will often get stuck in 'I can't' types of irrationality. The truth is you can do anything you set your mind to do. If you can imagine it, envision it, see it, sense it, or feel it happening, there is a way to do it. If you persist in holding and repeating a limiting belief, whatever the type of negative, you will keep yourself locked in that idea and continue perpetuating that belief.

If you set an intention inside of yourself to change your beliefs, and you monitor your thoughts, you will quickly be able to spot these most obviously negative, limiting types of thinking.

Irrationalities Based on Comparison

Another common type of irrationality is the comparison. Watch your thoughts for comparisons, words that measure things such as 'more' or 'less', 'better' or 'worse', 'stronger than' or 'weaker than'. Having thoughts that say, "My roommate is smarter than me," "Other people are more important than me," "He is better-looking than me," "I'm not as attractive as she is," or any other kind of comparison that makes you feel bad or less-than in any way does not serve you in the least. It is vital, when moving into a higher, more rational state of consciousness, to remember that we are all uniquely different. There is no better-than or less-than from the Loving perspective, only equality, and uniqueness. Let go of needing or wanting to be the best or the most whatever in the world, and simply focus on being yourself. You can absolutely be the best 'you' you can be. Just let go of measuring yourself up against anyone else. This does not mean that you cannot use others to inspire you; to the contrary. You will become much more inspired when you cease to compare and rather see the beauty, the skill, or the success in others and think, "I can have that, too."

Irrationalities Based on Right/Wrong or Good/ Bad

Another fairly obvious type of irrationality is beliefs that are based on 'good' or 'bad', 'right' or 'wrong'. This is what I call either/or consciousness – often referred to as black and white thinking – which says that something is either one way or the other. The truth is that often two things can exist simultaneously in the same space, and there are many, many shades of gray. For instance, in the old 'I'm right, so you're wrong' model, could it be possible that we are just in two different places on the learning track and that we both are operating from our own place of truth, relative to what we know to be right for us at this time? This would translate in right/wrong speak to say 'we are both right; let's just agree to disagree'. There are the old, perfectionistic beliefs like 'this has to be done the *right* way', 'I never do anything right', and 'people are supposed to know what's right.' Whose right way, mine, or yours? The Queen's? The Pope's? Krishna's? People who hold irrationalities based on the idea that they are right are often viewed as self-righteous, narrow-minded, or zealots standing on a soapbox. How about 'You need to be a good girl'; 'Good boys don't hit'; and 'If I am really, really good, then _____ (for example: Santa will come, the tooth fairy will visit, my momma won't die, my daddy will love me, etc).'

Then there is the flip side, who can tell me what is truly wrong or bad? Many people on the planet today hold dozens of these types of irrationalities out towards others who are different, leading to 'enemy' thinking and war mentality. 'Those people are wrong for _____.' Holding beliefs that other people are wrong or bad for whatever they are doing often leads to actions of againstness, shaming, punishment, vengeance, hatred, and violence. People will often engage in vindictive or hurtful behavior based upon some erroneous idea that they are somehow enacting justice. This is mob-mentality, vigilante, radical group, perpetrator type of thinking that only creates more suffering upon the planet. Then there are the wrong beliefs that are directed toward one's self; these are the ones that used to really get at me, beliefs like 'if someone is mad at me, it means I've done something wrong'; 'if I do it wrong, I need to feel ashamed of myself'; 'mistakes are wrong or bad'; 'taking care of myself is wrong and selfish; I need to put others first', 'it is wrong for me to _____'; and the oh-so-limiting beliefs like 'it is bad to _____'; 'I am a bad person if I _____'; 'because _____ thinks I'm bad, that means it is true'; 'bad people go to hell'; and 'if I do something bad, I deserve to _____ (for example: suffer, die, rot in hell, be punished, feel guilty, etc.)'. All of these are examples of just a small selection of the millions of irrationalities based on black or white, right/wrong – as one of my friends put it, 'it's my way or the highway'-type of thinking. Watch your thoughts for these, and apply lots of compassion on the inside when they appear.

Irrationalities Based on Extremes

Another type of irrationality that is relatively easy to spot is the extreme, which is a gross exaggeration such as 'always', 'never', 'nothing', 'everything', 'best', or 'worst'. This is the sort of thinking that resides at the furthest edges of the fear-based spectrum, so based in lack consciousness that it says that it's all or nothing; 'you *never* listen to me!'; 'I'm always the last person to know anything'; 'if I'm not the absolute best at something, it means I've failed'; and 'nothing I do turns out well - I ruin everything I touch.' Thinking in extremes will keep you stuck in fear and lack for certain. Why put yourself in a box with rigid, close-minded thinking such as 'always' and 'never'?

Irrationalities Based on Absolutes

The next type of irrational thinking is based on absolutes such as 'should', 'must', 'only', 'need to', or 'have to'. These are limiting because they are based on the extremely irrational idea that there is only one right or wrong way to do something. Ideas such as a lady must keep her knees together', a child should never speak until spoken to', 'I have to _____ right now', 'I need to lose weight before I can date', 'I'll only be happy when…' and, of course, the infamous 'you should know better' are all ultimatums that are saying that there is just one correct answer, only one way that can be, or only one way something is supposed to go. The truth is that there is an infinite number of possibilities of all that can occur as you are learning and growing. The idea that you 'should' or 'must' do something implies that there is just one correct thing to do, which brings guilt into play if you choose differently; if you can change the 'should' into a 'could', this will allow for your free will choice in the matter at any given time. You will begin to live free of guilt, knowing that there is a number of options. Instead of thinking, 'I should do the dishes right now', you could think, 'I could do the dishes right now'. This makes it Ok to decide to read a book at that moment and do the dishes later, guilt-free, knowing that there is no right or wrong choice – there are just decisions, what happens, and the consequences of your choice. Or, you could happily decide to do the dishes, feeling good and empowered about your choice rather than resentful because you feel like you *have* to do something and are powerless to choose differently.

Irrationalities Based on Judgments

Probably the strongest type of irrationality is based on harsh judgment. This kind of irrational thinking is critical, demeaning, and often involves a put-down of some sort towards self or others. 'I am so stupid', 'he is such an asshole', 'most people are totally ignorant', 'people can't drive worth a dang in the rain', '_____ people are evil' and the ever-popular 'I am guilty for being born'. These ideas are all examples of thoughts that are directly related to a feeling of judgment. People who regularly engage in this type of thinking and express it openly towards others might be viewed as prejudiced, biased, bigoted, or stereotypical thinkers. Most of us have these types of thoughts, whether we express them or not. While all feelings are completely normal and acceptable, what makes it irrational is when we turn a temporary, fleeting feeling into a 'being' statement. The verb 'to be' is an identifying verb that makes a statement about someone's or something's essence. So, thoughts or beliefs that begin with 'I am', 'he is', 'she is', 'we are', 'they are' or 'it is' are all saying that this is the way something *is* - that it is permanently so. If we identify ourselves or others based on temporary feelings or judgments, we are identifying with a lie or an untruth that does not serve our greater good.

In order for any statements that begin with 'I am', 'he is', 'people are', etc., to be based on rational thought, the statement would need to be indicative of the true essence of the subject getting identified in the thought. With the knowledge of our true nature as divine beings having a human experience of learning and growing, we can begin to let go of blanket statements about people, let go of prejudices, let go of stereotypical thinking, let go of believing our own judgments as 'true' and begin to live from a place that supports our true essence to thrive. When I catch myself in the 'I am' type of irrational thinking, I quickly forgive myself, state my new updated belief about my true 'I am' nature as a Loving being, and change the thought to an 'I feel' statement that is only temporary. Other ways to begin to update this kind of thinking include using words that separate the thoughts, words, appearances, feelings, behaviors, or actions of the subject from the subject's 'beingness'. For instance, instead of thinking, "He is a jerk," I might think, "He is *acting* like a jerk right now... and I know he is really a divine being just learning and growing." Another example: instead of "I am ugly" or "I am fat", I might substitute "I *feel* ugly right now" or "I think I *look* fat in this outfit." A final example that can be life-changing: Instead of "I am sick", I would recommend using, "I *feel* sick at this moment" – this allows me to view it as temporary, rather than my identity or a permanent, fixed part of who I am.

These are some of the most common types of irrationalities. Each person's belief system is wired differently, based on what they saw, heard, and experienced as a child and what interpretations they made. Only you will be able to listen to your own thinking to determine if a thought is rational or irrational. Be willing to examine your thoughts closely to identify any fear-based, irrational, disempowering, or limited thinking.

Other, More Subtle, Irrationality

While irrationalities that have negatives like 'I don't have enough money', extremes such as 'I'll always be unhappy', right/wrong or good/bad ideas such as 'she's wrong' and judgments like 'he's a jerk' will get easy to spot once you become aware of them, many irrationalities are phrased with more subtle wording that can make them increasingly challenging to catch in the beginning. Ideas such as, 'it matters what other people think of me' or 'It's my fault that _____' can be tough to spot at first because they aren't languaged in negatives, don't have an obvious right/wrong, comparison, absolute, extreme, or judgment that leaps out. Yet, they are totally fear-based and completely irrational. The bottom line is that if an idea makes you feel bad or limited in any way, it's likely to be irrational. Be willing to persevere until you spot them all. You can do it. If you commit to clearing your irrationality and updating your belief system to newer, more supportive beliefs, you will soon be watching your entire life shift for the better right before your very own eyes.

Discovering an Irrational Belief Can Seem Shocking

Discovering that you have been holding an irrational belief can sometimes seem quite shocking, especially if you are very new at examining your own belief system. I can recall my earliest clear memory of learning that something I'd held as a true 'fact' wasn't true at all, and to this day, I can remember how shocked and discombobulated I felt to discover I didn't really know everything after all.

I was about eleven or twelve years old. My parents owned a tavern – all my siblings and I worked there – and we had live music on the weekends to entertain the crowd. There was a Country band playing one night, and the lead singer was a stunningly gorgeous, outrageously curvaceous and sexy blonde – think Dolly Parton with silky-straight long hair about six inches taller. This woman was like a Malibu Barbie come to life, and I literally couldn't take my eyes off of her. During a break, I overheard someone asking her about her grandchild, and my mind could not compute this. I approached her and said, "You can't be a grandmother! Grandmothers are old, gray, and wrinkled." She laughed a beautiful, tinkling laugh and assured me that, in fact, she was indeed a grandmother and that not all grandmothers are old, gray, and wrinkly. She showed me a picture of her granddaughter to prove it. I was stunned. I didn't know what to think. How could I have been so misinformed? Why didn't someone let me in on this sooner? How could I have been so blind and not known it? I was despondent for weeks, not about the actual belief itself – which, quite honestly, was very liberating as I'd certainly love to be a young-looking grandmother – but about the idea that I might be clueless about a whole bunch of stuff. That felt very painful to me at the time, and that was long before I knew to hold myself in compassion.

If you find yourself feeling discombobulated, disoriented, shocked, or freaked out in any way to find that what you'd always believed to be true might not be so, go easy on yourself. Be gentle with your self-talk. Be willing to reassure the small, basic part of you that feels like the world is rocking wildly and might tip over that this is Ok and everything related to your new level of consciousness is unfolding in divine-perfect order. And remind yourself: this awareness you are having right now is causing a paradigm shift, with the intention to shift your entire world view to a higher perspective.

Think about what the people had to go through in the sixteenth century when most of the population thought that the world was flat and that you could literally sail right off the edge. Let yourself off the hook for not knowing everything before you did; none of us knows everything. The fact is that we are all simply growing and expanding into higher and new levels of truth *all the time*. There isn't an end where it stops on a level that says 'Congratulations! You have arrived. Now you know it all and can stop learning.'

Thankfully, at this point in my journey, I am able just to laugh whenever I discover another irrational belief within my own consciousness. I am delighted to know the level of things that I know, and I am also Ok with the fact that there is still so much that is over my head. I trust I'm expanding into higher truth as swiftly as I am ready to receive a higher understanding.

Because I love going higher, I greet the opportunity to update my irrational beliefs with joy; I know every belief I align with Loving is bringing me one step closer to God-consciousness and the embodiment of Loving.

Be Willing to Examine Your Belief System Fearlessly
Now, I'll be honest with you; most people's belief systems are vast, sometimes complicated, and uniquely-wired mazes of intrigue. Don't let that idea stop you from taking a deep, hard, fearless look at your own beliefs. Know that you absolutely won't be able to view all of your beliefs instantaneously. Just relax. You have plenty of time. If you have an intention to move from a fear-based reality into greater levels of Loving, you can trust that whichever irrational beliefs you need to see first will come forward for your attention. Imagine unraveling a big ball of yarn; you have to start with the end that is present and visible, then you simply give a little tug and follow the thread, trusting that it will all unwind in its own order. Have trust in the process as you go about updating your beliefs. Start with whatever beliefs are most present and visible. Your consciousness will take care of revealing whatever thread of beliefs is to show up next for your process.

We store beliefs about everything that has crossed our awareness in this lifetime. The word 'everything' certainly covers a lot of stuff. Don't worry. Beliefs are usually grouped together in our mind by subject matter, so if you have any particular issue or challenge come up, you'd just be presented with the beliefs around that specific topic in whatever order they surface for your attention. You can think of your beliefs as separate files in your personal computer-mind, and the categories of beliefs as the folders where the individual files are stored. For instance, you may have a folder labeled 'relationships', another labeled 'money', another labeled 'physical health', and so on. The computer screen just shows you one open file from a folder at a time, so you don't need to stress about all of your other unopened folders. Make a commitment to yourself to update your belief system from fear-based to Loving. You can relax and trust that everything will unfold in divine-perfect order, simply starting with whatever folder of beliefs is currently on your mind most presently.

Ask Yourself, "How is this working for me?"

Once you have identified an irrational belief within your own mind's filing system, before your belief can permanently change, there is a crucial moment wherein you must make a conscious choice to believe differently. If you skip this little but mighty step, you will be banging your head against the wall because your head will understand your new belief while the rest of your body will still believe in the old one. Let me say this another way, if you don't actually feel or state to yourself, either aloud or inside of yourself, that you are ready to change, the old belief will still have power, will still be active and operating within your mind's belief system. You must actively, energetically *decide* to believe something different in order to update your belief file effectively.

A simple analogy could be pulling up a word document on your computer that says 'I will always be a failure.' You can take the time to delete that sentence and type the words 'I am now successful at everything I do.' Then you close the program without saving the new document. Guess what? In that file inside of your brain-computer, it will still say 'I will always be a failure', because you skipped the step of deciding to change. It would be as if the little reminder box popped up to ask 'Do you want to save changes?' and you clicked 'No

– do not save changes'. Energetically, you have to say 'yes' to the changes in your belief system – you must engage your free will choice and decide to change – in order for the new belief to click into place and replace the old information in your mind's file folder.

The way to do this is to ask yourself, each time you have identified an irrational belief, "How is this working for me?" If the answer is 'it's not going well', right there, you can decide to believe something different. This question is a pivotal point in your conscious evolution because it will give you the power you need to detach from the old belief and decide to embrace a new one. Here's how the question works:

Let's say I've just identified the irrational belief I've been holding that other people's needs are more important than mine. I then ask myself, "How is this belief working for me?" This question allows me to consciously examine my past to review all of the times I have put other people's needs above my own. I recall the time I didn't pick up my son on time because the friend I was out with wanted to stay out longer. I remember the times I didn't eat because my boss needed me to do something or my kids needed a ride somewhere last minute. I recall all of my feelings of resentment that everybody else's needs seemed more important than mine, and I feel angry inside that I allowed myself to treat myself so uncaringly for so many years. How is that working for me? It's not working well at all. In fact, I am over it. I am so done with that belief. I am ready to change that one. Right there, once I have consciously made a choice to change, I have access to a higher possibility for myself. I can now choose a new, more supportive belief and know that it will really stick.

By asking myself the empowering question, "How is this working for me?" I am giving myself the intrinsic motivation to change my belief for the better. When I take full responsibility for creating my own life, knowing that my beliefs create my reality, nothing is more motivating than examining my past results to spur on change. Here are a few more examples of this deciding moment:

John's Story

John comes to see me because he is feeling stuck financially. He has big dreams, yet somehow hasn't been able to achieve his goals. He vents his frustrations and comes upon an irrational belief that he'll never amount to anything. He recalls his grandmother telling him this, his father telling him this, and his fourth-grade teacher telling him this. I ask John, "How's that idea working for you?" John explodes, "It's not! It sucks!" Great. John now has the deciding power to change. He is clearly feeling ready. I ask, "What would you like to believe instead?" John immediately replies, "I can succeed. I am highly capable and I can amount to whatever I want. I can realize my dreams." Right there, John is ready to move into the process to update his belief file. He has identified the old, irrational belief. He has energetically decided to change it, and he has articulated a new, updated belief to replace the old.

Melinda's Story

Melinda is a client who is seeking support to stand up to an abusive ex-husband and controlling parents. As she is sharing her feelings, she discovers the irrational belief that she doesn't have a voice. She remembers her parents telling her not to speak unless spoken to, her grandfather proclaiming children should be seen and not heard, and her ex-husband telling her to shut up. I ask her, "How's that working for you?" Melinda bursts into tears and sobs, "It's not! I hate it! It's not true! I *do* have a voice, and I'm sick of people telling me that what I have to say doesn't matter!" Right there, Melinda is in touch with tremendous power as she decides to change that old, unsupportive belief for the better.

Randy's Story

Randy is a young man who has been referred to me for depression. As Randy is talking, he arrives at the awareness that he doesn't believe he can be happy because happiness is always out there somewhere in the future. When he was little, his happiness was locked into ideas of 'someday we'll go to Disneyland' or 'wait until Christmas'; when the holiday passed, he still wasn't happy, and he had to come up with another future fantasy of 'I'll be happy when _____ happens'. When I ask the question, "How's that working for you?", Randy is uncertain. He shares that he believes it is true that he will never be happy, that happiness is unattainable and will always be out of his reach. Here, Randy does not yet have the decisive power to update his belief system to a more supportive belief and claim himself as his own source of joy. There is clearly no access to a higher truth for him, yet, and likely there are more irrational beliefs that are standing in the way of his infinite access to joy. Because it is extremely important to trust the process of unraveling at each person's own unique pace, I do not push Randy to a higher level of truth than he is ready to receive. I ask, "Are you open to the possibility that you could be happy right now?" He replies that he would like to believe it is possible, but he just isn't sure he can. Here, I would recognize that Randy has not yet decided to make a change in his belief system, so he would not move on to updating his irrational belief. He may need to sit with his old beliefs for a while and explore how they have been impacting his life some more before he is ready to consider a better option.

Nina's Story

Nina has been referred to me because of chronic pain. After just a few minutes of sharing about her childhood, she encounters the irrational belief that life is extremely painful. I ask, "How's that working for you?" Nina begins to laugh. She laughs until she is crying and replies, "Obviously, not so great." I ask her, "Are you ready to believe something different?" She replies, "I really want to, but I don't know-how. All I have ever known is pain." Nina is open to hearing a higher level of truth, even though she doesn't know what that is yet. I explain that our beliefs create our reality, and that if she wants to create a life free of pain, all she has to do is decide to believe something different. She is the co-creator of her world, and she is a powerful manifestor, as her experience with a painful reality can attest. I ask, "Are you open to the possibility that life can be beautiful, joy-filled, wonderful, and so on?" She gets very animated and says, "Oh, yes! I am open to that." I ask, "What would you like to believe about your life?" Nina responds, "That life is safe, pain-free, and wonderful. That I now live in joy and experience gratitude and wonder every day." Right there, with her enthusiastic response, Nina has the power to begin to work her process to update her belief system to change the way she experiences life for the better.

These are just a few examples of the point of power in deciding to update an old, limiting belief for the better. In the third example, Randy wasn't ready to shift his point of view. Sometimes people get very stuck in their old perception of reality – they can only see the parade from street-level and do not believe that another view is possible even though the stairway is right in front of them with the door standing wide open. Understand that we create our own individual reality – literally – based upon what we believe to be true at the time, and sometimes what we create feels really, really real. People will say things like, "But it's *true*! Such-and-such really *does* happen to me all the time, so how can I believe differently?"

At one point in my life, my own irrationality kept me completely blinded; I thought all of it was true – every last defeating, depressing, disempowering bit of it. I still can recall the feeling of believing that my lack-and-limitation thoughts were set in stone, based on unchangeable, cold, hard facts. I can remember thinking things like, "Here we go again; this is happening again, so it must be true. It's a fact because it is my real experience." What I had to learn, and what you can learn, too, is that, yes, we do indeed have certain experiences, but things only happen the way that they happen at that moment because we *believed* they would happen that way first. Other people around us are having entirely different experiences in similar situations all the time. Understand that if you don't like something in your life, your power to change it can only come when you decide to change what you believe to be true about it. This is because your view of truth is relative to your current perspective. It is one of life's strange paradoxes because what you are experiencing looks real, feels real, seems real, and therefore you think it must be true. And yet, it will only continue to feel true if you continue to believe that it is so.

If you find yourself getting stuck on something that you really think is set in stone, yet you know it is limiting, and you're sick of creating that reality, try asking yourself, "Do I want this to continue to be true and real for me, or would I like to create a different outcome?" Don't rely on past or current outer appearances to determine your truth; appearances are deceiving because you can change your perspective almost instantly the moment you decide to believe something more empowering.

The highlight of my week is when a client calls to share

their miraculous story about how they changed a belief, and their reality instantly changed to reflect their new belief. You, too, can create a miracle in your own life. Dozens, even hundreds, of them if you wish. You simply have to believe that it is possible.

If you don't believe that something could be different, it won't be. If you are, at the very least, open to the possibility that things could change if you update your beliefs, then things can begin to change. If you can grasp this concept, really wrap your mind around it, you will become extremely excited about the infinite possibilities you can create in your own life.

When you encounter an old, irrational belief that is no longer serving you, I encourage you to get emphatic about changing it. Get excited about the new possibilities. Become adamant that you are shifting this old idea into a newer, healthier version. Be decisive. Make a clear, empowering decision that says, "That belief is no longer working for me. I am over that old idea. I am ready to change it for the better. I know that I create my own reality based upon what I believe is true. I am a powerful co-creator of my own life." The more energy you can put into your decision, the more determined you are to change, the more receptive you will be, and the faster you will integrate your new beliefs.

The Process of Transforming Your Belief System

Now that you can see how to go about identifying your old, fear-based, limiting, irrational beliefs and know that you must make a clear, conscious, energetic choice to change them, let's take a look at the process of clearing those old beliefs that are no longer serving you from your mind-files and updating them to new, empowering rational beliefs.

The process of clearing irrationality can be broken down into three stages:

Stage 1: Preparation
Stage 2: Processing
Stage 3: Closing

Stage 1: Preparation

Let's take an in-depth look at the preparation stage for working with your belief system, which is about creating a protected, Loving space in which to work with your beliefs.

The Preparation stage includes three parts; A: Protection, B: Invocation, and C: Breathing in Love and Compassion. You may be somewhat familiar with these if you have been actively participating in the exercises at the end of each chapter. Here, I will go into greater detail about how to go about preparing a safe and supportive energy container before you begin to work your process of updating your belief system.

Stage 1: Preparation - Part A: Protection

The first part of the preparation stage is to do some intentional energy protection to create a safe, Loving field. Sit or lie down in a comfortable position, spine straight, breathing naturally, and relaxing your body. Next, say a short protection prayer or set some conditions to surround your energy field with love and light.

A very simple, universal protection prayer works well. Say out loud, "The light of God surrounds me, the love of God enfolds me, the power of God protects me, the presence of God watches over me. Wherever I am, God is. So be it."

If you don't resonate with the word 'God' as the name for your source of Loving, setting simple conditions - out loud - is equally powerful. Example: "I set the conditions of love and light. I set the condition that all that occurs herein be only that which is in my highest and greatest good and in strict accordance with the will of the Loving. I set the condition that anything that no longer serves me will be lifted and transmuted into Loving. So be it."

What you are doing here with your protection prayer or conditions is simply placing yourself inside of a well-protected field so that you can work your process from a space of love and light. This automatically includes the intention that any negativity that you release as you are processing will be transmuted into energies of Loving for the safety and highest good of all concerned. However you decide to set the space of Loving protection around you is up to you.

Stage 1: Preparation - Part B: Invocation

After you have established your protective field, you can invoke a spirit's presence to be here with you. A simple invocation would be: "I call upon the presence of the Loving." Or, "I call upon the presence of Mother/Father God."

I like to invoke spirit's presence at three different levels, calling upon the presence of the Loving Source-energy or Mother/Father God, my guides and masters, and my own higher self or soul: "I call upon the presence of the Loving, my guides and masters, and my soul." This gives me the most support and guidance I can receive during my session with myself. You can also call in any specific guides, angels, master teachers, or other energies you have been working with by name.

Invocation is a powerful tool that must be used with clear intention to be effective. Sometimes people get carried away here and begin to invoke energies they've read about or seen in movies that do not serve the greater good: for example, a general invocation invoking your ancestors could bring in a highly volatile energy that could cause disturbance. Perhaps you have an ancestor or two that isn't a vibrational match. To avoid unnecessary suffering and keep your process safe, always set your protection of Loving first, then invoke only those energies that you are certain are in alignment with the Loving and of the highest order. When done with care and loving intention, invocation is an expedient, effective way of connecting with your source of higher power for a specific purpose. If you do not have grounded experience with using invocation, I suggest you stick with calling in only your Source-energy – the Loving, God, Universal Mind, or however you identify your Source. – and your own soul.

Stage 1: Preparation - Part C: Breathing in Love & Compassion

The last part of the preparation stage is to bring the energies of love and compassion into your physical body at the cellular level through your breath. In order to free yourself from old, fear-based, limiting beliefs, the energies of self-forgiveness must be applied liberally inside of your own consciousness. These two energies, love, and compassion, are the two ingredients that make up the experience known as forgiveness. The root 'for' means 'already', so the literal meaning of the word forgiven means already-given. What is already-given? Love and compassion are already-given. Love and compassion are two Source energies that are always available to all of us, but sometimes we miss out on feeling them in our past. Even though love and compassion are our birthright and have always been available to us, we may not have known we had access to them in our past, and therefore we suffered.

The process of applying self-forgiveness is just a process of taking the two energies of love and compassion back to a time when you didn't get to experience them. Time is not linear. If your adult spiritual self sends love and compassion to your five-year-old self, your five-year-old self will receive it. Suffering will be lifted as a result; as the suffering dissolves, both your five-year-old self and your adult self will experience a greater level of freedom and a lightness of 'lightening up'. This, then, is the process of enlightenment or making yourself lighter. In order to take the love and compassion to the parts of yourself that have missed it in the past, you must consciously connect with those energies at the cellular level.

First, establish a direct connection with your flow of Loving by setting an intention inside yourself to begin to feel and experience this Loving at the cellular level. Example: "I set the intention to access the highest level of Loving that is available to me at this time." Then breathe it in. Imagine, sense, see, feel yourself breathing in the highest level of Loving energy that you can access at this moment. Breathe in love. Fill your heart-center with love until it is overflowing with this Loving energy.

Now, if you feel challenged by this, it is possible that your heart-center has been shut down, shielded, walled-up, or that you have been operating on a low level of Loving. Know that you can gradually begin to open your heart-center by setting the intention to do so and repeating the process of accessing Loving until you can really feel it. Be patient with yourself. It doesn't have to happen overnight. Allow this to be a gentle, gradual process. For now, if you have trouble feeling love for yourself, just think about someone you really love, maybe even a pet, and fill your heart with the love you feel for that person or pet. If you don't have a pet or person for which you feel love, think of that thing that brings you the most joy or peace inside; it might be the ocean, a sunrise, a flower, playing a video game, or riding a shiny red motorcycle. It doesn't matter what it is; each of us has something that causes us to feel lit up inside. Visualize it, and feel yourself getting lit up with Loving inside at whatever level you can access currently.

Fill your heart to overflowing with this feeling. Continue breathing in love, breathing the overflow down to your toes.

Picture and feel yourself filling up your entire body with Loving energy. You can imagine the Loving in your heart as the sun and begin to feel the warmth and the light of the sun permeating every cell of your body. Fill your feet, your ankles with Loving. Light up each and every cell inside of your body. Breathe in Loving, filling your shins and calves. Breathe in Loving, filling your knees and thighs, until every cell in your legs has been flooded with love and light. Breathe in Loving, filling up your hips and pelvis. Breathe in Loving, filling up your abdomen and all of your internal organs with Loving. Breathe the Loving up your spine, filling your whole torso with light and love. Fill up your chest, your lungs. Take the Loving down to your fingertips, filling up your hands, your wrists. Breathe the Loving up your arms through your shoulders, your collarbone. Breathe in Loving, taking the Loving up your neck, filling your chin, your whole face, and finally your whole head with Loving.

See, sense, or feel your whole body lit up from within. Experience your cells all vibrating at a higher frequency. It may feel like your cells are buzzing or tingling. You may also feel warm, dizzy, or high. If it feels too high for you, set an intention to reset the energies to a more comfortable level so that you may stay present and fully engaged in the process. Know that if your energy is set too high, you may become ungrounded or will fall asleep. If this happens, just consciously set it a little lower next time. For this process, it is necessary to stay as present and alert as possible.

Now that you have accessed your Loving source at the cellular level, set an intention inside yourself to access the highest level of compassion that you can reach right now. For example, "I set the intention to access the highest level of compassion that is available to me at this time." Breathe in compassion, knowing that compassion is the energy of the divine Mother. Compassion is the energy that says, "It's ok, I hear you, I care" when suffering is present. Flood your entire being with compassion, taking it to your toes and filling your whole body up to the top of your head, just as you did with Loving. Wrap each and every cell in your body with compassion, paying special attention to any areas that need healing or feel tight or constricted in any way. Breathe in compassion until you feel yourself radiating this energy from every cell in your body.

As a time-saver, once you've done this breathing and visualization of lighting up all of your cells a few times, you can begin to condense this part, taking one deep breath of Loving to fill your lower body and another one to fill your upper body. Or, if you can have the visual or feeling recollection of being lit up from within, you can simply set an intention such as, "I now set the intention to be lit up with Loving at the cellular level." Taking in one deep breath, you will instantaneously be vibrating with the highest level of Loving in all of your cells. You can flood your being with compassion in the same way. I would only recommend condensing this part if you have easy access to love and compassion; if you are new to experiencing these energies in your body, take as much time as you need to breathe deeply and get these energies down into each and every little cell. The idea is to really *feel* and *experience* the energies of love and compassion in all of your cells.

Now you are residing in the space of Loving protection, you've invoked spirit's presence, and you are steeping in the energies of love and compassion – the energies that make up forgiveness – at the cellular level. From this space, you are ready to begin to work your process.

Stage 2: Processing

From the place of love and compassion, you are now ready to begin working your process of updating your own belief system. The processing stage is the active phase of the conscious healing process, which contains three parts; A: identifying, B: clearing, and C: updating beliefs. If you've been actively doing the exercises at the end of each chapter so far, then you'll already have a good feel for how this works. Here, I'll break it down so that you can do this process on your own whenever you have an issue which you would like to heal and resolve.

Stage 2: Processing - Part A: Identifying

The first part of processing involves identifying your currently-held fear-based beliefs.

To begin working on your process, allow your thoughts to focus on whatever issue is most pressing for you to heal or resolve. Think about your issue, applying your awareness to the whole picture. Where did this issue come from? What time in your life does it recall for you? How long have you felt this way? Be willing to look deeply at your suffering and flood yourself with compassion for all of the pain you have experienced around this issue. Wherever there is suffering, there are old, fear-based, limiting, irrational beliefs. Examine your suffering thoroughly, identifying all of the fear-based, irrational thoughts that you've commonly heard in your mind in regards to whatever specific issue you are exploring. If you're not certain whether an idea is irrational or not, remember that irrational thoughts feel limiting, tight, and want to keep you small or safe.

Your irrational thoughts will lead you directly to the beliefs you've been holding that have created your fear-based thoughts. Identify your irrational beliefs. What fear-based or limiting assumptions are you holding about yourself or your world? What misinterpretations of reality did you make based on what happened in your past in this area? Lastly, you can ask the pivotal question, "How's this been going for me?"

Once you have explored your issue fully, you can begin to let go of any fear-based, irrational ideas and replace them with new ones that will empower you.

Stage 2: Processing - Part B: Clearing

After you've done the first part of exploring your issue and identifying your irrationalities, you are ready to move on to the second and third parts of working your process, which go together. The second part involves clearing the old, outdated belief at the cellular level by stating it out loud as a forgiveness statement: "I forgive myself for buying into the irrational belief that _____." Really apply compassion inside of yourself as you let that old idea go.

Stage 2: Processing - Part C: Updating

The third part involves creating a new, updated belief and energizing it at the cellular level by stating it aloud: "My new updated belief is, I now know _____."

Make your new updated belief supportive, uplifting, and empowering. If it feels like too much of a stretch to state a truly liberating new idea, you can start by getting a crack of light into the darkness by stating: "I'm open to the possibility that _____."

I recommend going back and forth between the second and third parts, forgiving old, irrational beliefs & updating to create new, empowering beliefs, doing your best to update each belief you clear before moving on to the next. During any particular process, you may repeat these steps over and over again many times for different irrationalities before you feel clear of a particular issue. You may also decide to repeat the same forgiveness statement several times until you feel the energy lift with compassion and release from your body before starting your updated belief.

Sometimes, people get on a roll and make many

forgiveness statements back-to-back without updating; if this occurs during your process, do your best to create updated beliefs afterward for all that you cleared. And don't worry, if you miss updating any beliefs, the old ones will simply resurface for repeated clearing at another time. However you go about doing this process is up to you. You are the only one who can know how your irrational beliefs are wired in your own consciousness.

Stage 3: Closing

The third and final stage is the closing. This will complete your process and assist you with integrating all of the work you have just done. The Closing phase has three parts; A: Acknowledgement, B: Gratitude, and C: Grounding.

Stage 3: Closing - Part A: Acknowledgment

To close your process, take a moment to acknowledge yourself out loud for whatever you'd like – your courage, your commitment to yourself – whatever is present for you to say that will encourage you, honor your process and acknowledge your active part in your own transformation. You can start by saying something like, "I acknowledge myself for…" or "I honor myself for…" Whatever comes forward for you is Ok. Sometimes people want to do this part silently, but it is way more powerful if you can say it out loud. That way, every cell in your body can hear you.

If acknowledging yourself feels awkward or uncomfortable for you, it simply means that you have had a hard time in the past giving yourself credit where credit is due. Do it anyway, no matter how challenged you feel. As you do this more often, the part inside you that hasn't felt good in the past will begin to soak up the appreciation and begin to blossom. Your source of love, attention, acknowledgment, acceptance, appreciation, and approval is inside you. You can only experience these qualities on the outside to the degree you cultivate them internally. Give yourself the time and attention you deserve by acknowledging yourself; you are so worth it!

Stage 3: Closing - Part B: Gratitude

Next, spend another moment expressing gratitude and disconnecting from the energies you invoked at the beginning of your process; you can thank God, your higher self, your guides, the Loving - whomever you invoked at the beginning of your process. Expressing gratitude for the healing you experienced will take you to an even higher vibration, ensuring that you up-level to the maximum degree that is possible at that moment. You can say, "Thanks and blessings to God... Thanks and blessings to my guides... Thanks and blessings to my higher self..." etc. If you pause between thanking each energy you have invoked, you may hear/feel a blessing in return as that energy disconnects. Disconnecting from these energies does not mean you are cutting yourself off from their ongoing presence or guidance in your life in any way; it is more like you have asked them to be present on a cosmic conference call for an important meeting, and now the call is over. You are simply ready to say goodbye and hang up the phone. Just like your phone battery is still on when you aren't using it, you are still always 'plugged in' to the Loving and connected to spirit regardless of whether you have purposely invoked spirit's presence.

Stage 3: Closing - Part C: Grounding

Finally, end by grounding your energies into the Earth to build and hold a larger container of energy for your expansion. You can do this in any number of ways. Make a declaration to ground; example: "I am now grounding and anchoring my energies, strengthening and expanding my energy container to hold my new, higher vibration of being." If you are a sensory person, you may simply sense or feel sending your energy through a grounding rod that extends from your base chakra (located at your perineum between your legs at the base of your spine) down deep into the center of the Earth. You will have a sense when you have gone deep enough. If you are a visual person, you can picture growing tree roots deep and wide, connected, and strongly rooted in the Earth. If you are a sensory person, you can put your bare feet into grass, dirt, or sand, feel your connection to the Earth and image growing roots, or you can hug a large tree and send your energies into a tree which is strongly rooted. If you're kinesthetic, you might like to dance, stomp your feet or bang a drum to ground your energies after expanding. You could also do a yoga posture such as down-dog or forward fold, putting your attention downward with both feet and hands to the floor. Find a way to ground and connect to the Earth in a way that feels authentic and works for you. There is no right or wrong way to do this, so have fun experimenting with it.

Again, your intention to ground and anchor your energy to build and strengthen your energy container is more important than your method. I use a combination of methods, depending upon where I am when I need to get anchored. If I am indoors, I picture a grounding rod going deep into the Earth or do a few down-dogs. If grass or sand is handy, I kick off my shoes and anchor to nature. When I have a large expansion, I go swimming in the ocean where my energy field has plenty of room to expand and connect with nature and All That Is. We are both physical and spiritual at the same time; just remember that in the process of enlightenment, to become fully realized, actualized, and integrated at every level, you must place an equal amount of energy down into the physical level as you have placed out into the spiritual.

The Universal Law of Manifestation states, 'As within, so without.'

Update Your Belief System & Transform Your Life

There you have the three stages of working your process to update your belief system. I encourage you to learn this process, get comfortable with this process, and use this process regularly as you go about the beautiful, transformational journey of creating a new belief system based in Loving. Updating your belief system from fear-based, limited thinking to Loving, empowering thinking creates an immediate, radical shift in the paradigm from which you will view and experience your world. I encourage you to take these stages, make them your own, and begin to up-level your belief system to the highest level of truth you can hold. You can modify the verbiage in any of these steps to suit yourself, yet I highly encourage you not to skip any steps.

All of the Steps to Updating Your Beliefs are Equally Important

All of the steps to each stage of this process are important; skipping any step will have an impact on your level of success in integrating your updated beliefs. For instance, if you skip the third part of the preparation and do not fill your cells with energies of love and compassion, you may only be giving lip-service to the clearing step. If we say a forgiveness statement from a place of depression, fear, anger, self-pity, apathy or self-judgment, the suffering does not truly lift; it simply circulates and settles back into our cells to let us know we are still holding judgment/irrationality in that place.

If, while working your process in stage 2, you skip the second part, the forgiveness statement, the old energies will not truly clear out of your cells. Sometimes, as people are quickly becoming aware of old, irrational thinking, they just make the decision to be done with the old and declare their new beliefs without ever verbally releasing the old, outdated ones with compassion. I've met dozens of people who have claimed to have updated their beliefs already, yet they wonder in frustration why the old, irrational thinking keeps popping up over and over again, like the pesky whack-a-mole game. Know that your fear-based thoughts will return as a reminder until compassionate self-forgiveness has been applied liberally, directly inside of yourself to the source of the old, fear-based belief. When enough compassion is applied (and it needs to be *felt* on the feeling level in order to work), the belief will fully clear, allowing room for new energies to take that place at the cellular level. Do not be afraid to clear the same belief a dozen times or more, either in one sitting or in many consecutive sessions; you will find that the belief has less and less power each time you clear it, until it is as thin and fragile as a piece of gossamer fabric, and you can see right through it to the truth. Keep clearing until the veil disappears, and you will be done updating that file once and for all.

Skipping the third part - stating the new, updated belief - during the processing stage means that you may have cleared your irrational belief using the second part, self-forgiveness, except your mind doesn't yet have any information in the file to replace the old belief. Know this: your mind computer will *absolutely* dig up old, deleted files when it comes to a moment of stress or panic if it does not know how to respond differently. I encourage you to state your new belief, out loud, boldly, as you work your process. Saying it out loud allows all of the cells in your body and all of the levels of your being to hear and resonate with your new, updated belief. Don't worry about the specific words; your intention is everything when creating a new belief. Then, write it down, and run it daily until it becomes a given in your consciousness.

Finally, the last stage of the conscious healing process includes disconnecting from your cosmic conference call and grounding, or anchoring, your energies to the physical level of reality. Both of these steps are brief but vital. Having a high level of spirit's presence invoked will cause you to be in an altered state of reality. While this is great while working your process, it is not a good idea to, for instance, forget to end the call and get in the car to drive. This could put you or others in harm's way. Unless you have been doing this awhile and have become acclimated to a very high level of energy, I encourage you to only invoke spirit's direct presence in a purposeful, meaningful manner when you sit down specifically to meditate, co-create or work your process. When you are finished, make a point of disconnecting from spirit by expressing gratitude with the intention to close the line.

Grounding is equally as important as disconnecting from the spirit's presence. Have you ever met someone who is flighty, flaky, disorganized, and unable to stay present or considered too 'out there'? These characteristics of spaciness can be directly due to a lack of grounding. You can do a great deal of clearing and updating, evolving rapidly into a higher level of consciousness. However, if you do not ground to the planet, you will begin to metaphorically fall over or float away. The rule of nature is that we must be as big at the physical level as we are at the spiritual. Just imagine a small glass, and then imagine trying to pour a whole gallon of water into the little glass. If the container is not big enough, the water is going to spill out all over the place. People have energy containers, also known as energy fields or HEF (Human Energy Field), and the higher we go up the ever-expanding spiral of consciousness, the larger our energy container must be at the physical, energetic level in order to 'hold' our new, higher vibration of energy. When you ground yourself after your clearing, your energy body will automatically expand into the Earth to accommodate your new vibration, allowing you to stay fully present and aware at the physical level of engagement. If you do not ground your energies, several things could occur. You may experience a state of dizziness, spaciness, forgetfulness, or otherwise feel disoriented. You may feel wonderful for a day or two, then experience a crash where you drop into feeling blue or depressed and lose the connection to your updated beliefs. This phenomenon happens over and over again for people who go on spiritual retreats or attend transformational workshops; they feel wonderfully high and then suddenly feel terrible, like having an energy hangover.

Unfortunately, many people who are teaching evolution are not yet anchored enough themselves to have a deep understanding of the importance of being equally as balanced with the involution of nature at the physical level. If you ever attend a mind-expanding event, be sure to do your own grounding exercise afterward, regardless of what the instructors do or do not advise. Do not worry about losing the high. While you will come down slightly as you ground, this is much better than crashing later and losing *all* of your high. The idea is to get to the point where you maintain that high *all the time*, where the state of highness you are able to access becomes your normal, natural state of being. This is the ultimate goal, but it is a process that takes time for most people. Once in a while, a person may take a huge, quantum leap during an instant enlightening experience. This is rare and not the norm, yet just in case it happens to you, it is helpful to be prepared by learning how to ground yourself.

After a powerful, mind-blowing type of transformational experience, a person may become unhinged and unable to cope with real-world details. There are many people currently living on the streets as a result of having ungrounded or instantaneous spiritually expanding experiences. In fact, author Eckhart Tolle shares his experience of spending two years on a park bench after his awakening experience. I am relatively certain that he spent much of those two years building his energy container and re-anchoring himself onto the planet after his extraordinary enlightening experience. Setting clear intentions of grace and ease can go a long way to ensuring you have a smooth and graceful transition into the new paradigm of Loving. And, just to be on the safest side and to avoid any unnecessary interruption to your life, just remember to ground yourself each and every time you work your process using compassionate self-forgiveness. Do this regularly, and you will grow energetically as you expand spiritually, staying in balance on every level of being.

To Integrate Rapidly, Read Your Updated Beliefs Daily

To more quickly integrate your new beliefs, write them down, and read them to yourself daily. When I was actively reprogramming my entire belief system, I carried a notebook around everywhere I went and read my new beliefs at stoplights, waiting to pick my son up from school, on tea breaks, and before bed each night.

My former mastermind partner began jotting her new beliefs down on index cards and reading them to herself anytime she had a moment throughout her day. Within a week of starting this habit, she had dozens of cards, and within a month, she was carrying around a huge stack of cards held together by a large rubber band. She joked that soon she would need a suitcase, but then an amazing thing began to happen. At about the 30-day mark, she began to say to certain cards, "That is so true. I *know* that!" and she was able to toss away those cards, which she really knew to be her truth. So, gradually, as she repeated her new beliefs daily, she integrated them completely, and her deck of note cards began to grow thinner and thinner.

Another student has taken to making audio recordings of his updated beliefs and listens to them while riding his bike. There are also flashcard apps you can download to work with your beliefs on your phone. Experiment with different ways to work with your new beliefs until you find the way that works best for you. The method you use to integrate your new beliefs isn't important; it's the commitment to actively running them that matters. The more you can affirm, declare, and own your new beliefs, the faster your belief system will make the shift into Loving, and the faster you will be residing in the joy and clarity of freedom.

Repeatedly Stating Your Updated Beliefs Supports Integration

Repeatedly stating your updated beliefs daily supports the integration of your new beliefs from understanding at the mind level into knowing at the cellular level. Think about it this way: if the 99.99% space inside of your cells is all filled up with the energy of your current beliefs, each cell could be likened to a balloon filled with air. The air quality depends on the vibration of the belief. Now, when we move through the self-forgiveness process, and we apply compassion as we update our belief, it is like infusing each cell balloon with fresh, clean air. The air will only stay clean as long as we hold the new, updated belief to be true in our own consciousness. The minute we let go of the new idea and begin running the old, more familiar, fear-based idea, the air inside each cell balloon is instantly polluted again.

Our cells are growing and dying *all the time*, randomly, throughout our body. The average span of life for a human cell is about three weeks. So, if I have spent an hour processing, and I updated a bunch of beliefs, for probably a few days, I will feel wonderful because I have clean, healthy air inside all of my cells. Say I forget to write down and repeat my new beliefs. Gradually, a few days would go by, and my old beliefs, which are still in my stored mind files until the updated version is fully integrated, creep into my thoughts. I then begin running my old, familiar programming – 'I am so stupid. I can't do anything right. I suck at this. Nothing ever works out for me. I don't deserve to succeed anyway, so why do I even bother, blah, blah, blah'. Right there, all of the great work I did a few days earlier is at risk. If I can catch myself running the old tape and quickly update to my new beliefs of infinite intelligence, worthiness, authentic power, and claim my innate capability, I can get back on track and keep the energy of my new updated beliefs running through my cells.

But say I don't catch myself falling back into my old pattern of self-bludgeoning, and I wallow in self-loathing for a few days. While I am busy beating myself up, ten percent of my body cells are dying and getting replaced. The newly-born cells are taking on the old, toxic energies of the old belief because there is no clean air present when the cell dies off. The brand new cells were not there when I worked my process around my updated beliefs, so they have *never heard* the new message. As a result, I now have parts of myself that are only running the outdated belief. If I run the old, negative beliefs for two weeks, I will quickly have more than fifty percent of my body buying back into my old, familiar, self-defeating story, and I will forget or discredit my updated beliefs. I would then need to forgive myself all over and update all of the same beliefs - again - until such a time I could keep the new ideas running for over three weeks.

When I run the new, updated idea regularly, catch myself if I lapse back into old thinking, and flood myself with extra reinforcement of my new beliefs, here's what happens: the cells inside my body will contain the information of both the old and the new beliefs, yet the air inside my cell balloons will be clean and clear, resonating with the newly updated belief. When a cell in my body dies off, the new cell will only take the updated belief. This is the process of evolution – *if there are two messages inside a cell when it dies, the newly-born cell will take the message that is vibrating at a higher frequency of energy.* If you repeatedly state your new beliefs to yourself regularly, your cells will take on this new idea as they regenerate. At some point, usually, about three to four weeks later, the old belief will drop off completely – it will be gone from your cellular coding – and the new belief will become your truth. You will have literally 'embodied' your new, updated belief.

Occasionally, there can be a stubborn, irrational belief that doesn't release even after several cycles of applying compassion, updating, and reading belief cards. This is usually a good indication that that belief is being run by a disowned aspect of your personality, a part that is still stuck in the shadows. When this happens, there are some other healing tools you can use to support the belief to shift; we'll cover this in a later chapter. More frequently, you will find that the majority of beliefs will begin to shift after a couple of weeks of running your updates.

Once a belief is your truth, you won't need to keep repeating it to yourself anymore because it will simply be a given. So, as you learn the tools of updating your belief system, I encourage you to really get into it fully, repeat your new beliefs daily, even several times a day, to ensure that you quickly integrate the new information all the way down to the tips of your toes.

Changing Your Beliefs Changes Your Life

As I applied love and compassion to myself and affirmed my new, empowering, healthy beliefs, my fear-based beliefs no longer had any hold on me, and my fear-thoughts gradually lessened. I would apply compassion to myself for having bought into the old belief and restate my new belief until the new, updated belief took firm hold. When I no longer had a particular fear-thought surface in my mind was when I knew the updated belief had fully integrated – the old thoughts never came back again. By changing my fear-based beliefs into love-based beliefs, I changed my thinking, which effortlessly changed my feelings, which led me to take different actions, which quite naturally produced different, more positive (thank God) results.

The change in my internal quality of life has been radical. It is as if by changing my belief system to align with Loving, I have rewritten my entire life story for the better and am now a completely different person living an entirely different life – my dream life. Sometimes, in remembering a story from my past, I can hardly even believe I ever thought that old way or felt that old way. People who know me now often do not believe the stories I've shared in my teachings. Workshop participants will say things like, "Really?! You did *that*? I find that hard to imagine." It cracks me up every time I look at how far I have come.

Changing your belief system changes your entire life. Not only have I transformed my life for the better, but I've also had the joy of witnessing hundreds of other people's lives change for the better as they've updated their belief systems to align with the Loving.

Changing Your Inner Reality Transforms Your Outer Reality

John went from sabotaging his own success to realizing his heartfelt dreams. Within a year of deciding that he could amount to anything he wanted, John's business skyrocketed, and he began reaching – even exceeding – his goals. He was able to achieve outer-level success doing what he'd always dreamed of doing, experiencing deep fulfillment as he accomplished long-term goals and set new ones. John is now affluent and thriving, doing work that he loves every day and filled with the knowledge that he can accomplish anything he sets out to do.

Melinda empowered herself and found her voice. She changed dozens of old beliefs about herself after deciding that she does have a voice and that what she has to say is important. She let go of allowing her parents and her ex-husband to rule her life and took full control of the wheel of her own human vehicle. She went back to school to do what she'd always wanted to do and no longer allows other people's opinions to affect her peace. She has become a strong, assertive, self-supporting woman who now knows and speaks her own mind freely. Melinda is delighted with her new life as she continues to grow into higher and higher levels of awareness.

Randy took his time exploring his old, limiting beliefs, discovering many layers of irrationality that contributed to his lack of happiness. He finally hit upon a belief that stated something like 'life sucks and then you die', and he realized that he had decided early on in life that he was powerless to change that idea. Once he decided he was not powerless, that he was, in fact, connected to the infinite source of power, he decided that he did have the power to change his mind. He claimed his power, and in doing so, he accessed inner joy for the first time ever. As Randy soaked in the joy, he instantly acknowledged happiness was indeed not 'out there in the future', but that he'd had access to it all along inside himself. Randy's depression lifted immediately, and he has been residing in joy ever since.

Nina embraced the concept that she was the co-creator of her own life – that she and only she had the power to decide what to believe. She chose to believe in joy instead of pain, liberation instead of suffering. She made an emphatic declaration that life was safe, joy-filled, and beautiful, and her physical pain began to lift from her body immediately. Within the week, she experienced long moments free of pain, which gave her the motivation to keep reaffirming her new, updated beliefs. Within a month, her new beliefs had integrated, and she was completely free of pain. Nina has been traveling and sharing her experience of joy and freedom ever since.

You, too, can be the co-creator of your own life. You have the power to completely overhaul your own belief system to change your outer level experience in life for the better. Your beliefs will directly lead to your results.

I learned that if I wanted to get different results in my life, I needed to change the first part of the equation – my beliefs. Now, if I want something to shift in any area of my life, instead of trying to change the answer (i.e., get a new boyfriend, move, change jobs, etc.), all I need to do is to look deeply at my beliefs in that area, update any irrationality, and watch the miracle take place in my outer world.

For Lasting Change, You Must Change Your Beliefs

What I have found, repeatedly, is that for lasting, life-long change, it requires changing my beliefs first, and everything else will naturally shift accordingly. If you want to change your outcome in any particular area of your life, you can learn to identify what belief or set of beliefs is producing your current life experience, decide if you want to keep it that way or not; if not, change your beliefs to a higher, more Loving level and watch your life change for the better. Here is the math:

Equation: Belief energy x itself x itself x itself = results energy

1x1x1x1=1

3x1x1x1=3
700x1x1x1=700
9000x1x1x1=9000

Understand that it is the vibratory level of belief energy that equals the outer-level outcome of manifested energy that we experience as the results in our life. This concept is really the key idea of the process of personal transformation. What this means is that changing behavior doesn't create lasting change, changing thinking doesn't create lasting change, changing feelings doesn't create lasting change. The belief system must change as well to support the change in behavior. This is why so many people quit smoking, only to begin again under stress. People quit drinking, only to begin again the first time they experience too much pressure or are faced with an old, unresolved issue. People lose weight and get in shape, only to go right back into old patterns of emotional eating the minute they let go of their strict fitness regime. People swear they'll never gamble or cheat again, yet somehow end up repeating the pattern over and over. People win the lottery and are just as broke as they've always been a year later. People practice meditation or positive affirmation yet still experience all of the same issues. Remember that our inner reality creates our outer reality. Only by changing our underlying belief system can we really transform our lives permanently for the better.

Updating the Belief System Quiets the Mind

After fully overhauling my own belief system, I found that my mind no longer had an on-going stream of chatter that I needed to try to suppress in order to experience a bone-deep peace and tranquility. Because my beliefs are now Loving beliefs, I am able to breathe in my knowing and come into stillness, experiencing a deep, profound silence where I exist in the space of infinite connection. How did I get there? It was a gradual process that accelerated as I cleared more and more of my old, fear-based beliefs and integrated more Loving, empowering beliefs.

Once a certain percentage of my beliefs were stemming from the rationality of the Loving, I became aware that I was actually residing in peace on the inside for longer and longer periods of time, so I no longer needed to practice 'getting there'. I simply needed to be. What this meant for me at the practical level was that I no longer needed to 'try'. I can drop into silent meditation at any given moment. My physical level yoga – or any activity I chose to engage in – can be done from a place of inner peace, tranquility, and stillness. I can have long moments of internal peace whenever I wish, and I feel joy and contentment in most of my waking moments.

Moving from Trying into Being

Know that you, too, can move from practicing these qualities to residing in them. Drop the 'trying' and just be. You can *be* the peace, *be* the joy, *be* the love you wish to experience. Just as judgment is the natural outcome of residing in the right/wrong reality, peace is the natural outcome of aligning your belief system with the Loving paradigm. By updating old, disempowering beliefs into new, empowering beliefs, you will quickly go from experiencing pain and suffering in the duality to holding in peace, residing in the Loving.

"How You Relate to the Issue Is the Issue"

One of the most significant changes I ever made which accelerated my own healing process was when I began to allow myself to have my feelings, to listen to myself with compassion, and to speak to myself in a loving, caring manner inside of my head, not only while working my process, but in every waking moment of my day. Two professors of the University of Santa Monica, Drs. Ron and Mary Hulnick repeatedly state, "How you relate to the issue *is* the issue." The first time I heard this phrase was in 2003, and I almost immediately grasped the truth of it. While I was focused on some external life problem, I would suddenly become aware of my internal self-talk relating to the external problem. Inevitably, I'd catch myself criticizing myself, berating myself, name-calling myself, 'shoulding' myself, or otherwise punishing myself in various abusive manners. What I discovered was that I had been perpetuating a familial pattern of abuse inside of my own mind. How I related to myself actually *was* the issue; the outer-level problems were just presenting me with opportunities to see how I was treating myself on the inside.

Since I had been a loving and supportive mother to my own children, it wasn't a stretch to begin speaking to myself the way that I had spoken to my own kids on a good day. As I gave myself a different sort of support internally, I was able to listen to myself in a whole new way, a way that enabled me to hear all of my old, irrational ideas from a compassionate perspective, which in turn allowed me to feel safe enough to unload all of the fear-based ideas and misinterpretations of reality. My supportive, loving, higher self was able to accept, to hear, to apply compassion, to act as a healing balm, and then provide new, updated, and healthier beliefs to replace the limiting ones. By relating to myself in a caring and gentle manner, my entire belief system was rapidly transformed.

Once I took dominion over my belief system, my general pattern of thinking changed without any effort on my part. My thoughts just naturally fell into alignment with my new, updated beliefs. For instance, when I cleared the old, irrational idea that I was stupid, my 'stupid' tape loop dissolved once I had fully integrated the knowing that I am connected to the source of infinite intelligence. From that point on, if an opportunity of learning something new presented itself, my thoughts would naturally be running supportive, encouraging messages like, "I can do this. I can learn anything I want to learn because I am connected to my Source."

For Supportive Self-Talk, Awaken Your Neutral Observer

In order to move into more supportive self-talk, you will first have to learn how to monitor your own thoughts. This is imperative because we want to be able to catch ourselves if we begin to run an old story while we are in the process of integrating a new set of beliefs. In order to be able to keep the energy of our updated beliefs resonating inside of our cells, we have to be able to actually *hear* ourselves when we begin to think the old, limiting thoughts. There is a part of each of us that is entirely neutral and detached from all that is going on in our lives. I call this part the 'neutral observer'. If you are not yet connected with this part of your own consciousness, I encourage you to set an intention inside of yourself to awaken your neutral observer right now. Begin to notice the part of you that is observing from inside. This part is simply watching you as you read these words, watching you as your thoughts stream through your mind. This part has no judgment at all of you whatsoever. Spend a few moments connecting to this part of yourself, and pay attention to your thoughts, watching them go by from a neutral perspective.

Once your neutral observer is awake and watching, you can now utilize this part inside of yourself in service to your own growth and transformation.

I use my neutral observer to let me know whenever I begin to think unproductive, unsupportive, or limiting thoughts. I ask my neutral observer to send up an immediate 'red flag' to get my attention whenever I have a fear-based, irrational thought. Once I receive the red flag, I can then either clear the limiting belief in-the-moment, or I can write it down and let my consciousness know that I'll clear it later. By using my neutral observer to alert me to my old, unhealthy thought patterns, which have come from my old, outdated beliefs, I have been able to quickly become aware of my irrational beliefs, identify them and update them, creating newer, healthier beliefs which lead to healthier thinking.

How My Neutral Observer Works for Me

Here's how it works inside of my own consciousness: I first visualized my neutral observer as a little guy sitting in front of a computer screen inside of my mind. The screen shows the stream of my thoughts, both the loud ones of my conscious mind and the softer ones of my subconscious mind. All of the thoughts appear in large print as they cross the monitor, so my neutral observer sees them equally, regardless of my personality's level of self-awareness. When a negative, limited, or fear-based thought crosses the screen, my neutral observer will immediately highlight the words on the screen in red, which automatically sends my conscious self an instant message alerting me to my own limited thinking. That is my neutral observer's job; to watch and to bring limiting thoughts to my attention.

Once something is brought to my attention by my neutral observer, it is up to me to decide what to do with that information. I could decide to do several different things at that moment: I might allow the limiting train of thoughts to continue for a moment and listen neutrally to these thoughts to gather more information about what I think or how I feel about a certain subject. I would definitely use this approach if the thoughts were new to me – if this were the first time this particular line of thinking or limiting idea had come to my attention. If I had the space and time, I might explore this line of thinking more deeply to discover all of the associated limiting beliefs surrounding this idea, juicing the opportunity to squeeze as much irrationality out of my own consciousness as I could.

If I were in the middle of another commitment when the red flag alerted me to a negative line of thinking, I would probably tell that part of myself that I had heard it and that I would get back to it at another time – as soon as possible. I would then consciously decide to place my attention on more positive, supportive thoughts as I went back to work or whatever else I had previously been doing before the thought was flagged. If I am diligent, I will write myself a note to get back to that particular idea, so I won't forget about it later when I have personal alone-time.

If the red-flagged thought was a recurring limiting thought that had already been brought to my attention in the past – one that had new, updated beliefs – I would respond to that thought in-the-moment by listening and then affirming the new beliefs. That might sound something like, "I hear you think you can't do such-and-such, that you aren't good enough; I really hear that, and I want to remind you that I now know that I can do anything I set my mind to do. I absolutely have the ability to learn how. I am innately good, whole and worthy of succeeding," etc. After I have heard and acknowledged the thought, there are several different ways my consciousness could go from here; I could react to my own updated thought with naysaying, skepticism or any other type of denial or negativity, I could react neutrally or I could react positively, falling into complete agreement with My new updated belief is, I know now, possibly feeling excited, energized or optimistic about it.

If I felt energy of negativity or denial running through my body, or heard a follow-up response that was scoffing towards my new, updated belief, this is a strong indication that there are more irrational beliefs around this particular subject that haven't yet been discovered. Sometimes, there is an entire nest of beliefs around one idea, and they are often tangled and twisted up together in such a way that if you find one, it will reveal the whole snarl-up. Sometimes, we find one limiting belief first and update it, and then when that one is triggered up again, we can find out there are many, many more irrational beliefs attached to that one, simply by observing our thoughts when we update just the one. If this happens, I write down the 'flagged' thoughts, as well as the subsequent thoughts rejecting, denying or questioning the updated belief, and make a plan to work my process around this issue at length, as soon as I can, with the intention to expose and update all of my limiting beliefs around the topic. Once I have cleared the entire nest of supporting beliefs, I will feel totally on-board with updating the beliefs around this issue for as long as it continues to arise in my consciousness.

If my internal response is neutral, my consciousness is hearing my new updated belief, and there is nothing else to do except observe and ask myself, "is there anything else?" Sometimes I will be guided to take it deeper, possibly do some more self-forgiveness around the idea. Other times, just restating my new updated belief is enough to completely dissipate the energy created by the flagged thought.

If my internal response to acknowledging the flagged thought and restating my new belief is joy-filled, enthusiastic and filled with 'yes' energy, I can rest easy and know that I am close to integrating this idea once and for all. The more time I spend reaffirming the truth of my new, updated belief, the faster I will drop the old one. Once I've updated the old belief completely, my thought pattern will change to create new, supportive thoughts that reflect my new updated belief.

As I have become more adept at working my own process of updating my belief system into alignment with the Loving,

I have become better able to deal with my 'red-flagged' thoughts completely in-the-moment. I am now able to listen to my thoughts, identify an irrational belief or old, outdated idea, apply compassion, experience self-forgiveness and update my belief to create healthier thinking in present time within moments. The more I apply these tools, the clearer my consciousness becomes and the closer I get to living in infinite Loving. If I could do it, you can too.

Having an Awakened Neutral Observer Accelerates Growth

You can use your neutral observer however you are guided. I initially visualized my neutral observer in front of a desktop screen, and that was in the 90's when desktops were still the common technology. You may come up with something entirely different, such as hearing a beep that alerts you to the text-message in your mind, or having an iPad app that allows you to observe your own thoughts. However you imagine this or perceive it working is up to you. I just encourage you to figure out an internal communication system that works. The most important thing to understand here is that you will not be able to make use of your neutral observer without connecting to this part of yourself and asking for assistance. It is up to you to decide what kind of role your neutral observer will play in your life, so ask this part, specifically, to show you the things that you are ready to become aware of, ready to heal and clear from your consciousness.

Having your neutral observer awake and monitoring your thoughts for you can accelerate your growth exponentially. When a part of you is still asleep or hasn't yet come to your attention, you will only be able to work with the fear-based thoughts that come to your awareness in a way that is loud and clear. These thoughts will be impossible to miss, because they are being blared from bullhorns. To the degree that you are still unconscious in this area, you might be missing out on the much greater percentage of your softer, sneakier, subconscious habitual thoughts. However, once you awaken your neutral observer and set an intention asking this part to monitor your thoughts for you, you'll get to hear everything that was running under the radar; nothing slips by the neutral observer. This means you might go from having a very minimal level of awareness about your limited thinking to having a heightened awareness overnight, having each and every negative, fear-based thought brought to your attention instantly.

You Can Set Parameters for Your Neutral Observer

For some people, this may be too much at once. They might feel overwhelmed or go into sensory overload. Understand that your neutral observer works for you; you are the boss, and therefore you and only you get to choose how much or how little information you would like to receive from this part of your consciousness. You have the power to set parameters for your neutral observer, knowing that this part of you is here to serve you with your growth. If you feel that full, instant awareness is too much to work with, you may decide to set your intention to any level of awareness you wish. You could set an intention to become aware of only those thoughts that are most relevant, vital, or important to whatever issue is your soul's top priority to identify and update. In this way, you would be able to work on one major issue at a time. You might ask your neutral observer to only point out severe lack-thoughts, to narrow it down to thoughts of unworthiness, or only red flag self-judgment. You can imagine that your neutral observer has a volume control or an automatic light dimmer switch that you could raise or lower to shed the amount of light you wish to receive at any given time.

There is no right or wrong way to do this. Personally, I

was so eager for freedom that I wanted to work as quickly as possible through my curriculum once I took responsibility for it. This meant that often I was bombarded with information; my neutral observer was red-flagging every other thought for my attention. There were a few times I felt I couldn't keep up, and I imagined turning down a volume switch, asking my neutral observer to tone it down a little. The information did slow down, I got caught up, and then I went back on full throttle. The universe never gives us more than we are ready to handle, and it is Ok to set the speed of your new awareness to a manageable setting.

Once you awaken your neutral observer, I don't recommend turning your neutral observer off. I did this once; I lapsed back into unconscious behavior and had a challenging time extricating myself because I was totally asleep at the wheel. I had to crash to wake back up again, painfully, before I could observe the wreckage I'd created in my unconscious state.

Remember, no one gets to skip or get out of their lessons; when I turned off my neutral observer, my lesson books began piling up behind me, just out of sight, and I was quite astounded at the crapload of homework that I had to catch up on the moment I reawaken my neutral observer.

If being aware of all of your unfinished curriculum feels daunting, don't worry! Just like college has semester breaks and summer vacation, you, too, can take a break from your spiritual curriculum whenever you need one.

Setting Your Neutral Observer to Take a Conscious Break

When I need a break from updating my irrational beliefs, I imagine setting my neutral observer's screen on a timer switch. This is just like having my computer reboot or restart at a certain time, a calendar alert on my phone, or an alarm clock set to go off at a certain time. I call this taking a 'conscious break'. A conscious break is necessary when we have been observing our own thoughts, diligently identifying and updating our irrational thoughts to the point we are tired, too serious, feel depleted, or perhaps overwhelmed with the extent of our own irrationality.

Rather than becoming stressed, depressed, or down about the beautiful process of enlightenment, take a break from your 'stuff' for a while and relax. Maybe you want to watch a movie without observing your own reactions, lay on the beach, or read a good book without getting distracted by your own thoughts for five minutes. Or you may want to veg out and not think or do anything. Start your conscious break by setting an intention and give yourself a time limit.

Here is an example: If I have been diligently and consistently updating my irrationality for days on end – mind you, this updating is happening on top of and concurrently with all of the other regular demands of a full life, work, shopping, kids, etc. – I might feel the need to take a break. I would call up my neutral observer and give him a two-hour break. It might sound something like this, "I call upon the part of myself that is in charge of neutrally observing my thoughts. I am giving myself a two-hour break to watch a movie. Please allow me to take a two-hour break, starting now, and begin monitoring my thoughts again in two hours, at ___ (state time)." Remember, the language you use is not the most important factor; it is your *intention* that is most vital. Give yourself permission to take conscious breaks as needed, and that way, you'll never have a reason to feel that you cannot deal with all of the information that is coming your way.

Take an Attitude of Joy as You Embrace Your New Awareness

Once your neutral observer is awakened, you will become fully conscious of your thoughts, feelings, and actions. This can sometimes be experienced as a painful stage in personal transformation. Sometimes, all of our many fear-based thoughts, lack-thoughts, judgments, and needs for healing are filled with pockets of pain and suffering. There may be traumatic or deeply painful memories attached to some irrational beliefs that you may have suppressed long, long ago because they were too painful to remember at the time. Know that you have the ability to decide whether or not to experience your transformation and updating of beliefs as painful and filled with suffering or as liberating, exhilarating, beautiful, light-filled, joy-filled, and infinitely exciting as you move into greater levels of freedom. Your attitude as you are observing the material that has surfaced for your attention within your own consciousness will determine whether or not you view the healing process as liberating or painful, joy-filled, or excruciating.

After having an 'Oh shit, here we go again; another bucket-load of crap coming up' sort of attitude towards my own irrational beliefs, I discovered that I didn't care to work through my material that way. I began to feel dread when I thought about unearthing more crap, and I started to attempt to avoid completing my coursework. This didn't support my desire for freedom. I finally learned that if I could greet my irrationality with joy and excitement, I could not only clear it more quickly, but I could hold in joy as I did my updating.

By using the support of my neutral observer, I was able to access joy from the highest part of myself and keep that running through my nervous systems energetically as I 'watched' myself having a painful issue come to the attention of my observer from a neutral position. I would feel a curious sense of detachment from my own triggering issues, maybe even watch myself getting mad or all worked up over something while the higher part of me was smiling inside

– even laughing sometimes – at myself as I became aware of another limiting belief or nest of irrational thinking. This totally lightened my learning process and enabled me to begin to respond differently, with excitement, each time a new issue would arise. Now, when an irrational belief surfaces for my conscious awareness, I think, 'Oh yeah! Bring it on. More freedom coming my way right now.' I joyfully leap at each opportunity to thoroughly explore my issues and update all of my beliefs in my highest and greatest good.

I strongly encourage you to take an attitude of joy, freedom, and personal liberation as you embrace your new awareness. With a joyful, humorous kind of attitude, discovering irrational beliefs within your own consciousness can be like discovering buried treasure. Dig for gold and silver. Mine those diamonds, emeralds, and rubies! This is the heart of transformational work – of self-realization – discovering where parts of yourself have been stuck out in fear-based, right/wrong thinking, and bringing those parts into alignment with the Loving. This is a beautiful process, so view it as such, and you will be able to greet your irrationality with joy as you unearth each treasure and transmute it into the gold known as rational thought.

I encourage you to awaken your neutral observer, monitor your thoughts daily, take note of any irrational thinking that comes to your attention, write them down, and spend a few moments each day clearing irrationality and updating your beliefs into a Loving, rational, supportive belief system. You are a divine child of God; the peace and stillness of having your thoughts aligned with the will of your soul is your birthright. I encourage you to be thorough and fearless in your clearing. You are so worth having the joy, peace, and clarity of mind that comes from rational thought.

Exercise: Claiming your Ability to Transform your Belief System

Begin by saying a protection prayer, setting conditions of love and light, and invoking spirit's presence.

Place your hands on your heart. Set an intention to access the highest vibration of Loving available. Breathe in the Loving and fill your body with Loving energies from head to toe. Then, set an intention to access the highest level of compassion. Breathe in compassion and fill your body with compassion from head to toe.

Repeat out loud any of the following that resonates, changing the verbiage as needed to reflect your own beliefs:

"I forgive myself for buying into the irrational belief that my belief system is a static, immutable set of beliefs that cannot be changed." "My new updated belief is, I now know my belief system is based on ideas that I cosigned long ago, and that I can decide to believe new ideas at any time. From now on, I get to ask myself, 'How's this going for me? Is this idea serving me to believe?' If an idea is not serving me, I can simply update it to an idea that serves me better."

"I forgive myself for buying into the irrational belief that changing my whole belief system is too _____ (hard, challenging, difficult, time-consuming, etc.)." "My new updated belief is, I now know changing my belief system is joy-filled, exciting, exhilarating, easy, liberating, an adventure, etc. I can have fun while I update my belief system."

"I forgive myself for buying into the irrational belief that the process of updating beliefs only works for other people, not for me." "My new updated belief is, I now know I can absolutely update my beliefs if I choose to do so. I am the co-creator of my own life, and I have free will choice. I get to decide what I can do, and I now know that I can update my belief system. I am so worth it!"

"I forgive myself for buying into the irrational belief that there are some old, fear-based beliefs that I will always have to live with – that these will never go away no matter what." "My new updated belief is, I now know I can update and integrate any irrational belief that I desire, no matter how much I have believed an old belief in the past, no matter how much energy, power or attention I gave an old belief in the past and no matter how long I believed an old belief to be true. I now know that the moment I identify a belief as 'irrational', I have the power to update it and transform my consciousness forever."

"I forgive myself for buying into the irrational belief that some irrational beliefs have power over me." "My new updated belief is, I now know I have dominion over my own consciousness. My belief system is a part of my consciousness. I get to decide what to believe; my belief system is a tool that works for me and has no power in and of itself. The only true power is Loving, and that comes directly from Source."

"I forgive myself for buying into the irrational belief that I need to fear examining my own belief system or fear what I may find when I do." "My new updated belief is, I now know fear has no power over me. My beliefs have no power unless I give them power. All of the power inside of consciousness is my own to place and focus as I choose. If I choose to take power away from a certain belief and transmute the power to an updated belief based in Loving, I have the power to do so. I place my trust in the Loving, and I am divinely protected as I clear and update my belief system with grace and ease, in joy and love and light."

"I forgive myself for buying into the irrational belief that I am not capable of transforming my belief system." "My new updated belief is, I now know I can do anything I decide to do. If I decide to transform my belief system, all I have to do is set an intention to do so, and the process will begin. I can transform my belief system and transform my life."

"I forgive myself for buying into the irrational belief that it serves me in any way to hang on to old, outdated ideas that are based in judgment, on comparison, on negatives, on 'should's, on lack, right/wrong, either/or, better than/less than, ultimatum, black/white, good/bad, or any other type of fear-based thinking for any reason." "My new updated belief is, I now know freedom is my birthright! I am love. It is now Ok for me to truly be the love in every way. I am easily and gracefully updating all of my old beliefs with new, clear, rational, joy-filled, empowering beliefs that put me in alignment with the will of my soul and allow me to fulfill my soul's purpose upon the planet to my highest divine potential."

"I forgive myself for buying into the irrational belief that it's not Ok to believe differently than my family, friends, loved ones, etc." "My new updated belief is, I now know each of us is 100% responsible for our own life; I get to decide what beliefs are best for me. My loved ones are in charge of their own beliefs. It is Ok for me to believe differently, and I am at peace."

"I forgive myself for buying into the irrational belief that I need to explain, justify, or pacify other people in any way in regard to my new updated belief." "My new updated belief is, I now know my belief system is my own. I get to decide who to discuss my beliefs with or not, and it is Ok to keep my process private. I am the only one who needs to know what I believe and to understand why I believe what I believe. It is alright for other people to become triggered or upset by my transformation; I now know that my own highest good is also the highest good of all concerned. Other people's upset is an opportunity for their own growth and upliftment. I choose to hold in peace and Loving."

Close your process by acknowledging yourself, expressing gratitude to spirit, and fully grounding your energy. Drink plenty of water.

CHAPTER SEVEN

Judgment – A Natural Outcome of the Right/Wrong Reality

Let's talk about judgment. First of all, is judgment your friend or foe? Have you ever heard the idea that judgment is 'bad'? That it is not Ok to judge? Most of you are likely familiar with that concept. For the first decade or so of my own spiritual journey, I, too, thought it wasn't Ok to judge, even though I'd been taught differently by my guides during my big awakening experience when I was eighteen. The idea that judging was bad was so ingrained in me that I had a challenging time integrating a different understanding. I tried everything in my power to stop judging. I denied my own judgment, stuffed it, repressed it, ignored it, pretended it wasn't actually happening, and above all else, judged myself as bad for every time I caught myself judging anyone or anything. Not only did it not work for me to deny my judgment, but it also compounded my judgment because I was judging myself for judging.

I encourage you to open to the possibility that judgment is your friend. Let go of the irrationality that judgment itself is bad, and begin to embrace your judgment. I have discovered for myself that judgment is the easiest and most handy tool for personal transformation. Yes, folks, you heard me correctly: judgment is a useful healing tool.

Judgment is a Natural Byproduct of Right/Wrong Reality

First, let's backtrack and take a quick look at how we humans arrived at the erroneous conclusion that judgments are 'bad'. I believe that we are all spiritual beings having a human experience. Being born as humans necessitates coming into whatever the mass level of consciousness is on the planet at the time of our entry. In our case, we were all born into a fear-based, right/wrong paradigm – a duality. Literally *everything* is seen as either 'good' or 'bad' in this level of reality. All judgment is simply viewing things as either 'good' or 'bad', with lots of subtle variances in the language. Therefore, thinking in terms of good or bad judgments is simply the natural human condition as seen through the eyes of right/wrong reality. Judgment is a normal, natural byproduct of right/wrong reality. When we are at the mercy of right/wrong reality, we cannot help but judge.

Now, the current human journey is about awakening to our own innate spirituality, growing into the awareness that there is another paradigm we can reside in if we choose – a paradigm of Loving. We all have the option of viewing life from the perspective of our soul, which sees things from the neutral perspective of Loving. People who have found a way out of right/wrong reality into the Loving reality and choose to reside there permanently are often referred to as masters. All of the world's religions are based on an attempt to worship, honor, recreate, or emulate a certain master's path to the Loving paradigm.

Labeling Judgment as 'Bad' is an Erroneous Conclusion

When someone who has reached their mastery speaks from that place of Loving and describes what it is like, the master describes this state of consciousness as a place where there is no judgment, no right/wrong. They describe a place of total acceptance, boundless Loving, and infinite compassion for all beings. What is crucial to understand here is that when the master speaks, this message is going directly into the ears of the humans who are still heavily engaged in right/wrong reality. Therefore, the interpretation of the message from the Loving into right/wrong reality often obscures the real teaching. The message goes into a different filter from the place it originates. Each one of us can only hear/see/view life from whatever set of filters/lenses we are wearing at that time. So, since the people listening to a particular master's teachings heard that the place of enlightenment is a place that has no judgment, from their right/wrong paradigm of thinking, they made an erroneous assumption that that meant 'judgment is bad'. This could not be further from the truth. These masters have been attempting to teach that nothing is bad, that we can begin to view it *all* as Ok, that everything is just an opportunity for growth and learning. This includes judgment.

It is pretty clear that people formed an inaccurate conclusion that because the masters who have reached enlightenment describe their state as a place where there is no judgment, it must therefore mean that judgment itself is 'bad' or 'wrong'. People concluded that we must not judge in order to get to this place with no judgment and that we are a bad person if we do judge. Many current spiritual leaders hold this as fact and are unwilling to even look at the possibility that they have come to an erroneous and unsupportive conclusion. Think about how silly this is really – the statement 'judgment is bad' is, itself, a judgment, so it is quite clearly still locked in judgmental, right/wrong thinking. Therefore, by default, this means that judging judgment as 'bad' is still judging, so there is no way out of the cycle of judgment for people as long as they hold this strong belief of 'bad'.

I have personally witnessed many people stuck in the belief that if they simply *stop* judging, that they will suddenly or eventually be transported to the unconditionally Loving paradigm, achieving instant enlightenment. Unfortunately, it doesn't work that way. The truth of the matter is that judgment is the natural outcome of existing in the right/wrong framework of reality. From the soul's perspective, this is neither good nor bad; it just *is*.

Owning and Accepting Judgment is the Ticket to Freedom

Whether we like it or not, we are currently residing in a space of right/wrong reality where everything is seen through the eyes of good/bad – in other words, everything within our perception is connected to a judgment of 'good' or 'bad', right or wrong. There is no way around this; the only way is through it. Owning and accepting our judgment is actually the ticket to freedom from judgment, incredible as that sounds.

Once you acknowledge that you may have reached the erroneous conclusion that having judgment is bad, what can you do with the new idea that judgment is just a normal part of the human condition based on right/wrong reality? You can begin to look at judgment differently. You can begin to see your judgment as a powerful tool for change. You can begin to see it as the *way* to change. You can then utilize your own judgment to get to the place of non-judgment. What you can begin to see as your truth is this: each time you become aware of a judgment, you can clear that part of your consciousness that is operating from a right/wrong perspective and bring it into alignment with the Loving perspective. By owning your judgment and clearing it, you are able to actually change your own perception, which will lead you to a shift in viewpoint or a paradigm shift.

The goal here is to get people who are living in the right/wrong reality to move to living in the Loving, going from having lots of judgment about everything to having no judgment about anything. The key to this transformation is to embrace your judgment, greeting every judgment as an opportunity for growth. Judgment is a healing tool, and if you can see and acknowledge its value, you can use it to quickly move into living a life in the neutrality of Loving, free of all judgment.

Using Judgment as a Healing Tool

How does judgment work as a healing tool? Judgment acts as a direct arrow to show you the specific place in your consciousness where you are holding something stored in right/wrong reality in your body/mind at the cellular level – you either view something as 'good' or as 'bad'. To the degree you judge something good or bad, you will hold that judgment at an equivalent vibratory rate, energetically, within your cells. The stronger the level of judgment, good or bad, the lower the frequency of energy you will hold towards that thing. When you follow the train of thought of your judgment, the trail will show you exactly what irrational idea or ideas you need to clear in order to view that thing from the Loving perspective. The moment you change the viewpoint from the right/wrong reality into the neutrality of the Loving, the vibration of energy stored at the cellular level shifts. Then you can let your judgment go by clearing it out of your consciousness and replacing it with your new truth. By clearing your judgment, you will experience an instant shift into a higher vibration of consciousness as your energy body transforms. It is an easy tool to utilize once you learn how it works.

Before I explain the steps to utilize this healing tool, first let me clarify one thing: when I am using the word 'judgment' here, I am speaking about judgments attached to negative energy or positive energy, not neutral judgment, which I call discernment or evaluative judgment. How can we tell the difference between a negative or positive judgment and neutral discernment or evaluative judgment? Easily. The answer will come immediately upon checking in with your emotional state by checking your internal feeling barometer. If you feel triggered, upset, annoyed, disgusted, or irritated in *any way*, then there is a negative charge of energy present. If you feel good in a personality-based way, such as self-righteous, better-than, smug, overly proud, superior to someone, or if you feel overly happy, excited, or manic, there is a positive charge of judgment present. If a thought makes you feel off-centered in any way, judgment is present, as I am defining the word today.

Some people think that they are only out of balance when they run negative judgments; in reality, positive judgments are just as unbalancing as negative judgments. True discernment comes from a place of total neutrality, and when you reside in that place, all of your thoughts are in energies of peace and Loving. This is the feeling that yoga or Tai Chi teachers would describe as feeling 'centered'. To promote clarity, from here on out, when referring to the term 'judgment', I will be using it to mean the kind of judgment that is attached to a feeling of good or bad, right or wrong. When referring to the neutral kind of judgment, I will use the word 'discernment' instead of judgment.

One helpful way to visualize how this works on a feeling-level is by picturing a pendulum – like the kind on a Grandfather's clock. Imagine it hanging down the center of your body. You can imagine the pendulum as your internal barometer. If you are residing in Loving, your pendulum will be still and centered, hanging in a completely neutral position in alignment with the Loving. This place of stillness is the place of internal peace. If your pendulum is not straight up and down, you are residing in the right/wrong reality because the swing of your internal barometer will be in either good or bad territory, which shows judgment is present. Having strong swings of judgment can also be referred to as 'war mentality' because the internal barometer is always pushing against something, which creates more againstness or struggle in the external world.

When the pendulum swings one way, that demonstrates the feeling of negative judgment; when it swings the other way, it represents the feeling of positive judgment. Once you begin to really tune in to your own feeling-barometer, you will easily be able to tell if you are in judgment or neutrality. When you are in neutrality, you will feel very steady and centered with your body completely at peace. When you are in judgment of something, you will feel upset, distressed, self-righteous, manic, indignant, scathing, angry, uncomfortable, annoyed, or any other feeling that takes you out of your place of complete peace and contentment. Believe it or not, your most basic desire is to live in peace. As much as we've bought into stories of great drama and experienced roller coaster rides of up and down, good and bad, more than anything, each of our souls yearns to come into the peace, acceptance, and stillness that is available only in the neutrality of the Loving. To get there, we first have to clear out our bags of judgment.

A great visual for describing the actual energy of judgment is to see it in bags placed inside baskets upon a double-sided scale. The scale does not have to be balanced. Some people are carrying more weight on the positive side, and some hold more weight on the negative. These two kinds of people are often referred to as optimists and pessimists, or people who see the glass as half full or half empty. It matters not whether someone's judgments are stored on the side labeled 'good' or the side labeled 'bad'. Whichever basket it is stored in, judgment is still judgment, and both kinds carry a weight that keeps us locked into right/wrong reality. Some people seem to have mostly good judgments or mostly bad judgments, and in actuality, they may be holding a very strong judgment on the other side that is simply going unvoiced.

For instance, a man may be bitterly unhappy, always complaining and judging everyone and everything as 'bad' or 'wrong'. He may also have an internal judgment of the opposite; everything he believes is good or right, even though he may not expound on that. Another person could seem very happy and positive, always going on and on about all of the good in the world. This person may seem to have an optimistic outlook on life but may actually be just as stuck in judgments on the negative side as the unhappy person. People who are strongly entrenched in right/wrong reality are often deeply invested in it. They have placed so much 'stuff' in their baskets of right and wrong that they are stuck, weighed down with the burden of their beliefs. These people have a hard time moving through life due to the weight of their baggage, as they have to drag their scales of judgments with them wherever they go. They often live inside of tiny boxes as a result of their heavy and restricting belief system.

People who have very little in the baskets of right/wrong judgment will have more freedom, live lighter, and travel faster. These people are able to do more in life as a result of their lightness and higher level of mental and emotional flexibility. People who have managed to empty their baskets of right/wrong judgments are enlightened; they are free of any stuff or baggage that weighed them down in the past and now see everything through the eyes of Loving.

By applying the tool of owning your judgments, you have the opportunity to see and acknowledge that you are carrying a scale filled with bags of judgments. Then you can look into your bags of right and wrong and identify what you have placed inside there. Each judgment will have a weight attached to it. The weight of various judgments will feel different, and it will be based upon the emotional energy you gave it at the time you stored it in your bag. Some judgments feel extremely heavy and have created a huge burden of suffering to drag around. Other judgments are lighter and may cause less suffering. All judgments, regardless of which side they reside, cause a drain in a person's energy to carry. Regardless of the size or weight of any particular judgment, none of them are much fun to lug around. Once I understood that I could utilize my own judgments as a tool to release them, I recognized that complete freedom from judgment is possible.

Here is possibly the most important point I can make when speaking about judgment: having a scale filled with bags of judgments is neither 'good' nor 'bad', from the spiritual perspective; it is simply what occurs to humans in a fear-based, right/wrong reality. If you are born on Earth, judgment happens. It is crucial to the process of enlightenment to come to peace with your scale of judgments.

Resist the Urge to Bypass Your Bags of Judgment

Many people who realize that peace is possible will attempt to disown their scale of judgment. They hear that there is no judgment from the place of mastery and quickly decide to deny or ignore their own baggage in the hopes that by denying their load, they can reach that beautiful place of enlightenment faster. This is what is known as doing a spiritual bypass. A spiritual bypass is an attempt to reside in a place that is free of baggage before one's baggage has been properly claimed, sorted, and consciously recycled. People who choose to bypass their judgments don't actually get to reside in peace; although they will often spend quite a bit of time pretending to feel at peace, faking feeling at peace, and often even irrationally convincing themselves they are, indeed, at peace.

Have you ever known anyone who is attempting to fake peace when in actuality, they are still residing deeply in judgment? A person could be smiling brightly, yet you can practically see, sense, or feel their unresolved anger or judgment pulsing behind their teeth or swirling across their face. Have you ever experienced being on the receiving end of that sort of inauthentic expression? Or, is this something you have tried to do yourself? Deny or avoid your judgment in an attempt to be free of it? Be willing to look deeply at yourself.

Here is the issue with bypass: when we put down our bags without owning them, they don't actually detach from us. We create a string or a line of energy to our bags that necessitates that we are dragging them around wherever we go, no matter how desperately we wish to be free of them. When our baggage is hanging out behind us, out of sight, all sorts of disasters occur in life to let us know that we are behaving irresponsibly. People will be tripping over our lines right and left, or taking our bags and holding them up in front of our face saying, "Excuse me – isn't this yours?" Not only do we create bigger messes when we deny claiming our baggage, we eventually get very tired. If we do not pick up our bags and take responsibility, we might even make ourselves sick. It requires a great deal of strength to hold all of our bags of judgment out in againstness. Some people will die in suffering before owning their bags, and they'll simply get to drag them along on into their next incarnation.

Eventually, no matter how long we avoid or deny our baggage, we all must take full 100% responsibility for our own bags of judgment if we wish to move to the next level. To utilize the profound power of using our judgments as a healing tool, it is vital that we take the stigma of 'bad' off of having judgment in the first place. If we can accept that we created our bags of 'good' and 'bad' judgments as a natural and normal outcome of getting born into the right/wrong Earth-plane reality, we can claim our baskets of judgments willingly. Then, once we declare that they are indeed our own, we can begin the transformational process of releasing our judgments by transmuting them from energy trapped in the right/wrong reality into energy of Loving and neutrality.

I encourage you to own your judgment fully. If you have not already done so, claim your baggage! Own that you have internal scale-baskets filled with bags of all sorts of judgments. Pick up your baggage and feel its weight. Get an idea of the size, shape, and feel of the bags of judgment you've been carting around for years. What is in your bags of judgment? Do you judge certain kinds of people, maybe certain behaviors or personality traits? Do you judge people based on their wealth or lack of wealth, their accent, their clothing, or what kind of car they drive? Do you judge people who are judgmental or people who attempt to force their opinions on others? Do you judge social media or the government? Get interested in the contents of your baggage.

Identifying your bags of judgment is a liberating experience. Don't be afraid to claim your bags. These bags are filled with tremendous amounts of stored energy. This is your energy. The great thing about energy is that it cannot be destroyed; it can only change forms. What this means is that you have the power to change or transmute all of the energy that you have put out into your bags of judgment. You have the power to transform your judgment into Loving. This is an energetic recycling process, also referred to sometimes as 'spiritual alchemy'. You have the power to be a catalyst for creating peace on the planet, simply by owning your judgment and then transmuting it into Loving. Utilize the power that is stored inside your judgments. See it as a hidden treasure. It is more valuable than gold.

The Active Process of Judging

As a noun, judgment is an energy-substance in the form of weight inside a bag or basket on a double-sided scale labeled 'right' and 'wrong'. Now, let's take a look at the process of how we acquired our bags of judgment in the first place, which happens through the active process of judging. Judging as a verb is an action. When we judge something, depending upon how much investment or feeling we put into it, we are actively determining how much energy or weight to place upon the stuff that will become our judgment.

Two Types of Judgment: Self-judgment and Projections

There are different ways to judge: Judging yourself, judging other people, judging your circumstances, and judging things and situations outside of yourself. Directly judging yourself creates 'self-judgment', and judging other people, places, or things creates 'projections of judgment'.

Self-judgment is usually pretty easy to identify once you begin to admit you do it constantly. Before I became conscious of my self-judgment, I had a running stream of judgment playing like background music inside my head every waking second of every day. It was like listening to an old familiar tape recording, same judgment different day. My 'stupid' tape went something like, "I am so stupid! *Why* did I just do that?! Why didn't I do that differently? I should have known better. I am *so* dumb. I am pathetic. I'm such a loser! If I had a brain, I'd blow up. I *cannot* believe I did that. I am such an idiot! I'll never learn. Why do I even bother? I am hopeless." And so on.

I had a few different tapes that could be played, depending upon the given situation. In addition to 'stupid', there was one for 'blame', one for 'victimization', one for 'failure', one for 'unattractive', and several other equally disempowering scenarios. Each tape I played in my head would create an endless loop, so if I was playing, "I am so stupid", I might hear that loop several dozens of times within a very short time if I didn't consciously intervene and change my focus.

What kind of self-judgments do you have? Do you ever play any old recordings that repeat themselves frequently or recur even occasionally in your mind? If so, list the topics of your recurring tapes.

Or, have you become aware of your self-judgment and are now in control of your internal background music? If so, congratulations! Wherever you are in regards to your own level of awareness of your self-judgment, it is all Ok. Remember that having judgment is the normal and natural byproduct of growing up in the fear-based right/wrong duality where everything is seen as either 'good' or 'bad'. Remind yourself that by bringing your judgments to your own attention, you are giving yourself access to a powerful healing tool towards your freedom.

Self-judgment

Self-judgment sometimes begins with an 'I' statement, such as 'I am so stupid'. Other times you will hear it in your mind as if it comes from a parent, teacher or other critical party, 'You are so stupid'. Whether it begins with 'I' or 'you' in your thoughts or speech, what makes it easy to spot is that it is evident that it is directed inward, toward yourself. A projection of judgment is when you are having a judgmental thought about someone or something else. This would come into your thoughts or speech in the form of a third-party statement such as, 'He is so stupid', 'She is such an idiot', or 'That dress is hideously ugly'.

Clearing Self-judgment

Clearing self-judgment is a simple process of transmuting the lower frequency of energy that is holding in the right/wrong reality into the higher frequency of energies of the Loving reality. This is done by consciously applying love and compassion to the judgment through the process of self-forgiveness and following up by stating the truth from your soul's perspective. The energy of compassion applied internally will actually neutralize the judgment energetically, and the statement of truth will then transmute it into a higher frequency, thereby lifting the old weight from your body and lightening your energetic load internally at the cellular level.

Example of Clearing Self-judgment:

"I forgive myself for judging myself as stupid." Take a deep breath and let this idea go. "The truth is that I am sourced from the Loving and am therefore connected to the source of infinite wisdom. I have instant access to infinite intelligence. Anything I want to know, I need only ask my higher self. I will be given direct knowledge or guided to the answer or solution. I am infinitely intelligent and wise beyond measure." Breathe this in.

Projections of Judgment

The truth is all judgment of others is ultimately really self-judgment; a projection of judgment is just a defense mechanism that we use to deflect some of our feelings of self-judgment off of ourselves. Why would we do this? Well, our essence is really Loving. We are sourced from infinite love, and our true nature is to act and feel Loving at all times. So, when we feel bad inside of ourselves, it goes against our soul's true nature as a Loving being. This doesn't feel good, doesn't feel in alignment, so our psyche unconsciously tries to deny this bad feeling by blaming it on someone or something else. If we can put it out there onto someone else, we won't have to feel so bad, and we can deny we judge ourselves. This defense mechanism works great as long as we remain unaware, asleep, and steeped in the right/wrong reality. When we awaken to our Loving nature as spiritual beings, it becomes time to get out of denial, take personal responsibility, and to begin owning all of our projections of judgment. Once we begin to identify our projections of judgment and self-judgments, we can begin using our judgments to heal.

Self-judgment sounds like negative, unkind, unsupportive, critical words that come into your thoughts as 'I am' or 'You are' statements. Self-judgment is fairly obvious. Basically, if you are feeling bad about yourself in any way, the chances are good that you are running some sort of self-judgment or negative self-talk inside of your consciousness that you can hear within your thoughts if you tune in and listen. Projections of judgment happen when whatever negative self-judgment you are running is too quiet, too suppressed, or too uncomfortable for you to deal with openly and consciously. The good news is, once you understand how projection works, you can immediately bring your judgment out into the open and begin to work with it consciously. Let me give you a specific example of how this works.

I was slender for most of my life, and while I was neutrally aware of many different body shapes and sizes, I held no judgments toward others about their body size. During my pregnancies, naturally I gained weight. With my first pregnancy I gained over 90lbs, yet I simply viewed my post-partum shape as the normal, natural outcome of growing a baby inside of my body. My body effortlessly and naturally lost the extra baby weight after I stopped breast-feeding, returning me eventually to my pre-pregnancy size each time. Since weight was a non-issue for me, I held no judgment about this inside of myself. Or so I thought...

A handful of years ago, I was standing in line at the grocery store behind a very large woman in a pink muumuu. As I placed my goods on the conveyor, I looked at her and thought, "Wow. She is really *fat*." Now, I could have done a spiritual bypass and convinced myself that that was simply a discernment of fact, yet I knew the difference on a feeling level. I felt the energy of judgment coursing through my body as I thought those words, and this caused a sick feeling in the pit of my stomach. My feeling-barometer had swung into the negative and was loudly beeping, 'Off-course. Off-course.' It didn't feel good to hold that projection of judgment towards that woman, so I immediately owned it, saying inside of myself, "This is about me. This woman is presenting a mirror for my healing." As soon as I owned the projection of judgment, I sent the woman in front of me energies of love and gratitude, thanking and blessing her for showing me that I had a judgment stored in my consciousness. My feeling-barometer dropped right back into neutrality, and I felt much better inside, even as I was now aware that I had some inner work to do around this issue.

When I got home that day, I was determined to face my self-judgment. Taking a big, fortifying breath, I quickly took off my clothing and stood in front of the bathroom mirror. Sure enough, there was a ring of pudge around my middle that I'd been steadfastly ignoring and avoiding, hoping that if I didn't acknowledge it, it might just go away. My arms were thicker, especially my upper arms. My bottom looked bigger & wider than I'd ever seen it. Without my fully-conscious awareness, I had gone from very slim to somewhat heavier than I'd ever been in my life. Obviously, this was something that I had begun placing judgment on inside of myself.

Doing my best to view this situation with neutrality, I thought about my recent lifestyle and reflected on how this change may have come about. A couple of years earlier, I had gone from having an active lifestyle to spending more time in a sedentary position as I began counseling and writing full-time. I was now sitting for up to eight or ten hours a day, rather than running around as a mother, teacher, waitress, nanny, dancer, and generally very active person. I hadn't compensated for my lack of activity in any way, such as doing more exercise or joining a gym. This lack of physical activity had begun over a year and a half earlier. Wow! That was a long time for my body to go without any exercise. No wonder I had stored a bunch of body fat around my middle. I owned this fully and viewed myself with compassion for my lack of self-awareness in this area.

By looking deeply at my projection of judgment, I realized that I had been unconsciously judging myself as 'fat' for months now, but it had been such an uncomfortable feeling that I had been stuffing and denying my own feelings of judgment. I'd begun avoiding mirrors, dressing and undressing more quickly than usual, and exhibiting other weird behaviors to avoid thinking about my less-than-comfortable new body size. Deep down, under all of my denial, I had been saying to myself, "I am getting fat. Ugh! These pants don't fit. Look at that stomach – that's disgusting. Yeesh! I look awful!" I had been running a constant tape of self-judgment about my body shape, but I'd had the volume turned down so low I could barely hear it – that is, until the universe was thoughtful enough to place the woman in the pink muumuu so close I couldn't miss the opportunity to hear my own judgment.

In order to fully own and clear the projection of judgment,

I first had to clear the irrationality that 'fat is bad', which I didn't even know I had. Next, I had to forgive myself for judging myself as 'fat', and to forgive myself for judging myself as 'neglectful' for neglecting to pay attention to my body. As soon as I forgave myself for judging myself, I was immediately able to move into action about it, coming up with a plan to do some regular yoga and fit some walks into my daily routine. By owning that projection of judgment, I brought valuable awareness to myself and was able to move my life forward in a healthier, more Loving direction.

When we stay stuck in our judgment, we are staying stuck to whatever it is that we are judging. We are saying, *"This is the way it is."* From this place, there can be no movement, no change. Believing 'I am fat' keeps me totally stuck in 'I am fat'. If I can take that out of right/wrong reality that says 'fat is bad', I can see that it is Ok that I grew a little tire around my belly; there were logical reasons for it. The reality was I was doing absolutely nothing to support my metabolism and everything to slow it down. I had stopped dancing every day and hadn't been doing any form of exercise on a regular basis, and on top of that, I had begun eating bread, eating out at restaurants more often, and eating way fewer fruits and vegetables than I'd previously been used to eating. After many years of an active lifestyle, I had suddenly become more sedentary; from the place of discernment, I could objectively see that my calorie intake was now larger than my caloric output – of course, I had gained some extra weight.

From a place of non-judgment, matter-of-factly accepting my weight gain as normal and Ok, now I had the power to do something about it if I wished; my body weight had become a temporary situation that was completely reversible. All I had to ask myself is, "How is this working for me?" Now that I was aware of my judgment, it was no longer working to stay sedentary. Was I able to change my body shape? Yes. I was empowered to begin to be aware of my body and take better care of myself. Now, instead of remaining stuck in unconscious judgment of myself, by owning my judgment fully and detaching the energy of 'bad' from around it, I was able to become fully responsible (able to respond) and chose to respond in a different way to create a different outcome in my life. Most importantly, I was able to stop putting myself down and feel good about myself again, which made me feel ten times lighter almost immediately.

Owning Projections of Judgment as a Healing Tool

Here are some steps to use when applying the process of owning projections of judgment as a healing tool.

Step #1: Awareness – Pay attention to your thoughts and feelings; notice when you feel triggered or upset.

Step #2: Identification – Identify or label the projection of judgment; examples: "Lady is *fat*." "Driver is *stupid*." "Husband is acting like a *jerk*."

Step #3: Ownership – Own the judgment as your own; claim "this mirror is about *me*."

Step #4: Self-exploration – How does this judgment (fat, stupid, jerk) resonate as a judgment inside of me? Have I ever thought this way about myself, past or present? Have other people ever called me this or judged me as this? Do I judge this as 'bad' or not Ok in anyone else? Do I believe that God judges this as 'bad' or not, Ok? How's holding onto this judgment working for me? Be willing to examine your own consciousness fearlessly.

Step #5: Self-forgiveness – Free yourself from the judgment by applying the energies of love and compassion. Take the judgment from right/wrong good/bad reality into the grace of the Loving. State the truth from a neutral perspective of Loving.

Step #6: Blessing – Give thanks and blessings toward your mirror. Feel gratitude for the healing opportunity this projection of judgment has provided for you.

Let's use another example and go through the steps.

Example of Owning a Projection of Judgment - Cheryl's Story:

Cheryl felt irritated and annoyed by her husband all the time, and although she knew it was really petty stuff, it was becoming too frustrating for her to ignore. She felt ridiculous, even admitting her judgments because her husband was such a wonderful man and a great, supportive partner. She didn't know *why* she felt so much irritation towards him.

I assured her that the feelings of judgment were normal and Ok and that this did not at all mean that her marriage was in jeopardy; we simply act as mirrors for each other in relationship when our stuff is ready to surface for healing. Then I asked her if she was willing to explore the judgments she'd projected onto her husband, knowing that it is Ok to judge and that her judgment could be used in service toward her healing. She was very willing to move forward, eager to stop feeling irritated with her husband.

(Step #1: Awareness) First, I asked her what was it about her husband that annoyed her the most right then? She instantly replied, "His stinky socks!" Apparently, Cheryl's husband was an athlete and had a habit of removing and leaving his sweaty socks in inconvenient places like on the living room couch.

I asked her to judge her husband's behavior around the stinky socks, as much as she could judge it. (Step #2: Identification) She laughed and readily complied, "Irresponsible. Uncaring. Gross, dirty, sweaty, smelly, icky, disgusting, filthy, yucky, impure, unclean."

Ok, great, then I asked her if she was willing to own

this projection of judgment that her husband's socks were mirroring. (Step #3: Ownership) She said, "Yes, of course, if it will make this irritation go away!"

Next, I asked her what most people find to be the most challenging part of the process, "How do these judgments resonate inside of you? Have you ever felt these judgments – irresponsible, uncaring, gross, dirty, etc. – toward yourself?" (Step #4: Self-exploration) At this point, Cheryl looked shocked and burst into tears, nodding her head 'yes', that she had often felt that way toward herself in the past. She shared that these words brought up painful, long-forgotten judgments she'd felt toward herself as a teenager who had spent several years abusing alcohol and not caring who she had sex with when she was drunk. These judgments brought up painful feelings of shame and self-loathing she'd been bottling up for many years. She remembered waking up many times in strange places, not remembering how she'd gotten there. She remembered the shame she'd felt knowing she had slept with a stranger but didn't remember anything that had happened. She remembered the smell of her vomit in her hair, on her clothing, and she recalled how much she had hated herself in those moments. All of the judgments were there – she had judged herself as 'irresponsible, uncaring, gross, dirty, sweaty, smelly, icky, disgusting, filthy, yucky, impure, and unclean'. She dug deeper and judged herself even more as 'drunk, addicted, promiscuous, hateful, loathsome, worthless, oblivious, disconnected, despicable and slutty'.

She cried it all out and eventually moved into compassion for herself as an unhappy teenager. (Step #5: Self-forgiveness) Cheryl was able to access love and infinite compassion for herself and take it back into her memory to the years when she'd felt so disconnected from her source of Loving. She bathed herself in compassion in her memories of drinking, of waking up stinking and sweating, unaware of her whereabouts, saying things like, "It's Ok. I was just learning and growing. I was doing the best I could at the time." She applied love and compassion to the part of herself that expressed self-hatred and came to the conclusion that she had always loved herself; that part of herself just wanted better for her and knew she was worth more than that unhealthy lifestyle. She forgave herself for each judgment she had placed against herself, knowing she was not really any of those things; she'd only *felt* and *acted* like those things, and that at the being level, she was not her feelings or actions. She stated the truth about herself – that she was, in fact, a divine being, simply having a human experience which had included drunken behavior, and that her essence has always been Loving. She had been doing the best she could at that time, learning and growing, and from her soul's perspective, she has always been pure, innocent and clean. She freed herself completely of this old weight she'd been unknowingly suppressing for years.

She was radiant by the time she finished letting go of all of the self-judgment and washing herself with compassion. (Step #6: Blessing) She moved naturally into gratitude towards spirit and her husband, thanking and blessing her husband for providing her with the mirror to do such profoundly deep healing work. She felt a tremendous load had been lifted, and she was at peace inside. Who knew that her husband's stinky socks could result in a purging of many years worth of self-hatred? This is the healing power of owning a projection of judgment.

Cheryl continued to take full responsibility for her judgments and, over the next few months, eventually cleared every projection of judgment she'd been holding towards her husband. Cheryl became calmer, more centered, and Loving, and as a direct result, her marriage improved dramatically.

Owning Projections are Part of the Process of Enlightenment

The process of owning your projections of judgment is a liberating and life-changing experience. To the degree you can own your own projections of judgment, you are taking responsibility for your own baggage. Once you fully claim your bags of judgment, then it becomes up to you to determine how much baggage you want to continue to carry around daily. If you want to lighten up, to become more enlightened, you can clear your judgments through the process of self-forgiveness.

When forgiving self-judgment, the key is to simply acknowledge that the judgment was just a temporary feeling, not who you really are; who you really are is a divine soul, and you have always been Loving on the being level. It is also important to acknowledge to yourself that it is Ok to have felt the judgment, as judgment is a very normal and natural outcome of living in a fear-based, right/wrong paradigm.

Phrasing Your Self-Forgiveness Statements using 'As'

When applying self-forgiveness to clear your judgment, make sure you phrase your statements specifically using the word 'as' followed by the judgment or labeling word. It is important to avoid using 'being' words when making the self-forgiveness declaration, because, on the being level, we are pure, Loving consciousness, not our judgmental thoughts or words. Let me give a specific example:

If the judgment is 'stupid', avoid saying 'being' statements like this, "I forgive myself for *being* stupid", because on the being level, you are not stupid. Avoid any tense of the being word, such as, "I forgive myself for *having been* stupid," "I forgive myself for times I *was* stupid," "I forgive that I *am* stupid," "I forgive myself if I *should ever be* stupid in the future" etc. You have never been, nor will ever be, stupid on the being level. Nor have you been or ever will be any other judgment you may have identified with in your lifetime. The verbiage is extremely important when clearing judgment, because when you use any form of 'being' words, what you are essentially doing is creating more of that.

'Being' Words are Co-creative Words

The words 'I AM' are powerful, identifying, co-creative words that create your reality in every given moment, so I encourage you to begin to only use them in positive, empowering, and self-supportive statements. Use 'being' words freely when you update your new beliefs or state your truth, claiming things like "I AM connected to my source of infinite intelligence. I AM the Loving."

To help to dis-identify with particularly strong judgments, start to use the words 'thinking', 'feeling', and 'acting' instead of 'being'. You can begin to do this in your own stream of consciousness if you learn to observe your own thoughts. The next time you catch yourself thinking something like, "I am so stupid," cancel that thought and think, "I felt stupid for a moment there, and I know I am not my feelings." This will immediately help to separate you from the self-judgment and will allow you to quickly move into letting the judgment go; "I forgive myself for judging myself as stupid. The truth is that judgment was just a temporary feeling. I am really a Loving being, and I am connected to the source of infinite intelligence, infinite wisdom. I can learn how to do anything I want to do."

Self-judgments Attach Themselves to Irrational Beliefs

In my experience, irrational beliefs almost always have self-judgments attached. Now that you know how to update your beliefs, you can begin to see and identify all of the self-judgment that has been stored up along with each limiting belief. For instance, my irrational belief that 'I was an unlovable child' had dozens of judgments attached; I judged myself as bad, unworthy, unlovable, unloved, less-than, despicable, pitiful, guilty, deprived, on and on. My irrational belief that 'women need a man to support them' led to judgments of unsupported, incapable, less-than, sexist, weak, pathetic, needy, undeserving of equality, undeserving of prosperity, undeserving of independence, and so on.

Once you spot an irrational belief and update it, I encourage you to dive deep and juice the judgment for all it's worth. Judgment is like gold! Judgment is stored energy that shows you something that has been locked into right/wrong reality inside your own consciousness. Remember that when you apply love and compassion to your judgments, a kind of spiritual alchemy takes place that immediately transmutes that old, stored energy into a vital and powerful healing force. The energy cannot be destroyed; it simply changes form. In this case, the judgment takes on a new, higher vibration of Loving and can be used in service to the entire world.

You Are a Powerful Being of Light and Love

You are a powerful being. Know that each and every time you update an irrational belief, clear and transmute the surrounding judgment, or own a projection of judgment, you are taking a step forward on your soul's path toward the completion of your soul's lessons, coming one step closer to fulfilling your own unique destiny upon the planet. Since we are all one at the level of consciousness, each time you clear one judgment or update one belief, the entire whole of humanity takes one step forward up the evolutionary spiral of consciousness. Take full responsibility for your judgment; own your projections of judgment, transmute your judgments into Loving, and watch your entire life and the lives of everyone around you change for the better.

Exercise: Claiming Judgment as a Valuable Healing Tool

Begin by saying a protection prayer, setting conditions of love and light, and invoking spirit's presence.

Place your hands on your heart. Set an intention to access the highest vibration of Loving available. Breathe in the Loving and fill your body with Loving energies from head to toe. Then, set an intention to access the highest level of compassion. Breathe in compassion and fill your body with compassion from head to toe.

Repeat out loud any of the following that resonates, changing the phrasing as needed to reflect your own beliefs:

"I forgive myself for buying into the irrational belief that judgment is bad or wrong." "My new updated belief is, I now know judgment is simply the normal, natural response to residing in the fear-based, right/wrong reality. I now know that I will continue to judge things to the degree that I continue to reside in the right/wrong paradigm, and that I can gradually cease to judge by moving my consciousness into the neutrality of the Loving paradigm."

"I forgive myself for buying into the irrational belief that if I have any judgment, it means I'm not a good person or a spiritual person." "My new updated belief is, I now know I am innately good, and that I am innately spiritual, regardless of any judgments I may have made or may still be carrying. It is the nature of right/wrong reality to create judgment. I fully accept myself as good, innately spiritual, and Ok for having judgments."

"I forgive myself for buying into the irrational belief that it is a sin to judge, and that I'll be punished for having judgment." "My new updated belief is, I now know to sin simply means to 'land off the mark'. There is no punishment for landing off the mark from the spiritual perspective; there is only an opportunity for growth and learning, then course-correcting.

All punishment resides only in right/wrong thinking inside of myself. I now let myself off-the-hook. I forgive myself! I am an innocent child of God."

"I forgive myself for buying into the irrational belief that I should suppress my judgment and pretend that I am totally non-judgmental." "My new updated belief is, I now know that suppressing my judgment is called doing a 'spiritual bypass'. To the degree I pretend to be free of judgment, I am actually passing up the opportunity to clear my judgment, heal, and integrate the parts of my own self that have been trapped in judgment. I now know that the only way to truly free myself of judgment is to identify my judgment, own my judgment, accept my judgment, and forgive myself for the judgments I have placed against myself and others."

"I forgive myself for buying into the irrational belief that my judgments about myself are really true." "My new updated belief is, I now know that I am simply a divine being having a human experience of living in the right/wrong paradigm. I now know that on the being level, I am pure love, compassion, and innocence. I can now view my judgments as temporary thoughts and feelings based on my irrational, fear-based beliefs. I can now update any beliefs that are no longer serving me, and I can clear any judgment related to my old, unsupportive beliefs."

"I forgive myself for buying into the irrational belief that it is best not to acknowledge any judgments I might have." "My new updated belief is, I now know the only way to get out of the right/wrong paradigm is to acknowledge the parts of my consciousness that are still stuck thinking in terms of right/wrong. By identifying and owning my judgment, I can use my judgment as a powerful healing tool to shift my entire consciousness out of right/wrong until I am fully residing in the Loving paradigm."

Close your process by acknowledging yourself, expressing gratitude to spirit, and fully grounding your energy. Drink plenty of water.

CHAPTER EIGHT
Embracing Disowned Aspects of Self

Now that we have covered some of the basic principles of creating a belief system based on rationality and spiritual truth let's take a more in-depth look at what has occurred inside our mental and emotional bodies as children born into a fear-based, right/wrong reality.

Sub-personalities are a Normal, Natural Outcome

When a child is scolded, punished, criticized, shamed, blamed, or otherwise judged or treated as 'bad', the child's personality will fragment, developing into different aspects or what are called sub-personalities in psychology. It is as if the main personality cannot deal with having a 'bad' part, so it pushes that part away from what it views as the 'good' or acceptable self, disowning the so-called 'bad' part in order to feel any level of comfort or self-acceptance. This is a normal, natural, instinctive psychological protective coping mechanism that helps children survive. The child will do this unconsciously over and over during the formative years, sometimes to the point of having no parts left that it views as 'good'. These disowned parts are also often referred to as the shadow self or the dark side of the self. Having lots of the personality stuck out in disowned sub-personalities – stuck in the dark – creates an illusion of separation, feelings of 'not good enough', unworthy, and so on, often leading to what has been termed 'low self-esteem'.

Part of the awakening and healing process for us as adults involves gathering up all of our different aspects and bringing them into the light of our heart, into the compassion and acceptance of the Loving. This is the process of integration. Once a person begins to integrate the various aspects of their personality into their heart, they begin to feel more whole, joyful, and content. They begin to hold themselves in higher and higher esteem until they are one with their source of Loving.

One Underlying Issue: The Feeling of Separation from Source

There really is only one real underlying issue that is at the root of every problem that humans face, and that is the feeling of separation from our Loving Source-energy. If you look at modern psychology, each and every diagnosis involves a separation at the level of the personality. We have all experienced a certain level of separation from our Loving Source within our personality, depending upon how we related to our circumstances as a child. Understand that there is nothing wrong or bad with having aspects of ourselves that we've put in the dark. It is actually a normal, healthy way for the psyche to relate to the harshness of the right/wrong reality. The psyche must protect itself at all costs. It is actually a basic survival instinct and nothing we have any control over as children.

People can become very triggered by the idea that they might be viewed as having a mental health issue. If you have sensitivity about this sort of thing, I highly encourage you to just laugh this idea away. In my experience, I have never met a human who has not had a degree of personality separation, so you could say that until we go through the process of integration, we could *all* be viewed as headcases. Thankfully, most mental-level disease - where dis-ease simply means 'lack of ease' or lack of peace – can actually be fairly manageable to heal once a person becomes conscious; as soon as a person is ready and willing to take responsibility for themselves, they can choose to begin the process of updating their belief system to more Loving, healthier ideas and inviting their various parts out of the shadows.

Again, there is only really ever one issue that all people face, and that is the illusion of separation from Source. The labels that have been adopted by modern psychology are a way of describing how a particular personality has coped with that feeling of separation. A diagnosis of bipolar or manic-depressive is simply describing two very strong, opposing sub-personalities. Schizophrenia is just a name for multiple, severely disowned aspects. Depression is usually related to one strongly-suppressed aspect that feels very bleak, powerless, or despairing. Anxiety disorder is an aspect or several aspects that are stuck in fear. Most people have lots of different aspects that have been disowned, whether or not they have ever been given a psych label.

My advice is that if you have ever received a label of this sort, know that you can decide to view the label as a temporary situation, rather than a fixed state, and begin owning the separated parts of your own personality. If you are currently on any type of medication, please seek professional care before changing your dosage in any way. I have seen many clients that have successfully weaned themselves off of their medications over a period of time after diligently clearing their irrational beliefs and self-judgments, and it is important to understand that weaning from medication is a process, not a one-time event. It requires commitment and close supervision by a qualified professional to ensure the health and safety of the client. If this is something that you are interested in doing, I encourage you to do it responsibly with awareness, support, and tremendous self-caring, knowing that physical bodies do better with gradual change. And, there are some instances where an aspect is so severely detached that it may present a danger to self or others to attempt to change a prescription. Attend to your healing and clearing first, holding the knowing that you are not your prescription. Know that it is absolutely possible to detach from any medical labels and see yourself as whole right now regardless of where you are in the healing process.

Whether or not you have ever received any sort of labeling, you are still very likely to have some disowned aspects of your personality who are waiting to be brought into the light and the Loving. How do you know if you have a disowned aspect of your personality? That is easy. If there is any part of yourself you'd like to change, any part of yourself you dislike, or any behavior or thought pattern that isn't supporting you, chances are excellent that you have an aspect of yourself that is residing outside of the Loving.

Why do you need to know about aspects or sub-personalities in order to evolve spiritually? Simply put, *all* of your parts must be brought into the light in order for you to up-level into a higher vibration. The process of enlightenment is often called self-realization or self-actualization because you must realize – 'make real' or 'make actual' – every part of your own self in order to feel the wholeness of your being. Looking at the various parts of your personality is a simple, straightforward way of getting real. For me, the more information I gathered about my own consciousness, the easier it was for me to shed light on my old patterns of unhealthy behavior, identify my irrational beliefs, and clear all of my self-judgment.

The bottom line is that your soul does not want your sub-personalities to stay stuck suffering in the dark. Your soul wants nothing more than for all parts of you to be seen, acknowledged, and accepted, to be brought into the light, and to live in the Loving along with all of your other already-accepted parts as one. Your soul does not want you to stay small, stuck, or hidden in any way; as long as there is any part of you that continues to hide, avoid, ignore, deny, defend or otherwise deflect your issues, these parts will be clamoring inside of you for your attention.

If we choose to act like the ostrich and put our head in the sand, it doesn't stop our sub-personalities from wreaking havoc upon our life; to the contrary! Ignoring our sub-personalities or repressing them can cause them to act out in bigger ways. When that happens, we feel totally out of control in our own lives. It is as if someone grabs the wheel and takes over driving our body vehicle. Have you ever had that happen? I can own that I've had that happen *way* more times than most people would be comfortable admitting.

There were times I snapped at people in anger that seemed to just fly up out of left-field. Times I dropped into a depression and couldn't even respond to my own child's question. Times I had so much resistance I couldn't force myself to do something if my life depended upon it. Times I said mean things for unknown reasons that I immediately regretted. Times I did things that made no sense to me at that moment. Times I sabotaged relationships and jobs for no apparent reason. I could fill volumes on the subject, but you get the idea.

The news is filled with reports of people's errant behavior; the child molester whom everyone agrees 'seems like such a nice guy'. The upstanding cop who beats his wife in private, the married minister who seduces vulnerable members of his flock, the teacher who has a flaming affair with her middle school student, the prim secretary who cuts loose in Vegas, and so on. These are all stories of people who have had the experience of a disowned aspect of their personality jumping into the driver's seat and taking over control of the wheel. It happens all the time, for there is no way to suppress a disowned aspect, no sure-fire way to control a part of ourselves that we've been suppressing from coming to light.

Now, those were examples of dramatic behavior, yet each of us experiences our own degree of separation uniquely. You may not be an abusive spouse, but you may occasionally scream at your children in a way that you instantly regret and feel bad about. You may not be a child molester, but you may have some level of guilt or shame around sex that causes you to feel less-than in some way. You may not be anorexic/bulimic, but you may notice that you use sugar, wine, coffee, or cigarettes for comfort or to alleviate stress or boredom. You get the idea. For myself, once I understood that I'd been repressing parts of my own personality for years and trying to change my unhealthy behaviors to no avail, I took a deep breath, metaphorically bit the bullet, and took full responsibility for all of my parts of my own personality, no matter what.

What I discovered was that there was no way to get around the fact that I had parts of my very own personality that were definitely *not* in alignment with my soul's purpose or even in line with my own core values and rational beliefs. After steeping in pure joy during my out-of-body awakening experience, beyond anything, I wanted to feel totally at peace within myself again. I wanted to live in that sense of peace and freedom, and I knew it was possible; not only was it possible for me to live in peace, but it was also actually imperative for me to do so in order to fulfill my life's purpose. And yet, I was excruciatingly aware that there were parts of myself – *lots* of parts – that weren't experiencing peace. Initially, the idea of exploring and accepting these parts was pretty uncomfortable because for so long, I had judged them as 'bad'.

Understand that at the level of the soul, no part of ourselves is viewed as bad or wrong. However, to the degree that the part has been pushed away and labeled as 'wrong', 'bad', or 'unacceptable', it will continue to act out in such a way as to prove its own lack of worth and lack of acceptability. In other words, poor behavior is the natural and inevitable result of ignoring or suppressing disowned aspects of self. If we keep a part of our personality in a dank, dark prison of despair, how could we possibly be surprised when that part responds like a fugitive?

Embrace Disowned Parts with Compassionate Acceptance

As crazy as it seems, the only way to make peace with every part of your personality is to reach out with love and embrace the disowned aspects with compassionate acceptance. That means you must embrace the fugitive part of yourself; no matter how dirty, disheveled, or smelly he appears in your mind, you simply open up your arms and invite him into the Loving. As he gradually gets used to the light, he will begin to adapt himself to the warmer air, he will start to feel better about himself, start to care better for himself, and quickly move from smelly and dirty to clean and well-kempt. This is what happens when we embrace our darkest parts.

For some people, this may feel like a big stretch. It is Ok to start with baby steps, maybe begin with sending the fugitive a letter in prison, or go visit the cell block before allowing your aspect to be paroled. You can start in whichever way you feel comfortable connecting to these parts that have been put in the dark. Remember, there is no right or wrong way to accept your aspects. I highly recommend, however you go about this, to not take it so seriously. Be light about it.

Discovering your disowned aspects of self, or sub-personalities can be likened to an adventure, like a treasure hunt! I encourage you to approach this topic with as much excitement and humor as you can muster. The funnier you can make this, the easier it is to accept and integrate all of your parts into your Loving self. You can start by exploring the personality traits you see as your main personality, your 'good' self, or the face you show the world when you are out in public, at work, or wanting to be viewed at your best.

Your Main Personality – the Face You Show the World

Your main personality traits will have traits that you feel good about, characteristics of yourself that you like, or maybe that you think others like. Behaviors of your main personality will be socially acceptable if you are a social person. If you are living your life seeking approval from one main source outside of yourself, the behaviors of your main personality will include whatever behaviors you believe will be acceptable to the person or persons who you have viewed as your source of Loving. Your main personality will usually include all of the parts of yourself that have gotten approval or praise from parents, teachers, or bosses over the years.

My main personality included traits such as kindness, politeness, caring, good humor, helpfulness, good grooming, the ability to follow directions, good listening skills, and mild creativity. My major motivations for my behavior included wanting to be liked, needing to be seen as 'good', seeking approval, avoiding punishment, avoiding shame or embarrassment, and wanting to fit in. My main feelings when I acted 'good' were feelings of safety, security, inauthenticity, fakeness, stiffness, falseness, lacking guts, weakness, fear, stupidity, neediness, dumbness, resentment toward myself, etc.

What are some of the personality traits and characteristics that make up your main personality? What are some of the major loving motivations? What are the main feelings related to the behaviors of this part of your personality? Write them down if you feel inclined.

Exploring Your Disowned Aspects or Sub-personalities

Next, you can begin to explore some of your disowned aspects of self. These sub-personalities are the parts of yourself that you sometimes wish you could change, don't like about yourself, maybe are uncomfortable with, or even loath. There are many different ways to go about acknowledging your disowned aspects; some people like to give them real first names such as Benedict or Ruth; others call them by the major feeling or behavior, such as The Procrastinator or Depressed. You could also make up a funny name with both, such as Doubtful Deb or Nervous Ned. However you go about doing this is Ok; there is no right or wrong way to explore your personality, so just do whatever you are inclined to do here and trust the process. The main goal of exploring your disowned aspects is to bring them into your conscious awareness. By becoming aware of these different parts of yourself, you will be literally shining a light on your previously disowned parts and beginning to own them, taking them from unconscious to conscious.

When I explored my personality, I found a whole group of sub-personalities that I'd felt uncomfortable with for much of my life. Here are a few disowned parts of my own personality that I identified, explored, and brought into the light:

The Avoider - My biggest sub-personality was called The Avoider. This part of me was afraid of moving forward in life, didn't like facing issues or conflict and basically just wanted me to stick my head in the sand rather than deal with my fears. She was always disheveled, had snarly hair, liked wearing old, worn clothing, disliked grooming, and resented the time it took to shower and wash her hair. She had a 'why even bother' attitude about self-care. Traits included acting messy, unkempt, uncaring, fearful, unconscious, protective, in denial, stubborn, determined, and resistant. She had patterns of avoiding by reading for hours or days on end, taking naps, eating chocolate, and generally distracting me from whatever issue was currently at hand. If she couldn't find another way to avoid something she didn't want to do or face, I would become physically ill and end up in bed with a high fever. The Avoider allowed me to miss almost every ballet performance I was terrified of giving, skip church as a child, miss deadlines for auditions and college applications, leave countless projects unfinished, ignore my credit card debts, not file my taxes on time, and otherwise avoid taking responsibility for much of my own life. Major loving motivations of behavior were self-protection, fear of failure, fear of commitment, and fear of conflict. Major feelings included feeling disappointed, ashamed, bad, wrong, weak, inadequate, unworthy, disgusted with me, and dread of taking my head out of the sand and facing whatever I'd been avoiding.

The Helper - My most codependent aspect was the part of me that needed to help others, usually to the detriment of myself. This part of me felt it was my job, my responsibility to take care of everyone else's business but my own. Traits included acting caring, sympathetic, bossy, controlling, manipulative, judgmental, and self-righteous. The Helper had behaviors of advising, interfering, and doing things for other people, sometimes without even asking them if they wanted my help. Major motivations for behavior included needing to feel needed, to prove that I was useful, and to get attention or acknowledgment. Major feelings included feeling superior/inferior, unworthy, anxious, fears of 'not good enough', and self-hatred.

The Know-it-all - The Know-it-all was the most hated aspect of my own personality, a part that would come out, again and again, no matter how much I'd try to suppress her. Traits included acting superior, authoritative, assertive, snobby, rude, controlling, confident, self-centered, self-righteous, and oblivious. She had the behavior of correcting people's grammar, pronunciation, or usage while they were speaking, often interrupting people to tell them they were wrong or to clarify what she thought was a relevant 'fact'. Major motivations included a huge need to feel right, needing attention, and needing approval. Major feelings included feeling embarrassed, mortified, vindicated, better-than, self-righteous, indignant, angry, and ashamed.

Sexy Cyn - This was the part of myself that needed to feel like she was attractive or sexy. Traits included vanity, naivety, inauthenticity, and self-centeredness. This part would come forward if I ever had the opportunity to go out at night, go on a date, go dancing, etc. This part was very vain, and felt uncomfortable unless wearing mascara and a push-up bra. Sexy Cyn had behaviors of glancing in windows to make sure she looked Ok, sucking in her stomach to appear skinnier, speaking in a higher tone of voice, and generally trying to appear sexy or attractive at all times. Major motivations included needing to be loved, needing to be liked and accepted by men, wanting attention, wanting to feel 'good enough' and 'worthy' of attention, and wanting to be seen and acknowledged. Major feelings included feeling insecure, unworthy, embarrassed, pathetic, fake, stupid, less-than, ugly, unacceptable, unwanted, undesirable, unlikable, and a lack of confidence.

Sarcastic Cyn - This was my major 'offensive' defense mechanism, which I employed if avoiding conflict didn't work. Traits included acting sarcastic, mean, brutally honest, blunt, courageous, judgmental, compassionate, caring, protective, cynical, impetuous, spontaneous, funny, and creative. Sarcastic Cyn would respond with a dig, a put-down, or a joke to deflect any perceived criticism towards herself or someone close to her. Her energy was rather momma lion-ish; like a fierce mother protecting her cubs, she would unsheathe her sharp claws at any suspected threat. Major motivations included self-protection, protecting her family, or protecting loved-ones from pain or judgment. Major feelings included feeling fearful, defensive, small, helpless, angry, bad, not good enough, and inadequate.

The Yeller - The Yeller was a part of myself that I disliked intensely but didn't seem to be able to control. Traits included acting loud, uncaring, bold, defiant, vindictive, creative, strong, and powerful. She would come out whenever I was really angry or very upset about something, usually toward my partner but occasionally toward my children. She would just scream whatever was on her mind uncensored, without caring about the consequences of her words. She would then feel contrite and say 'I'm sorry', but that never really made her feel any better about losing control. Major motivations were trying to control, trying to defend, seeking justice, venting anger, and expressing self-righteousness. Major feelings were feelings of sorrow, tremendous shame, blame, self-hatred, despondency, inadequacy, embarrassment, fear of self, anger, resentment, and stupidity.

The Hitter - This aspect was a tiny part that didn't show herself very often, yet she was quite powerful. Traits included acting strong, controlling, authoritative, courageous, stubborn, and mean. She would only come forward as a last resort if yelling didn't work, and I was at an absolute limit. Behavior was a strong, right-handed slap across the face of whoever was not obeying my boundary. This behavior happened three times in my life, once as a teenager and twice as a young adult. The first two times it happened, I shoved this part deeper down into the darkest recesses of my consciousness, as it was so incredibly painful to own up to. The third time, I decided to take responsibility, own my shit, and make a change. Major motivations included trying to control or defend. Major feelings included deep shame, sorrow, regret, mortification, fear of self, self-hatred, and self-loathing.

These were some of my previously disowned aspects, and I can tell you – thankfully – that I've successfully integrated each one of them. By identifying their characteristics and exploring them fully, I was able to heal and transform each of these parts of myself that had been stuck out in the dark, feeling judged and unwanted. I now have new, more supportive patterns of behavior and healthier responses in place of the old, destructive behaviors. I have also owned the positive qualities that each of these aspects represented for me, and I've cultivated new traits in areas that were lacking. I identified and owned all of the self-judgment related to the feelings of these aspects, and I now feel deeply peaceful and utterly comfortable in my own skin.

It was life-changing to notice that my very best traits were actually connected to parts of my character that I'd labeled as 'bad'. All of my strength, power, confidence, courage, boldness, honesty, creativity, and compassion were wrapped up in parts of myself that had been beaten, punished, blamed, yelled at, criticized, scolded, and shamed as 'wrong', 'bad' or 'unacceptable'. The parts I judged as 'good' or 'acceptable' to show in public actually turned out to contain the weakest parts of my own character – my codependencies, neediness, self-doubt, insecurities, and such were all motivating feelings behind the so-called 'good' behaviors of my main, public personality. By identifying and claiming *all* of my parts, I was able to fully own my own strengths and to begin to act with self-confidence and authenticity in almost every moment of my life.

Coming into Peace is an Inside Job

Understand that we cannot 'lose' any part of our personality; rather, we can transform ourselves to become even greater as a whole. The natural tendency from the right/wrong perspective is to get mad at, kick, or punish the part of ourselves acting out of alignment. We yell at that part, want to kill that part or try to get rid of that part that we judge as 'bad' and blame for all of our problems. In order to transform, we must come to see that all we are really doing by hating a part of our own self is, in fact, perpetuating the cycle of abuse and violence. If we want world peace for our children, we must first come to reside in peace within our own consciousness. Coming into peace is an inside job.

If you want to end the mirror of war in your outer-level reality, you must first stop the war that is going on within your own consciousness. The only way to do that is through applying love and compassion to the parts of your own self that you've been warring with – the parts of you that have been stuck in suffering.

Think about it this way; the parts of your consciousness

that you've disowned for whatever reason are like little children who have been locked in the dark closet, imprisoned in the cold cellar, stuck in the attic, or trapped in a cage. Quite naturally, if you were to come upon such a trapped child, the child may be crying in rage, throwing a tremendous tantrum, hissing, and spitting. Would you, if you discovered such a child, respond by kicking the child back while she was down, causing her to fear you and run back into hiding again? No way. You wouldn't abuse that child, would you? You are much too caring and compassionate, right?

And yet, that is indeed what most of us do. What we have been programmed to do and what has been modeled for us to do is to berate, scold, reprimand, and punish that already-abused child in our own harsh self-talk. We kick ourselves, call ourselves mean names, and criticize ourselves to no end whenever one of our aspects appears in our awareness.

Think about your own self-talk. How do you relate to yourself in your own thoughts when you make a mistake, when you judge that you've 'blown it', when you fall back into addictive behavior, or when you behave in a way that you don't feel so good about? Are you in any way perpetuating a cycle of abuse and somehow justifying that it is Ok to treat yourself this way?

To identify your unsupportive self-talk, it becomes necessary to engage the support of your neutral observer. If you haven't already done so, you can activate this part of yourself by setting an intention to do so: "I set the intention to awaken my neutral observer to monitor my thought." Once you are comfortable actively observing your own thoughts, you may begin to notice a constant stream of chatter going on underneath whatever may currently be holding your conscious attention in any given moment. What is that chatter anyway? For me, it was an on-going stream of worry-thoughts, criticism, lack-thoughts, and self-doubt thoughts being constantly presented to me throughout my day. My disowned aspects had so many personal insecurities; they felt so uncomfortable that they just couldn't keep quiet. All of my various aspects were clamoring for my attention, all the time, so my mind was a chaotic barrage of fear-based thinking.

In any given moment of my earlier life, my inner Know-it-all/Perfectionist was criticizing my every action. My Sexy-Cyn was worried about her appearance. My Avoider was bogged down with feeling incapable and unworthy. My Helper was busy telling me all of the zillion things I needed to do for everybody else to prove I was good enough. My Yeller was constantly feeding me guilt, more guilt, and then even more guilt because no matter what I did, I'd always be bad, shameful, undeserving, and basically guilty for being born. All of this was occurring simultaneously. This is just to name a few aspects and their personal trips. Living inside of my head was like having a waking nightmare.

My old, fear-based thought-pattern went something like this: 'Ugh. You look terrible today. I do, don't I? That's what you get for staying up until 2 am—you idiot. You deserve to feel like crap. It's all your fault. You need to exercise more—what a slug. Go to the gym. Do some yoga. I can't. I'm too tired. What difference would it make anyway? I have already lost my muscle tone. You're so stupid. You can't do anything right. You should never have stopped dancing. I sucked. Yeah, but at least you were fit. Look at you now. You look like shit. You are a loser. Who is going to want to even talk to you? You're pathetic. I need to go to the grocery store. Shit. I don't have enough money. I can't afford that today. I never have enough. The kids need new shoes, new clothes. I can't take care of them like they deserve. You are a terrible mother. I know I am a bad, awful mother who cannot even support my own kids. You need a man in your life to support you. The men in my life don't support me. What man would want to support me? I am an unlovable, unworthy, stupid piece of crap. You should cook a casserole for so-and-so who just had a baby. I don't have time to cook for anyone. You need to be a good friend. It's expected. Ok, how am I going to buy what I'll need for this casserole? I can't afford that. You don't need anything. Just take such-and-such off of your list. Everyone else comes first. Yeah, right. I don't really need anything. I'm not important.' And so it went.

This would be a small sample of the kind of thoughts that would stream through my mind unchecked. Notice that there were parts that were speaking to me second-person, addressing me as 'you', and then there were parts that were speaking first-person, making 'I'-statements. The parts that speak/think in terms of 'you' are usually sub-personalities that are as-yet unclaimed, and the parts that speak/think in terms of 'I' are usually parts of the self that have been consciously identified or belong to the main personality. These parts will have an internal dialog going that can include many differing opinions and voices.

Now, when I initially began to monitor my own thoughts, if I noticed a negative voice chiming in strongly, I might have reacted to that aspect something like this: if the aspect thought, 'You are so stupid. You can't do anything right. I hate you!' I may have jumped in with, 'Be quiet! I'm not going to give you and your negativity the time of day. Just shut up! I don't need to listen to you. Ignore. Ignore. Ignore. Breathe deeply. Om….' Rather than actually addressing the issue that the aspect was presenting, which was that there was a part of my own consciousness that was running beliefs and self-judgments about perfectionism and clearly locked in right/wrong thinking, I was simply attempting to deflect the real issue, avoid the issue, and basically sweep the issue under the rug. I wanted to change my thinking by willing myself to just not think those thoughts anymore. This method got me absolutely nowhere.

Cultivate Supportive, Nurturing, Compassionate Self-talk

I want you to consider a different, more supportive way to relate to yourself from within. Imagine that the part of your consciousness expressing negativity is a small child, crying and raging in despair, and simply kneel down, open your arms to the child, and begin to pour on the love and compassion. Compassion is a very nurturing and mothering energy that soothes. Imagine yourself saying things like, "It is Ok to cry. It's Ok to feel the way you feel. I am here with you. Everything will be alright. I love you, no matter what." Become a Loving parent to that child, and give that child everything that they had been missing. This is how I suggest you begin to treat yourself on the inside, with loving kindness and tenderness no matter what aspect of yourself you may be confronted with at any time.

There is no way to 'get rid of' a part of yourself, and, just like you would not consider murdering the suffering child who had been locked in the closet, it is important that these parts of your personality stop getting the message from you that you wish they would die. If you wish a part of yourself would die or even just go away, this causes a tremendous lack of trust within parts of your own consciousness. If you have been very mean to yourself or otherwise hard on yourself, it may take some time to repair the trust internally before your parts will be open and trusting with you.

Know that the moment you begin to pour on the Loving, healing will begin to take place. Trust can be built. Amends can be made. If you come clean with the part you've been used to abusing, express your new awareness, take full responsibility for your own pattern of self-talk, and let that part know that you want to connect, that you are ready to listen and understand, I can practically guarantee that your aspect will want to share with you. From there, you can begin listening and learning about this part of you that has been locked away or in hiding, and you will begin the process of integrating this part of your own personality into your conscious, healthy, rational higher self.

Listen to Your Aspects with Compassion

Here is an example of what listening with compassion to an aspect of yourself could sound like; it is an internal mental dialog where your higher self asserts sovereignty rather than allowing the sub-personality to simply take over the wheel of your internal body vehicle:

Aspect: "You are so stupid. You can't do anything right. I hate you!"

Higher Self: "Wow, you sound really mad…"

Aspect: "Mad? Are you freaking kidding me?! I am furious! You ruin everything. You don't do anything right."

Higher Self: "I really hear that. You think I'm stupid and can't do anything right. I hear you. What makes you feel that way?"

Aspect: "Because you blew that job! It's all your fault."

Higher Self: "Hmm… sounds like you think it's not Ok to make mistakes."

Aspect: "It's *not*! Mistakes are bad. People who make mistakes are stupid idiots."

Higher Self: "I really hear you think that…"

Aspect: "It is true! Mom, Dad and Grandma all said so. They said I was a bad, stupid girl." (cries)

Higher Self: "It's Ok… Go ahead and cry it out. I hear that they said that… that must have really hurt your feelings. I want to assure you that you are innately good no matter what and that it is absolutely Ok to make mistakes. Mistakes are how we learn. In fact, we are all smart enough to learn from our mistakes if we want to. You are innately good and innately smart. You are plugged into the source of infinite wisdom. You can learn anything you want to know."

Aspect: "Do you really think so?"

Higher Self: "I know so. We are brilliant."

(Aspect smiles and moves in closer to Higher Self, closer to the freedom of the Loving)

By learning how to respond inside of yourself to the parts of yourself that have been previously disowned, abused, ignored, neglected, put-down, punished, etc., you will begin to reel these parts into your own heart and feel whole. How you respond to your suffering parts will determine the rate at which you integrate all of your various aspects. The more self-acceptance you can hold and give to your aspects, the better they will begin to feel about themselves. The better they feel, the easier it will be for them to share their suffering with you, and the easier it will be for you to hear their pain. If you can hold the knowledge that we are not our behaviors, this is very helpful towards cultivating compassion and self-acceptance.

Every Part of Yourself is Beautiful and Loving in Nature

Every part of yourself is beautiful and Loving in nature, regardless of how you were treated as a child, how you responded to your environment, and how your disowned aspects have been coping by acting out in unhealthy patterns of behavior. Every part of you is a divine, Loving being in a body at the level of Source-energy, and therefore every part is essentially Loving. Your disowned parts are simply needing and craving your own love and attention, wanting more than anything to be included in the whole of who you truly are. You are not your behavior, and your unhealthy behaviors were patterned after some gross misinterpretations of reality. Have compassion for yourself for whatever judgments or irrationality you bought into as a younger person that caused your aspects to act out. Once you can bring your aspects into the light of self-acceptance, you can begin to identify their strengths and weaknesses, knowing that you can fully claim and cultivate the positive qualities these aspects represent and that you can consciously grow in any areas you discern are weak.

I did not lose the strength of my Hitter, although I no longer ever feel the urge to hit people; instead, I can whack a ball out into center field during a family softball game, do fifty squats, or drive a tennis ball across the court with my strength. I now have the strength to persevere when things seem challenging because I know how strong I truly am. I did not lose the vocal power of the Yeller, although I no longer ever feel the need to yell at people; instead, I have powerful projection which I can utilize when speaking in front of large audiences. I claimed the wisdom and confidence of my Know-it-all, the compassion and caring of my Sarcastic Cyn, the determination and perseverance of my Avoider, the courage of my Hitter, and so on. By bringing all of my hidden parts into the light, I was able to see that I actually had more strength, power, creativity, and wisdom than I'd ever given myself credit for. From that point on, I could express these traits openly and freely, rather than having them attached to only a few unhealthy behaviors.

By letting go of viewing these parts as 'bad', 'wrong', or 'shameful', I was able to quickly see how I'd developed all of those old, unhealthy patterns of behavior. Many of these behaviors were modeled for me as a child by my parents or siblings. I didn't know any other way to respond in those instances, and I did the best I could at the time to cope with whatever was occurring in my world. From there, it was easy to ask myself, "How's this working for me? Is this pattern of behavior serving me to continue in any way?" The answer was always 'no', so this supported me to choose new patterns of behavior that were more self-supportive. I also noticed that every aspect had an underlying Loving motivation; every part of me that had been judged as 'bad' was really just trying to either protect me or to get my needs met in some way. These motives are natural, normal, and built-in methods for survival at the most basic level. By seeing that these parts of my personality were the natural outcome of being raised in my particular environment, in my particular level of fear-based reality, with my particular set of irrational beliefs, I was able to simply embrace each and every part of myself as Ok and totally acceptable from the learning perspective. Accepting all of my parts allowed for rapid healing and integration of my personality, leading me to completely transform my life in every way for the better. Now, I feel whole and complete, all parts of me are in alignment with the will of my soul, and I move forward in life with joy, authenticity, and courage. This is the power of being willing to explore my own personality diligently.

Now it is your turn. You can begin by identifying the parts of yourself that you are uncomfortable showing the public, behaviors you don't particularly care for, the feelings you don't like to feel, parts that you have judged as 'bad', or parts that you feel are your weak points. Take your time with this, writing down traits, behavioral patterns, motivations, and feelings of each different part of your personality you can identify. Maybe draw a picture of that part, or cut out a character that reminds you of that sub-personality. However you go about doing this is Ok; I just encourage you to do it! Explore your own character fearlessly and with humor, diligence, and commitment.

Have Fun Exploring your Various Aspects

Exploring your various aspects can be illuminating as well as highly entertaining. This process does not need to be dull, boring, or painful in any way; in fact, it can be as fun or entertaining as you can make it. I highly recommend making it a comedy.

One of my Own Your Shadow workshop students had an aspect she named 'Jeb' who she vividly described as a large, overweight hillbilly with a big beer-belly hanging over the front of his pants, plumber's butt, and a wad of tobacco in his jowl. He had judgmental and prejudicial behaviors toward others while remaining perfectly oblivious to his own projections of blame and judgment, and her description of this character was hilarious. Not only was this funny for other people to hear about when she shared her story with the group, but she also used humor to lighten her own healing process, literally laughing uproariously every time she mentioned this aspect. By being able to laugh at this part of herself, she began to soften her attitude, let go of her defensiveness, own her projections of judgments, clear her self-judgment, and also see that this part of herself she'd named 'Jeb' had some traits that were quite wonderful. He lacked self-consciousness, he didn't care what anyone else thought, he was able to let it all hang out, he was honest with his feelings, he had oodles of self-confidence, etc. You see, no part of the self is really bad. There is no such thing as 'bad', from the soul's perspective, so it becomes part of the healing journey to find the parts that we've labeled as 'bad' in the past, reach out to them and then reel them into the Loving where we can reap the benefits of having all of their strengths.

Once you discover what has motivated your behaviors

for each aspect, then you have the power to look at each part, identify the irrational beliefs that were motivating these behaviors, update the beliefs, and clear the surrounding self-judgments. After the irrational beliefs have been updated and the judgment has been transmuted, your behaviors will quite naturally begin to shift, as there will no longer be a reason or a motivation in place for continuing that particular behavior. The new motivation for the new, updated pattern of behavior will reflect your highest, most rational, most empowering, and Loving understanding, allowing you to fall into alignment with your higher self, to align yourself with the will of your soul. Upon doing such, you will become free.

Integrating Your Disowned Aspects of Self

For integration to happen, communication needs to begin to take place between the part of you that knows your truth and the parts of you that are still residing in the fear-based, right/wrong reality. Most people think that it is very difficult to change, that their personality is set in stone, and that they will always be the way they are. This idea is based on an irrational belief that we are static, unchanging beings. Nothing could be further from the truth. We are always learning, always growing, always evolving, and expanding if we follow our natural instincts. Your soul is guiding you to integrate all the parts of your personality so that you can expand to reach your highest potential. Know that you can change any part of yourself for the better.

To the degree that we have parts of ourselves left hanging in the dark, there will be obstacles to our success and fulfillment on various levels and in different areas of our lives. It is as if a part of us is holding us back from reaching all of our dreams. That part doesn't really want to hold us back; it cannot help holding us back and putting up obstacles to our success as it is doing so to get our attention. It is saying, "Hey! Wait for me!

You can't leave without me." We can't move forward without that part on board.

You Cannot Get to Where You Want to Go in Pieces

Think about a train with electronic doors; the train cannot move on until everything is safely through the door. On the platform of life, no matter how many times the direction may blare, "Stand clear of the doors!", if a part of you is hanging back on the platform, your train to your next destination will not be able to depart. Just like elevators, planes, and trains, you have parts that need to be all the way on board before you can take your journey to your next level of growth.

From your soul's perspective, it is Ok to hang out in lower levels of awareness with many parts in the dark; there is nothing wrong with this. You just won't be able to get to another level until you become more aware. Once you become aware and begin to up-level your life, it becomes necessary to integrate those previously disowned parts in order to get to where you really want to go.

Think about your own life. Where do you wish to move forward? Think of every area in your life, including but not limited to: relationships, family, friendships, health, self-care, sex-life, fitness, finances, standard of living, living environment, hobbies, recreation, travel, creativity, free time, and any other area that is important to you. Now, think about your issues and obstacles in each of those areas where you desire to move forward. Whatever issues are present for you will lead you directly to discovering what part or parts of yourself need your attention in order to be brought onboard into the light so that you can move forward freely.

Basically, it is as if you have been denying your sub-personalities their boarding passes, thinking things that could be interpreted to mean to them, "I don't like you. You cannot come with me." In order for the plane or train to be able to get you where you desire to go on the next leg of your personal journey, you must be willing to hand over the passes, acknowledging all of your parts, which will send a different message that will say to that part, "You're with me. We're in this together. I won't leave without you." To get your parts on board, you must first be willing to admit they're yours.

Working With a Disowned Aspect

The first step in working with the disowned aspects of your personality is to identify your various parts, which we covered earlier in the chapter. If you haven't yet taken the time to identify some of your sub-personalities, I highly encourage you to do so now so that you can follow along with the rest of this chapter. You can start with just one. Pick any aspect of yourself that you'd like to begin to integrate, and list personality traits, patterns of behavior, underlying loving motivations, and feelings of this particular part. After you've identified an aspect, the next step is to acknowledge it as yours. Give it a boarding pass.

Before going within to work with one of your sub-personalities, I recommend you start by setting your protective field of love and light, invoke spirit's presence, then breathe in the energies of love and compassion. This will put you in the best possible space to work with whatever comes forward for your healing. You can review this part in chapter 6, stage one, under the preparation stage of updating your belief system.

For this next part, you can read through the paragraph first, then follow along by doing the process yourself. Experiential learning is the only way to see if this process will work in your own life. I encourage you to go for it!

Identify a Disowned Aspect; Visualize Your Aspect

Once you have prepared your energetic space to work with your own consciousness, go deep inside, eyelids closed…

imagine that part of yourself – see, sense, or feel this aspect. Notice how the aspect appears in your consciousness. Once you have observed this part for a moment, reach out to your part with an attitude of caring, openness, friendship, and compassion. See if you can get close to this part of yourself physically in your imagination, maybe by giving the part a hug, hold hands, or whatever show of love and affection comes most naturally to you. If the aspect isn't ready to receive your affection, be respectful of that, and give your aspect a little space.

Establish Healthy Communication with this Part of Yourself

Next, say whatever you are guided to say to begin to establish healthy communication with this part of yourself. Disowned aspects need to hear things like, "I see you," "I hear you," "I acknowledge you," "I accept you," "I will always be with you," and "I love you." There is no right or wrong way to connect with a part of yourself, so simply speak from your heart, telling that part whatever you most want to say. Then offer to listen, asking if there is anything this part of you wants you to hear. This can sometimes be the most challenging part, as often what our disowned aspects have been through involves pain and suffering. Some of the stuff our aspects have been suppressing can be pretty intense and heavy. Sometimes an aspect might feel very angry and may feel betrayed by you. It is not uncommon to hear things like, "I hate you," "I don't trust you," "How come you let that happen to me?" and "What took you so long?" Respond with pure compassion, just pouring on the Loving. Remember, this is a part of yourself that has been hurt, beaten, criticized, and otherwise abused in the past, so be sure you speak with care and respect, no matter what kind of response this part may offer in return. As you respond with Loving compassion, be observant as to how your aspect responds to your Loving. Some aspects will soak it in like a sponge, and others will initially deflect it.

Be Patient and Loving with this Part of Yourself

Be patient if a part of yourself is not ready to receive your Loving care. Understand that it has been a long time that this part of you has been stuck out in the dark suffering, and it may therefore take a little time and perseverance on your part to heal. Do whatever you can do at the moment to create a bond with this part of yourself. This may require lots of listening while this part of yourself vents. Be sure that you are coming from a strong, neutral position of compassion as you listen to your aspect, knowing that whatever you are hearing is not good or bad, right or wrong. It is simply some information that this part of you needs to share with you for your awareness and healing. The more neutral you can be while listening, the more supported and safer this aspect will feel to unload with you. Trust your guidance about how long to listen. Sometimes an aspect that has been unheard and unsupported will continue to pour like a broken faucet. Know that you will not be able to fully heal and integrate this part in one day. When you feel you have given enough time listening, respond with compassion. Then gently inform this part of yourself that you have to go now and that you will definitely be back to hear more soon.

Get as Close as You Can in Your Imagination

If your sub-personality soaks in the Loving easily, you have the green light to apply more Loving liberally. I recommend getting as physically close and affectionate to this part of yourself as you can in your imagination. Hug yourself up. Wrap your arms around this part of yourself and pour on the compassion. If this aspect appears young or small, you can sit down and hold this part of you on your lap in your mind's eye.

Young parts love to be rocked, stroked, sung to, or otherwise comforted. Spend as much time as you are guided to spend with this part, then ask if there is anything else they need from you. Sometimes, aspects will respond to this question with things like, "I just need to know you love me" or "Don't leave me." Reassure this part of you that you do love them so much and that you will always be connected in the Loving. Let this part know that you are now awake and listening, fully available to meet their needs. Give your part whatever they need to feel Ok and supported at that moment.

Make Closure when Finished Working with an Aspect

Once your process with your aspect feels complete, you want to be sure to make closure with that aspect. If you forget to make closure, the thoughts, feelings, and behavioral patterns of that aspect will be 'up' for you; you might find yourself suddenly acting or thinking from the perspective of your sub-personality, rather than operating from your adult, spiritually-connected, higher self. When proper closure is made, that aspect will be able to rest peacefully, knowing that it does not need to act out in any way to get your attention, as it is already being tended to fully by you consciously. Making closure allows both you and your aspect to feel that safe boundaries are being set during the healing process, which is very important for establishing the bond of trust between the highest part of you and all of the aspects of your personality.

To make your closure with an aspect of yourself, create a safe, loving environment in your heart – a sanctuary. You can do this based on whatever you intuitively feel would be best for the particular aspect that you are currently working with. For instance, a very young part may feel most comfortable in a children's park or in a playroom filled with toys. An older aspect may appreciate a comfortable couch, the beauty of nature, maybe the beach, or a meadow filled with flowers. I grew up in the woods, so no matter what age my aspects were, each different part of myself felt most comfortable deep in the woods surrounded by trees. If the aspect you are working with is still very shut down or depressed, you can create a safe cocoon-like space or a cozy bedroom space – just be sure to leave a crack of light or a nightlight on so that Loving can trickle in. We want to leave our aspects with more access to light than they had when we first connected.

To create your sanctuary, simply breathe into your heart-center and then visualize – see, sense or feel – the environment you wish to create appearing right inside your heart. You can use your imagination to make up an environment, or you can re-create an environment you've seen before from memory. However you choose to do this is fine. Some people are way more visual than others and will see their sanctuary in living color with hundreds of details. Others are more sensory, auditory, or feeling-oriented, so their environment may consist of feelings of warm sunlight, fuzzy blankets, smells of the forest, sounds of music, birds singing, or running water. Your sanctuary could also just contain feelings of safety, love, and compassion. However you sense it is just fine.

Whatever you end up creating, it is important to know that it is your intention to create a safe and Loving sanctuary for your aspect that is most important. Remember that when we initially begin to work with an aspect, the aspect has been stuck out in the dark and cold, usually in an environment of pain and suffering. The feelings of the old environment will be slightly different for each aspect, but it is pretty much a given that you won't find your aspects residing in a protected space filled with love and light. Therefore, it is up to you to take your aspect out of the old environment of suffering and into the Loving protection of your own heart.

When you have finished creating the space of protected

Loving in your heart, bring your aspect into the sanctuary and make your closure with this part of yourself. Thank this part of you for coming forward for your healing. Let this part know that you are available for listening and that you'll be checking back in soon. Close with whatever words come naturally to you; whether you say, "I love you," "See ya soon," "Goodbye," "Blessings," or "Have fun" matters not. There is no right or wrong way to make your closure with a part of yourself. It is your intention to make closure that is most important. When you have finished making closure, take a deep breath, and bring your awareness out of your heart and back into your mind.

End your process by following stage 3, the closure process, from chapter 6, acknowledging yourself out loud, giving thanks and gratitude to spirit, and then grounding to anchor your healing in this higher vibration of energy.

Notice How You Feel After Working with Your Aspect

When you are finished working your process with this aspect of yourself, notice how you feel afterwards. Most people experience a deeper connection within themselves. Some people feel joyful, elated, or lighter; others simply feel more centered inside of themselves. Know that whatever you experienced is Ok and that the more you can connect with your various aspects, the closer you will become to your true divine nature.

Develop an Ongoing Relationship with Your Aspect as Needed

After you have established contact with a part of yourself, then you can begin to develop a relationship to become intimate with this part of yourself in order to heal and integrate. You can develop your relationship by cultivating bonding time together. Check in with your inner guidance about how often to connect with your aspect. With a more challenging aspect that needs a lot of love or reassurance, you may be guided to check in every day, maybe upon waking in the morning or just before going to sleep. Five minutes a day is often all that is needed to let a part of you know they are loved. With an aspect that clearly needs lots of listening or attention, you may make a plan to make time to listen to this part once a day, once a week, or once a month, depending upon how often you are guided to work with this part of yourself. You can try setting an alarm for 10-15 minutes to start with, then adjust your listening time as needed. Trust your instincts as to the timing of your process.

Some aspects don't have much to say – especially very young aspects – but they still need your undivided attention, nurturing affection, or support. Spending time with a previously disowned aspect does not always entail listening; your time could involve quiet holding time, speaking from a higher perspective, singing to your aspect, rocking or soothing your aspect, or playing a game together. Whatever this part missed out on – whether it was affection or attention or safety or simply just acknowledgment – is going to be what this part needs to receive from you in order to heal. If you go with the flow, you will easily be able to determine what each part of yourself needs in order to integrate fully into your Loving self.

Don't worry if you happen to forget about checking in with an aspect after bringing it into your heart. The great thing about the awakening process is that you can always trust in the process. If your consciousness is ready for you to do more work with that part of yourself, that aspect will bring itself back into your awareness so that you may continue to apply more compassion. The aspect may call out to you, and it may stir an awareness inside of you in the form of a gentle nudge or reminder where you might think, "Oh, yeah…

that's right, I haven't checked in with that part of myself in several weeks. I'll do that right now." Or, if you don't hear or choose to ignore the reminder, you may find yourself suddenly thinking, feeling, or behaving from the perspective of that sub-personality. It can appear in a short, subtle way or come up for you big-time, whatever is needed to get your attention back to applying the compassion to this part of yourself. If this occurs, go easy on yourself. It is all part of the learning process. There is no right or wrong way to integrate a previously disowned part of yourself into your Loving, highest self. However it occurs, however much time it takes, it is all Ok from the spiritual perspective.

Sometimes aspects are so ready to be integrated that they will simply jump into your arms to be held, say how they feel, and then melt into the compassion of your Loving heart. Other aspects may take a few visits to integrate, and some may require an ongoing commitment on your part to fully heal and assimilate. Only you can know what the various parts of yourself will need. And only you can give it to yourself. Remember, healing is an inside job.

Healing Takes as Long as it Takes

When people consciously become aware of a previously disowned aspect of themselves and begin their healing, they will often question, "How long is this going to take?" The answer is that it will take as long as it takes. The only way to know is to check in with your aspect. If an aspect has more to share, there is likely more compassion needed or more information that you need to learn towards your healing. Since this part of you has not been allowed to reside in your conscious awareness up until now, the only way to learn what you need to know about this aspect is to invite this part to share and then listen or apply whatever is needed. You can simply keep working with each aspect as long as there is more healing to be done.

Follow your aspect's lead as to what is needed during the time you spend together. There are usually three different types of energy that will come forward as an aspect shares: feeling energy, irrational beliefs, and judgment. If there is feeling energy present, time is needed to either listen to feelings or apply compassion, attention, or comfort to meet the aspect's previously unmet needs. If there are irrationalities present and ready to be updated, you can update the limiting beliefs this part has been running. If there is self-judgment or a projection of judgment present, you can own and clear the judgment. There may be one type of energy present, there may be two out of three, and there may be all three present. Work with whatever is present to the best of your ability.

When you check in with the aspect at the end of your process to ask, "Is there anything else you need from me?" and the reply is, "Nothing," or there is no reply, you will know you are close to being fully integrated with this aspect. I suggest making your closure with this part of yourself as guided above, and then checking back in with that part in a few days. If the aspect still feels separate from you when you check back in or has more to tell you, this is an indication that there is more work to be done with this part of yourself. If the aspect is nowhere to be found, seems very faint, or simply smiles happily at you and is residing in perfect peace within the sanctuary of your heart, this is usually a pretty clear indication that your work with this part is complete. If the aspect is quiet and peaceful yet still visible in your imagination, simply open your arms and enfold this part of yourself into your heart. When your work is totally and fully complete, you will see, sense, or feel this part of you simply melt into the oneness of your Loving heart. This feeling, when it happens, is an indescribable feeling of joy and contentment. Right at that moment, you will feel more whole and more complete than you have ever felt before. This is the process of integrating a part of yourself into the greater whole of you. Once the final integration occurs, you will no longer have to connect with this part of yourself because what used to feel like a separate part will simply be *you* in every moment.

Integration is Complete When Separation Ceases to Exist

How you will know the integration of an aspect is complete is when there is no longer any sense of separation; the separation has ceased to exist, so the separate sub-personality ceases to exist. Know that this does not mean that the essence of the aspect is gone; it has simply changed forms. You can liken this process to visualizing drops of water around a puddle on a smooth surface. The surface tension can represent the Loving, pulling the separate drops toward the bigger puddle in the middle. As the individual drops touch the water of the central puddle, the drops cease to exist as 'drops' and become one with the rest of the water. While the water that was in each drop is still present and measurable inside the greater whole, the title of 'drop' no longer applies. It is all simply water.

If You Want to Integrate Faster, Make More Time for Yourself

As each of your aspects integrates, you will let go of identifying them as separate and just feel like a fuller version of 'you'. When this happens with a part, you will simply drop the label and no longer need to work with this part, which will feel completely normal now and part of your whole. By that time, the irrational beliefs that had been motivating that aspect will have been updated, the negative thought-patterns that the aspect had been running will have transformed into positive, healthy thought-patterns, the feelings that the aspect had been repressing or expressing in an unhealthy manner would have been emoted in a healthy way and transmuted into Loving, and the unsupportive behaviors that that aspect had been using will have been reprogrammed into healthy, self-supporting behaviors. You will have fully claimed the strengths of the aspect, and be aware of any weakness, and cultivating these into strengths as well. This process takes as long as it takes, and if you are feeling impatient or urgent about it in any way, the easy solution is to make more time for yourself. The more time you can spend with yourself in working your process, the faster you will integrate your various parts into the whole of you.

Once you understand how the personality is developed, it is actually a very simple process to begin to connect with the parts of yourself that you've been criticizing, resisting, denying, disliking, fighting, repressing, or however you've been relating to them in the past. The key to healing is to dialog with them; each and every time a part surfaces to your awareness, respond to that part with compassion and understanding, no matter what. Once you have identified an aspect and are consciously working with this part of yourself, you can accelerate the process by spending extra time listening and loving this part of yourself up. If you can learn to respond with compassion to the parts of yourself that have been suffering, these parts will quickly heal and integrate into your heart, coming into alignment with your highest truth and into alignment with the will of your soul.

Identify, own, and claim all of the parts of your personality. Embrace all parts of yourself with love and compassion, knowing that every part of you has simply been doing the best that you could with the knowledge and tools you had at the time. Accept yourself fully and watch yourself begin to deeply transform in ways you've never even dreamed. By accepting and embracing all of your parts fully, you can truly *become* the person you've always been meant to be.

Exercise: Claiming your Disowned Aspects of Self

Begin by saying a protection prayer and/or setting conditions of love and light and invoking spirit's presence.

Place your hands on your heart. Set an intention to access the highest vibration of Loving available. Breathe in the Loving and fill your body with Loving energies from head to toe. Then, set an intention to access the highest level of compassion. Breathe in compassion and fill your body with compassion from head to toe.

Repeat out loud any of the following that resonates, changing the phrasing as needed to reflect your own beliefs:

"I forgive myself for buying into the irrational belief that there are any parts of my character that are bad or unacceptable." "My new updated belief is, I now know all parts of my character are innately good and acceptable, despite how certain parts may behave. I now accept myself fully."

"I forgive myself for buying into the irrational belief that there are parts of my personality that need to stay hidden." "My new updated belief is, I now know every part of my personality is a lovable, intrinsic part of my wholeness, and therefore every part of me deserves to be brought into the light."

"I forgive myself for buying into the irrational belief that I need to get rid of part of myself in order to change my behavior or to become enlightened." "My new updated belief is, I now know all of my parts are needed to make up the whole of my being. I now know that my behavior can only change when I love and accept myself fully first. I will always contain all of my parts, and my various aspects can be integrated into my being until I reside in complete wholeness in alignment with my soul."

"I forgive myself for buying into the irrational belief that there is something wrong with me for having disowned aspects of my personality." "My new updated belief is, I now know having disowned aspects of my personality is the natural outcome of having been raised in a fear-based, right/wrong paradigm. The parts of myself that were judged as 'bad', 'wrong', 'unacceptable', 'sinful', or 'not good enough' have been pushed away as a natural defense mechanism. I can simply accept that that occurred and know that I am whole on the being level."

"I forgive myself for buying into the irrational belief that I'm broken and need to be fixed or changed in order to be acceptable." "My new updated belief is, I now know I am whole and fully acceptable just as I am. All of my parts are connected in the Loving, and I am perfectly acceptable just the way I am, wherever I am in my process."

"I forgive myself for buying into the irrational belief that I need someone else to accept a certain part of me before I can accept it myself." "My new updated belief is, I now know I can accept every part of myself fully, no matter what anyone else thinks. I am the only one who needs to accept me in order for me to feel totally and completely acceptable."

"I forgive myself for buying into the irrational belief that I am at fault for causing certain parts of my personality to behave a certain way." "My new updated belief is, I now know there is no blame or fault from my soul's perspective. I can trust that everything that has occurred has had a reason, and I trust that everything is unfolding in divine-perfect order in my own highest and greatest good. I let go of all blame. I am innocent as I grow and learn. I am doing the best that I can at every moment."

"I forgive myself for buying into the irrational belief that I need to feel bad, guilty, ashamed, humiliated, or embarrassed about certain parts of myself." "My new updated belief is, I now know all parts of me are Ok and innately good, no matter how they might appear in the right/wrong reality. Since I've never done anything wrong from the spiritual perspective, I let go of all judgments that I've held toward myself based on the illusion of 'wrongdoing,' and I now move into freedom inside of myself. I am an innocent child of God, simply doing my best as I learn and grow."

"I forgive myself for buying into the irrational belief that I ever need to repress, avoid, deny, hide, ignore, berate, or punish aspects of my personality ever again." "My new updated belief is, I now know that only Loving kindness, caring, and compassion can heal my wounded parts and that by treating myself caringly, my behaviors will naturally shift as I learn to come into alignment with my true Loving nature."

"I forgive myself for buying into the irrational belief that I need to fear that someone may find out about what I've done in the past and judge me as bad." "My new updated belief is, I now know I am not my thoughts, feelings, or behaviors. I am not my body or personality; I am a divine being of love and light. I am innately Loving, and everything I've ever done is acceptable from my soul's perspective. I am innocent. I now free myself from all fear and self-judgment. I now know that other people's judgment is simply a reflection of their own unresolved issues and has nothing to do with me. I am free."

"I forgive myself for buying into the irrational belief that I am my label of _____ (example: Depression, Anxiety, Bipolar, ADHD, etc.)." "My new updated belief is, I now know I am a soul in a body having a human experience. I choose to dis-identify with any and all labels that have been given to me, knowing that who I am is totally separate from and much greater than any label. I can now simply use labels as information about parts of myself that are seeking the light. I know that I am whole, and it is now safe for me to accept all of my parts as innately good."

"I forgive myself for buying into the irrational belief that mental illness is incurable and that I will always have my diagnosis/issues for life." "My new updated belief is, I now know the only issue ever is separation from God/Loving/Source. All issues are curable by simply coming into alignment with my natural state of being as a whole, divine, Loving child of God."

"I forgive myself for buying into the irrational belief that mental issues always have to be heavy and serious, and I need to take my healing process very seriously." "My new updated belief is, I now know it is Ok and in fact a healthy thing to laugh at myself, to find humor in my irrationalities and to have fun with exploring all of the parts of my personality. Laughter keeps things light, and healing is a process of lightening up, letting old judgments lift up and off to reveal my true divine essence. I am a being of light and love, and I now allow humor to flow through me as I use healing laughter as medicine."

End your process by acknowledging yourself, expressing gratitude to spirit, and fully grounding your energy. Drink plenty of water.

CHAPTER NINE
Releasing Emotional Energy

We are all divine beings attending Earth School to learn and grow. While at the soul level, we exist as pure consciousness, we take on a multi-dimensional energetic form when incarnated into human bodies. In the physical realm, our being-energy exists in overlapping layers, or bodies, of energy. The first and densest layer is our physical body. The second layer is our mental body, which contains our beliefs, judgments, and thought-form energy. The third layer of energy is our emotional body, which contains the energy of all feelings we are having currently and any old emotional energy that we have stored during our lifetime.

In this chapter, we'll focus on the third layer of the Human Energy Field – the emotional body.

When a person is in full alignment with the will of their soul, they will be using their emotional energy as simply a feeling-barometer, knowing that they are not their feelings.

We have feelings, our feelings are separate from our true self, and we are not at the mercy of those feelings. Our feelings are there to give us information about what is in alignment with us at any given time, as well as what is not in alignment with us at every moment.

When you can learn to utilize your emotions as simple information, you will stop being ruled by old, familial patterns of emotional, habitual responses. Not only can you stop allowing your unresolved emotions to run your life, but you can also actually change your unhealthy habitual emotional patterns of response into healthy, neutral patterns of response, no matter what the situation.

Emotion Equals Energy in Motion

To become healthy emotionally, you must first begin to learn to use your emotional energy in a healthy way. Let's look at what emotion actually is to begin. Emotion can be looked at in two parts – 'e' and 'motion'. The 'e' stands for energy. So, e-motion means energy in motion. To emote, therefore, means to express, or move, the feeling-energy. The energy must *move* to be released; if you do not express your feelings, the emotional energy will stay trapped in your energy field, repressed yet still vibrating with as-yet-unreleased power.

Each Emotion Resonates to Its Own Specific Frequency

Emotional energy is power, so for every feeling that has been stored, shut down, stuffed, denied, pushed under the rug, etc., there is personal power there, just waiting to be claimed and put to good use. The vibratory level of the latent power will be resonating with whatever emotional energy is stored. Each different emotion resonates to its own, unique frequency; just as the keys on a piano keyboard each create a different sound, each emotional line of energy creates a slightly different feeling-response.

For every general emotion, there is a whole scale of depth. For instance, with the feeling of loss, there can be anything from a slight feeling of sadness to bone-deep, excruciating grief towards the loss. There may be many levels of grief between the two. For the line of emotional energy labeled hatred, there may be anything from a feeling of dislike to thoroughly despising someone; the lowest level of hatred is the feeling of self-loathing.

So, what this means is that if you have some old, stored emotional energy, it is going to be vibrating at a certain rate, sending out a signal, so to speak, just as if it were a piano playing the same note, over and over and over again. This signal, or note if you will, will be attracting the same energy to resonate with it, just like a magnet, drawing in anything within range.

Have you ever seen or heard of a musician playing a string of one guitar in order to check if another guitar is in tune? If the guitars are in tune with each other, the untouched guitar's string will begin to vibrate in resonance with the played guitar string. A more dramatic example is the opera singer hitting a high note and shattering a wine glass. The important thing to understand with this example is that not every glass will break; only a glass that can make that same note will shatter. The sound any glass makes depends upon the size of the opening, depth of the glass, and how much liquid, if any, is in the glass. Two things that have the same vibratory frequency will be attracted to each other and resonate together. There is a universal law that states, "like attracts like."

Old, Stuck Emotions will Attract Like Emotions

What this means for you emotionally is that if you have old, stored emotional energy, you will be attracting, or resonating with, that same energy inside of other people. Others will mirror whatever you have going on, again and again, until you emote and clear that particular energy. When the stored feelings are unconscious, this can make for some very uncomfortable situations. The good news is that once you have the awareness, it is pretty easy to identify the old feeling simply by using other people as a mirror, and from there, you have the power to decide to release that old energy once and for all.

What emotional responses in other people really push your buttons? If there is an emotional expression that you judge so critically or one that sends you running out of the room or sounds like fingernails scratching a chalkboard to you then, yes, that is the one that is likely resonating with the same feeling you locked down decades ago and are still doing your darndest to forget. The more judgment you have towards another's demonstration of feeling, the more energy in this line of emotion you have probably repressed.

Feeling-energy often goes hand-in-hand with judgment, which is stored on the mental level rather than the emotional level. They are subtly different, and it is important to differentiate because the way they are cleared from a person's energy field is completely different. Feelings simply need to be emoted or released into motion. Feelings are like the bubbles in a bottle of soda that has been shaken up or steam in a pan with a tight lid; if the build-up of bubbles or steam does not get vented, there will eventually be too much pressure, and the top will blow. When people' blow their top' in anger, it is because their anger has been stuffed down too long, or there is simply too much of it to contain any longer.

Negative Societal Beliefs Surrounding Emotional Expression

The emotional body, in general, has gotten a pretty bad rap. Rather than seeing the incredible beauty of having a built-in feeling-barometer to let us know when something is on-course or off-course in our lives, some cultures have formed negative societal beliefs about emotional energy that are still affecting us in the present. These societal beliefs get taken on by individual families to certain degrees, and the beliefs get passed down through the generations of family members, becoming familial beliefs. There are a few cultures that honor the expression of feelings, especially grief for the loss of a loved one, but for the most part, the majority of us were raised to believe that it was bad, shameful, or weak to express our feelings.

Here are a few common examples of familial beliefs on the subject of feelings or expressing emotional energy: 'It's not acceptable to show emotion', 'expressing feelings is a sign of weakness', 'in order to be strong, I have to keep a stiff upper lip', 'showing emotion is shameful or embarrassing', 'only girls or sissies show their feelings; real men are stoic', 'big boys/girls don't cry', and 'showing emotion will bring dishonor to my family'.

Families who hold these types of beliefs around emotional energy will pass these ideas down to their children. The children will make all sorts of their own beliefs around the subject, depending upon how they respond to their parents' beliefs and modeling on the matter. For instance, if a very feeling-oriented child is born into a family that has strong negative ideas about the expression of emotional energy, that child will make some of their own beliefs on the subject in order to stay safe in that particular family environment. Some examples of beliefs the child might make are: 'My emotions are bad, wrong, irrational, etc. and I must suppress them at all costs', 'I am _____ (example: bad, stupid, shameful, guilty, wrong, embarrassed, etc.) for having strong emotions', 'something is wrong with me', 'it is unsafe for me to feel how I feel', 'it is unsafe for me to say how I really feel', 'my feelings don't matter', 'if I do express myself, I can expect to be punished', 'I am unworthy and deserve to be punished', 'I am unsupported by my family', 'My family does not love or accept me for who I am', 'I am a misfit', 'I do not belong or fit into my family', and 'I am unlovable.'

On the other hand, if a child born into a family with strong familial ideas about suppressing emotion is a more thinking-oriented child, the child will likely just take on the parental views as 'fact' and create their own beliefs to support and perpetuate these cultural or familial views. Some examples of beliefs the child might make are: 'feelings are stupid; only facts are relevant', 'if I have a strong feeling, I need to just stuff it down and ignore it', 'feelings are never to be aired in public', 'people who demonstrate feelings are _____ (example: dumb, unstable, overly emotional, idiots, immature, weak, etc.)', 'logical people are smarter than/better than emotional people', 'I should feel awful, embarrassed, and ashamed if I blow it', 'keeping a tight lid on my feelings means I'm strong', and 'If I ever lose it, it is because it is someone else's fault'.

In my own family, I received mixed messages about showing emotion. From my father, I learned that expressing feelings on most subjects was not Ok, except for mild expressions of affection. My father was not above a hug or a kiss hello after returning home from work, and I would lavish him with affectionate hugs until he'd reached his tolerance level and push me away. My father was very logical and analytical in his approach to life. If it wasn't a provable fact, it was complete and utter nonsense. He appeared calm and collected and was usually pretty quiet and introspective for the most part. This worked for him until he became angry, usually fortified by a little extra alcohol, and then he'd blow up with all the force of an erupting volcano. He was not able to take personal responsibility for his angry outburst when it happened, which was thankfully pretty infrequently. Instead, he blamed us, his family, for causing his upset, and therefore we were all deemed guilty for making our father so unhappy. We'd run around like frantic ants whose routine had been disturbed, trying to make it up to him in whatever way we could until he seemed content again. My father's anger would blow over fairly quickly, and we'd all breathe easier the moment it passed.

My mother was different from my father. She verbally professed to disdain shows of emotion, which she viewed as a sign of weakness. She rarely displayed affection, did not give out hugs, kisses, or loving words for the most part. Physical touch is my main love language, so I'd been super invested in getting a show of my mother's affection from as early as I can recall; my mom would stiffly endure my ritual goodnight kiss with a sigh or an eye-roll until I simply gave up on her returning my affection around age eight or nine. She had an outward, public appearance of a sharp, practical, logical, highly intelligent woman with a beautiful smile that rarely reached her eyes. At home, away from the public eye, my mom emitted a constant emotional distress signal, ranging anywhere from depressed or irritated to frustrated beyond belief, furiously angry and irate. Her general attitude seemed both bitter and resentful, and my siblings and I were charged with causing her anger daily. The moment we set foot outside of the house and appeared in front of a friend or neighbor, my mother's fake smile would appear, and we'd all know that that was our cue to pretend to be happy.

Before I go any further here, let me just share that I love both of my parents dearly. My parents have never done anything wrong; they've always simply done the best that they could, with the beliefs and tools and patterning that they had at that moment. In fact, all I have to do is picture what little I know of my parents' own upbringings, and I feel flooded with compassion for them both. They both had it much harder than I did as a child. When I reflect on their attitudes and behaviors in service to my own growth, I am holding the knowledge that they, too, have both always been learning and growing.

Both of my parents have also come a long, long way in their own personal evolution since I was younger, so what I share herein is not my current experience. My dad became more comfortable, open-minded, and less judgmental around other people's expressions of feelings before he passed.

My mom has become more open, warmer, and more in touch with her own feelings. She actually had a breakthrough and became more physically and emotionally affectionate when I had my spiritual awakening experience at age 18; the doctors hadn't known if I would survive after my long surgery from a ruptured appendix, so they told my mom I had a 50-50 chance of recovering. When I awakened the day after the surgery with my mom at my bedside, she burst into tears of gratitude and said those three magic words, 'I love you', to me for the very first time. From that day on, when I hug my mom, she hugs me back, and we have a closer, more honest, and openly-communicative relationship than we ever did when I was a child.

Be Willing to Look Deeply at Your Modeling of Expression

Regardless of what kind of relationship you have or had with your parents, and regardless of what kind of childhood you experienced, if you are willing to look deeply at the beliefs, ideas, and patterns of behavior around emotional expression that were modeled by your parents, neutrally, just as information and without placing blame out on them, you will gather tons of valuable insight into your own beliefs, thoughts, feelings, and behaviors. This information can lead you directly to your own needs for healing and clearing so that you may continue to grow and evolve in a positive, self-supporting direction, moving into greater alignment with the will of your soul.

Once I examined and better understood my own modeling around emotional expression, I was able to clear my irrationality and judgment around this, let go of my fears of expressing emotion, and come into healthier patterns of emotional expression in all areas of my life.

From both my mother and my father, I received the belief that expressing emotions was bad. I didn't buy into that belief wholeheartedly, but I did modify it to believe something like 'it is Ok to express positive emotions, like love, joy, excitement, affection, etc., and it is not Ok to express negative emotions like fear, sadness, anger, rage, etc.' My father's occasional outbursts were terrifying to me as a child. My mother's constant expression of anger, resentment, suffering, and disappointment punctuated with regular physical punishment led me to have an active fear and dislike of any expression of unhappiness, especially anger.

For many years, I continued to perpetuate the idea that anger was bad, scary, or harmful, and the companion belief that if someone was angry or upset with me, it was naturally my fault. I judged myself as a bad, guilty, terrible person who had done something horribly wrong to cause that other person to become upset. As a result of these two ideas, I would attract friends, partners, or situations into my life that would reflect and validate those beliefs over and over.

I can distinctly remember a life-changing incident with a friend where I finally shifted inside of myself enough to fully let go of both of these beliefs at once: I had made a commitment to attend an event with a close friend, and my childcare ran late. As I had three small children, with my youngest still in diapers at the time, I was not able to shower or dress for the evening until help appeared, so I wasn't ready to go when my friend arrived to pick me up. My friend seemed patient for a little while as I ran around getting dressed, and then suddenly reached a limit and exploded in anger towards me, blaming me for ruining the whole night. A barrage of judgments was dumped upon my head – I was deemed rude, uncaring, selfish, and mostly wrong. I was pronounced guilty of committing a grave, hurtful error for running late. I was told that I should feel bad, guilty, and ashamed of my behavior. My friend issued an ultimatum; I would need to repent for my sin, apologize profusely, and beg for forgiveness, or my friend would not forgive me. This was so reminiscent of what I'd heard for much of my childhood that it makes me laugh just writing about it!

It was a moment of temptation for me; I could continue to view myself as bad, guilty, and to blame for someone else's anger, or I could say 'no thanks' to the familial pattern of shame, blame, and guilt, and move on to something higher. What I know about feelings of shame, guilt, embarrassment, humiliation, and any and all other feelings related to feeling bad about something that has occurred is that we only experience any of these feelings to the degree that we have bought into right/wrong and good/bad thinking. If you understand that you've never done anything 'wrong' from the spiritual perspective, and nothing is 'bad' in your soul's eyes, then there is nothing to feel bad, guilty, embarrassed, or ashamed about, ever. I decided to declare my innocence as someone who is simply learning and growing, doing the best I can. I decided to move on from the pattern of guilt and shame.

At that moment, I told my friend that it was Ok to have feelings about my lateness. I could hear those feelings, and I would own that I had, indeed, been late. I was unwilling, however, to take on the responsibility for my friend's anger, upset, judgment, hurt, disappointment, etc., and I didn't care to have someone scream at me in that way. I wanted my friends to treat me in a caring manner, even when they felt upset. And, no, I would not grovel, repent, or beg for forgiveness. I knew that I was already forgiven because love and compassion are a fore-given thing – they are two energies that are already given to each of us in every moment as we are going through the sometimes-excruciating process of learning and growing. We don't have to *do* anything to get them. In this instance, I was able to feel love and compassion towards myself at the moment and not have to apply them to myself later. I simply soaked in the compassion that is my birthright and claimed my innocence. I knew, deep down, that I had done nothing wrong. I was just learning. Yes, I had landed off the mark, and I was willing to take full responsibility for that learning. What happened was what happened – my childcare ran late – and I simply had to deal with the subsequent consequences.

Later, I was able to review my actions, checking in with my feeling-barometer. I came to the conclusion that I had erred in making the commitment to attend the event with my friend in the first place. It was a commitment that was not realistic in my current role as a mom of three – any number of things could have come up to prevent my attendance that evening, so it would have been more prudent for me to have said 'no' to the invitation, knowing how important the event was for my friend. Then, my friend could have asked someone who was better able to commit to sharing this special event. I recalled saying something along those lines when initially asked, and feeling like my friend had negated my hesitation to commit and twisted my arm to get me to say 'yes'. In reflection, I realized that I had agreed to go not because I really wanted to go, but to please my friend. Look how that turned out! From that time on, I have had more clarity about what kind of commitments I make to others, knowing that my mothering role was currently my top priority and that when I acted to people-please and ignored my intuition, it never turned out well.

This was a huge moment of success for me, internally, because, for one of the first times ever, I accepted myself fully without making myself bad or wrong – and subsequently beating myself up over it for days – when something went in a less-than-perfect direction and someone else blamed me as wrong. I let it be Ok for myself to be fallible without seeing myself as bad or wrong, to appear fallible in front of someone else, and to still stick to the knowing that I deserve to be treated and spoken to in a caring, respectful manner no matter what.

By forgiving myself for the irrational belief that I must be to blame or at fault for causing someone else's anger, claiming the updated belief that each of us is 100% responsible for our own feelings of anger, my fear around other people's anger just dissipated. I discovered that I no longer needed to feel sad, hurt, scared, upset, alarmed, or triggered in any way by another person's anger. This was a big win for me at the time.

Over the next few years, I embodied my new beliefs to the point where I have become non-reactive in the face of someone else's anger. I have even had the opportunity to stand up to someone screaming in my face without feeling any trigger at all, and I have been able to simply listen then set a boundary from a neutral position. Now, I know that nothing has the power to upset my peace, and other people's anger or upset is simply a reflection of their own unresolved issues. Another person's anger has nothing to do with me.

Other modeled behavior that I took on included unconsciously having my feelings and opinions spilling out all over the place like my mother, blaming other people for those feelings, and, if those feelings were particularly strong or angry, bottling or suppressing the angry feelings or resentments until I couldn't keep the lid on any longer and blowing my top, just like my father.

As a result of my familial emotional programming, in the past, I exuded a constant, low-level vibe of unhappiness, dissatisfaction, resentment, guilt, shame, embarrassment, and dislike of myself. Simultaneously, I had access to parts of myself that were outwardly caring, affectionate, kind, and supportive of others. When I first became aware of my own emotional suppression and stored negativity, I had so much judgment around the irrational belief that negative feelings were bad that it was a little challenging at first for me to admit to the level of underlying negativity I'd been feeling and emitting for my entire life.

But the hard truth was that many people I liked and admired didn't want to be around me. And the people who were attracted to me at that time tended to be highly critical, judgmental, complaining, stressed out, or otherwise miserable themselves much of the time. I was ready for mutually supportive, joy-filled, emotionally stable, and radiantly healthy relationships in my life. I had to own that my inner reality was creating my outer reality and that if I wanted to attract a different sort of person into my life, I'd need to *become* that different sort of person first inside of myself.

The first order of business was for me to accept *all* of my feelings as Ok. Once all of my feelings were acceptable, it became easy for me to simply allow my feelings to emote. From there, I learned healthier ways of emoting or expressing my feelings.

Examine Your Emotional Patterning as a Child

Think about yourself as a child. What messages did you receive around the subject of emotions or feelings? What was the modeling like around the expression of feelings? What were the familial beliefs? What were the societal or cultural beliefs? I encourage you to spend a few moments writing these down now.

Next, take a look at how you responded as a child raised in that particular environment. What beliefs did you take on as your own? What beliefs did you reject? What modeling did you pattern yourself after? If you did not easily fall in line with the familial or cultural beliefs, what beliefs did you make about yourself as a result of your childhood experiences? If you bought into any of the familial or cultural beliefs around the expression of emotion, how has it been going for you? I encourage you to write down any beliefs you may have unconsciously taken on, as well as any beliefs you formed on your own around this subject now. Be willing to look deeply at yourself.

Exploring Healthy Ways to Emote Your Feelings

Before you can begin to update any of your old, unsupportive beliefs around emotional energy and create a new pattern of expression, it is important to learn what a healthy expression of emotional energy looks like, sounds like, and feels like. This is so that you can create new, healthier beliefs and patterns for yourself in this area. Let's face it; most of us did not receive healthy modeling in the area of emotional expression.

Healthy emotional expression includes holding in the knowing that we are each 100% responsible for our own thoughts, feelings, and actions. When you are certain that you are fully in charge of your own feelings, you will no longer be able to verbally spew them out in blame onto others.

Energetically, this means that you will retain ownership of your own feelings for the entire time it takes for you to emote them. You will keep the energy of your feelings to yourself within the bubble of your own human energy field, without having the need to dump, slime, or ick anyone else.

Acknowledge Your Feelings Internally as Emotions Surface

As soon as you take 100% responsibility for your own feelings, you have the power to begin to express them differently. As a starting point, acknowledging your feelings on the inside is a way to hear yourself and validate your own feelings without involving anybody else in your process. As an emotional feeling bubbles forward, you can simply own it, saying inside yourself something like, "I feel upset."

Label the Feeling that is Present

The moment you have recognized the feeling of upset or noticed that your feeling-barometer is pointing 'off-course' inside of your own body, you now have the power to identify or label the feeling that is present. You may then say inside of yourself, "I feel _____ (example: hurt, angry, sad, frightened, bad, guilty, ashamed, etc.)." This can be viewed by you as a practical, rational, and neutral act – just like checking the thermostat on a hot or cold day to see what the temperature is like – all you are doing is checking in with and 'reading' your internal feeling-barometer. Instead of noting the degree of hot or cold outside, you are simply labeling the feeling, recognizing the particular line of energy frequency or 'emotional temperature' running through your body environment at that moment.

Listen and Validate the Feeling Reflectively

Once you have identified the feeling by giving it a label, you can respond internally to the feeling. Feelings simply need to be heard, so the more you can validate or hear the feeling coming up, the faster the emotional energy will dissipate. Listen to your feeling, allow it to speak internally, really hearing what the feeling is telling you. The feeling may say something like, "I feel so irritated. Irritated and annoyed. Urg. I feel irritated and annoyed because everybody keeps interrupting me, and I just need space to get this paperwork finished." Dialog with the feeling. Reflect back to yourself, whatever you are feeling. "I hear that. It's Ok. My feelings are valid. I'm feeling irritated and annoyed because no one is honoring my request to be left alone right now." As soon as the feeling energy is heard and validated, it will usually dissipate, and you will feel more centered.

Take Time to List the Irrational Beliefs & Judgments

If you have the time in-the-moment, you can take it deeper to get to the underlying irrationality as well as any judgment that may be creating your 'off-course' feeling-response. Remember that your natural state is one of peace and Loving, so if something is upsetting your inner peace, your feeling of upset is a pretty good indication that you are running some sort of irrational belief or judgment that is stuck in right/wrong thinking, which has created your feeling of suffering.

An easy way to discover the irrational beliefs underneath any particular emotional response is to simply make a feeling statement and fill in the blank.

"I feel irritated because _____" and "I feel annoyed because _____" Listen patiently, and keep listening until all of the 'becauses' have run their course. The more information you can get on the line of feeling-energy that is up for you, the more irrationality and judgment you can clear from your consciousness.

In this example, the limiting beliefs may be something like

"No one respects my requests," "My needs aren't important to other people," "People are disrespectful," or "Nobody ever listens to me." None of these ideas are rational or based on a supportive, Loving reality; when you encounter beliefs like these that are creating feelings of suffering, you would want to update them to create more empowering, self-supporting beliefs in order to manifest a better internal and external experience.

The judgments that may be attached to the feelings could be something like, "People are *disrespectful*," "I am *unsupported*," "I am *unimportant*," or "I am *unworthy of being heard*." These judgments are not based on spiritual truth; you would want to clear any and all judgment around your feelings until you can view the situation with total acceptance and neutrality.

If you are at work or in a public setting, you likely won't have the space or privacy to work with your feelings in the moment. If time and space is an issue, you can say to the feeling silently inside of yourself, "I really hear you feel irritated and annoyed. I will be sure to address your feelings soon." You may want to write yourself a note about it, reminding yourself you want to explore that feeling deeper when you get home from work or maybe over the weekend when you will have more time. I recommend that you make some regular time for yourself to do this because clearing out old, suppressed emotional energy is a big part of personal transformation. The more time and space you give to yourself to do this, the faster you will evolve and move into emotional freedom.

When you write down the irrational beliefs and judgments, you can either work your process then and there, updating your beliefs and clearing your judgment using compassionate self-forgiveness, or make a point of setting aside some time for yourself to do it later. Know that if you just express and validate the feeling-energy without addressing the underlying cause, this same line of feeling may surface again and again in the future until you are ready to clear the irrationality.

Remember the equation of beliefs: our beliefs lead to our thoughts, which lead to our feelings, which lead to our actions, which creates our current outer results, what we see or experience as our reality. So, your feelings (which reside at the emotional level) are simply an out-picturing of your thoughts (which reside at the mental level) whose sole purpose is to bring your awareness to what you are creating in your life based on your beliefs. We are meant to be conscious co-creators with our souls, creating a world of peace, joy, and unity. If there is something inside of you that is not residing in peace, your feelings are there to point a direct arrow to whatever it is that needs your attention and compassion.

If, for whatever reason, you do not get to intentionally go back into the feeling to listen to more, no worries. The underlying belief that has led to the thinking which causes that particular feeling to arise hasn't yet been cleared from your field, so that same feeling will simply surface again and again until you take the time to listen deeper.

Go Deeper into the Feeling in Your Own Time

Once you own the feeling and label it, you can begin to get tons of valuable information from that feeling, especially if it is an old, familiar feeling that has been a recurring theme in your life. In general, with feelings, the more intense or 'over it' you feel, the readier you are to heal and resolve the underlying issue. When you make the time and space, you can facilitate your own emotional expression in a number of ways. Start by placing yourself in a protected field of energy, invoking spirit's presence, and breathing in love and compassion. When you have invoked your protection and the Loving, you can sit quietly and tune in to the feeling. Connect with the feeling, feel it fully. See if you can notice where the emotion is stored inside of your body. Then you may want to give it a voice by asking the feeling to speak. You can hear it speak internally, or you may wish to vocalize it out loud. Either way is Ok. I would encourage you to do whatever feels in alignment for you. There is no right or wrong way to do this. Allow the feeling to express fully – to emote, which means to move the energy through you. Once you have finished expressing your feelings, apply compassion to the part of yourself that just shared.

Venting Emotional Energy Through Write & Burn

If there is a great deal of emotional energy stored, you may want to vent it out onto paper and then burn it. I encourage you to do this on loose notebook paper or in a spiral notebook in which the pages can be easily torn out. Avoid using a journal or a special notebook for this process. This type of writing is different from journaling creatively, brainstorming, writing poetry, visioning, or writing about ideas or aspirations, all of which you would likely want to keep. Here, with this process of write & burn, you will be allowed to give your feelings free rein to vent and simply cut loose, knowing that no one will ever read what you have written.

Express your feelings as they come out onto the paper without censoring a thing. Allow it all to be Ok. Every feeling is completely acceptable. Don't worry about spelling, legibility, capitalization, grammar, punctuation, or anything you may have learned in the past about the proper form of writing. None of that matters here, as no one will ever read it – this is strictly a tool for releasing the old, stored energy, so the idea is to let your feelings flow without thinking or impeding the flow in any way.

Know that when you are venting in a responsible, healthy manner, you can hear and accept everything without attaching any judgment to yourself for having felt that way.

From a neutral perspective, your feelings are simply providing you with useful information. Juice the information-gathering by squeezing out every last, little drop of energy. Your feelings may include profanity, blaming, name-calling, finger-pointing, judgment, self-pity, and any other expressions of upset. Know that it is *all* Ok to vent and that you are taking full responsibility and ownership by expressing it in a most healthy manner.

Once you are finished writing, breathe in compassion. Imagine filling all of the newly-emptied space in your cells up with the healing energy of compassion. Apply compassion to yourself for whatever came forward during your writing. Breathe in deeply and steep in Loving. Make a note of any particular irrationalities or judgments that were attached to the feelings on a separate piece of paper or in your healing journal, if you have one.

When you are finished venting onto paper, resist the urge to read it. I suggest burning it immediately or otherwise destroying the writing by shredding, throwing in the dumpster, or putting it into your compost bin. If you leave the paper in your space, you will be retaining the energy that has been dumped out on the pages as well. You may inadvertently take the old energy back into your body, and, if so, you would have to release it from your system all over again if you wanted to be free of it. To avoid taking it back in, do your best to get it out of your space as soon as possible.

When you burn/destroy the paper, do it with the intention to transmute the energy into Loving. This will neutralize whatever emotions came out on the page, as well as use the energy that was stored in your body for the greater good of mankind. If you are in a space where you absolutely do not have a way to destroy the paper in-the-moment, you can put it in a box or folder marked 'burn' and set an energetic protection around the box or folder to neutralize the contents until you have the opportunity to burn it.

If you do choose to store writings to be burned, I highly recommend you treat the box or folder with reverence. By this, I simply mean put it somewhere safe, don't let it stay out in the open where someone else may open it. Make sure you know where it is if you move, so you don't have to find it later in a strange box and accidentally reread it when unpacking. If that were to happen, and you suddenly found a file labeled 'burn', I would encourage you to simply burn it directly and resist the temptation to open the folder to see what was in there. Rereading an old 'write & burn' could be likened to having a splinter removed and then purposefully sticking it back into your body after the wound had already healed – it makes no sense and serves no purpose to read over something you have already released from your field.

If you have been using a journal to vent old, painful emotions in the past, I strongly encourage you to burn your old journals. If there is writing you wish to save mixed in with emotional venting, set strong conditions of protection and neutrality before reading through your old journals to pull out the parts you wish to save. I would recommend copying the parts you desire to keep into a different journal and burning the original, as emotional energy will be contained on the page if there was any degree of emotional release or dumping involved anywhere in the journal. You can also use a voice recorder to read the parts you wish to keep and transcribe them later. Bottom line – keep your environment free of any old, unproductive, unsupportive, painful, or negative emotional energy.

Electronic Write & Burn – for Emergency Use Only

If you do not have a pen and paper handy, or you aren't able to burn or safely dispose of your writing, you can do electronic 'write and burn' on your computer, in an email, on your phone or iPad – with caution and clear intention beforehand. Simply vent onto the keyboard, then hit 'delete' after completing your dump, setting an intention to wrap the whole thing in compassion. The reason I caution you to use this only in an emergency is that the computer will store the writing somewhere, even after it is deleted from the memory. This writing could, therefore, 'appear' somehow at a later date. Also, I have heard of all kinds of cases where this type of electronic vent was sent to someone inadvertently. Sending this type of writing will absolutely create unnecessary pain, suffering, and snarl-ups if that happens. The best way to do your write & burn is in a setting in which you are confident that none of the energy will leak out onto others before it is transmuted into Loving. Therefore, if you do choose to use an electronic device to write and delete, I encourage you to do so mindfully.

Finding a Safe Space to Verbally Vent in Solitude

Doing a write & burn is one way to vent old, stored emotional energy. Another way is to find an isolated space or a noisy space where no one will pay you any attention, and vent your feelings verbally, out loud. You could do this down by the ocean into the noise of the surf. You could do this under a crowded freeway overpass. You could do this in a soundproofed room. You could do this in a car, parked out in a remote area with your windows rolled up, in a noisy parking garage, or parked anywhere during a loud rainstorm. If none of these options are attractive or available, you could also create your own 'safe' environment to vent by playing some loud music to drown out your voice, either at home or in a vehicle. This option is dependent upon time of day, appropriateness of the situation, and so on – use your discernment to determine if venting verbally is in alignment wherever you may choose to do it. After verbally venting, respond to yourself from a place of compassion, allowing your higher, spiritual self to offer words of comfort and acceptance to the part of yourself that was expressing the feelings.

Verbally Venting with a Close, Trusted Confidant

You may also decide to verbally vent to a friend, a counselor, a minister, a mentor, or an otherwise safe person who can hear your feelings neutrally without taking any of them personally. I only recommend doing this with someone you trust implicitly – someone that you feel very safe to be vulnerable and open with. It would need to be someone who would keep your feelings confidential and not use them as family gossip or fodder for the break-room gathering at work. When you know you are 100% responsible for your own feelings, you will be much less likely to allow that energy to potentially leak out onto someone else. If you do feel the need to share, choose your listener wisely.

If you have ever had your feelings shared as gossip or a confidential sharing discussed by someone else without your knowledge or consent, you will know what I am talking about here. Because they are *your* feelings, and no one else's, it is solely up to you whether or not anyone else needs to know about them. The clearer I get in my own evolution, the less need I have to share my feelings with anyone. The exception is when I may decide to share my process with a couple of people I feel very safe and close with – my partner, my daughter, or one of my close friends. A high level of mutual trust with the person with whom I choose to share is mandatory for me. Usually, I share with a trusted friend when I really need to hear myself air something in order to work it through. Venting person-to-person gives me the opportunity to listen to my own upset while someone else holds a neutral, accepting space for me to process. After I give vent to my feelings, it is then a simple process to apply compassion to myself, clearing any irrational beliefs or judgments, and coming back into peace.

When choosing a person to hear your feelings, I encourage you to pick someone who is capable of listening with neutrality. What this means is that if your feelings of emotional upset were triggered up by your partner, I would suggest that you vent to a friend instead of asking your partner to hear your feelings. If your feelings were triggered up by a friend, you could ask your spouse or a different close friend to listen. Avoid sharing raw feelings with someone you are feeling upset with until after you've had a chance to emote. This will prevent you from giving in to the temptation to vent your feelings as blame, projection of judgment, or criticism of someone you love. And, if you do find yourself having trouble owning the feelings and go off in an expression of blame, your trusted, neutral listener will not feel harmed by your expression in any way.

Express Your Emotions Safely for All Involved

If your feelings are very big, old, or potentially harmful to yourself or anyone else, I strongly encourage you to find an experienced, qualified spiritual counselor or therapist who can hold in a high level of compassion in a sacred space so that you may safely vent. Suppose you don't currently have a counselor and have lots of old, repressed feelings that need to surface. In that case, I recommend finding a compassionate counselor who is trained in Gestalt or spiritual psychology.

Some people may recommend an anger management program for people who have lots of anger, and this may be a good short-term solution. Personally, I would recommend going deeper. In my experience, I have found that anger is usually just a cover for other feelings such as fear, hurt, disappointment, or resentment. Rather than learning to cope with having lots of feelings of anger, I recommend expressing the anger in a safe and Loving environment with the goal of getting underneath it to the real issues. Once the feelings are lifted in a space of compassion, the irrational beliefs and judgments that led to the feelings of anger will become self-evident. Beliefs can be updated, which will create new thought patterns to develop. New thought patterns will lead to different feelings. In other words, the anger could quickly become a thing of the past.

When, Where, and How to Emote Your Feelings is Up to You

If you have strong or potentially volatile feelings, the most important thing to know is that you always have the free will choice about when, where, and how to express your feelings. It is 100% up to you to decide when to vent or when to contain your feelings for a safer time. You are the driver of your emotional body vehicle. The more experience you have choosing when, where, and how to express your feelings, the easier it will become for you to decide to save them for later in a potentially unhealthy situation. I encourage you to begin to make self-honoring choices, and to choose radiant health and well-being for yourself and others by expressing your feelings in the healthiest ways.

Sharing Learning after Emotion has Passed Builds Intimacy

While I don't always share my feelings with another person in-the-moment, I will often share my learning after-the-fact, once I have released the emotional energy, worked through my process, cleared my judgments, and updated any irrationality that I'd been running.

Sharing what you are going through keeps you close to the people you are most intimate with; it allows them to better understand what you are going through and to connect with you on a deeper level. You can consider sharing your process as an extension of your true self, as a means of authentic self-expression of where you are in the present moment with whatever occurred in your recent past.

So, for instance, if I needed to take some space from my partner because a big, angry feeling surfaced and I didn't want to dump it on his head, I might tell him about it a day or two later in conversation, "Wow, I was really triggered up yesterday when blah-blah-blah happened, remember?" He would probably smile and raise his eyebrows and maybe laugh at me like, 'Yeah, how could I forget when you excused yourself and bolted from the room with steam coming out of your ears.' And I would share, "I figured out I was still holding the limiting belief that other people are supposed to do such-and-such a certain way, and if they don't do it my way, it means they don't care about me. God, it feels good to let go of that one", or whatever learning or awareness happened for me. If I have a big internal win or up-leveling, I celebrate it internally and almost always share it with the people that are closest to my heart.

What I don't do, for the most part anymore, is share my upset feelings in real-time while they are emoting from me in-the-moment. I've done this a few times in my past, and, trust me, it has never gone down well and has never been worth the suffering it created in the end. Sharing my emotion when it is 100% mine – especially if it is heated, challenging, or strong – does not serve my loved ones or me in any way. The exception is if my feelings surface while I happen to be in the company of one of my safe and trusted confidants; in this case, I feel free to let 'em rip. If I am in public or with my family, I respond to my upset feelings internally without dumping them out all over anyone who happens to be present

– most especially if one of those people happens to be the one who triggered my feeling of emotional upset in the first place.

Do Your Best to Resist the Urge to Dump Your Feelings

Do your very best to resist the urge to just dump your feelings out onto other people. Other people are innocent bystanders, no matter how very much you would love to blame, curse, and scream at them for how you are feeling. Understand that while your feelings are totally valid, they are for you and for you alone. Your feelings are not 'right' or 'wrong'; they are simply information that is showing you about something that is off-course in your world.

In my experience, the information from the feeling is almost always showing me where I am holding an irrational belief in my own consciousness. This means that my big feeling is based on something that is lodged in fear-based thinking, lack-thinking, limiting-thinking, right/wrong-thinking, or some other form of irrational thought. And so, my feelings are not based on what is spiritually true; they are coming up for me because there is something there for me to address, some issue to be healed, some fear or judgment that needs to be released, some dis-owned aspect that needs my attention, or whatever they are showing me that is out of alignment within myself for the express purpose to assist me in cleaning it up and move into greater alignment. Since my feelings are based on my own internal, irrational thinking, they are nobody else's business but my own.

If you have had a habit of sharing your feelings of upset with others, a good rule of thumb before you open your mouth to vent is to ask yourself, "What is my intention in sharing how I feel right now?" If your intention is to complain, defend, argue, make yourself right, justify your actions, seek vengeance, blame, shame, judge, criticize, or otherwise put another person down in any way, I would highly encourage you to stop yourself.

You may initially feel like you cannot possibly keep your feelings to yourself, and yet the first time you successfully prevent yourself from venting your emotional energy in an unhealthy manner, you will immediately begin to feel better about yourself internally. This lovely, on-course feeling that results from acting in alignment with your soul's will is much stronger than the urge to dump, and it will strengthen as you shift your pattern towards a healthier manner of self-expression. Everyone in your world will benefit when you make the decision to change your pattern for the better.

Understand that the only person who needs to know when you feel upset about anything is you. As long as you hear yourself and get the necessary information, that is all that matters. Remember the old saying, 'misery loves company'? This is one of the most irrational ideas of them all. It's like saying, "If one person is upset, let's make everybody upset, then we'll *all* feel terrible. Yay!" This is a mindset that has compounded the level of suffering upon the planet daily.

Think about it this way; if you were seriously injured and freaking out, would you want the nurse to walk into the E.R. and freak out with you? Just imagine that scenario for a moment – the nurse comes in and screams, "Ohmygod, ohmygod! Look at all the *blood!* Oh *no*! What are we going to do?! That is *horrible*, terrible, disgusting!" How would this help you? How would this serve your highest good? It makes no sense because when we are injured, we can be served best by someone who is holding in a calm, centered, clear-headed place of rational thinking.

The same thing holds true when we feel emotionally injured or traumatized; we are best served by having those around us remain centered, neutral, and rational. Yet somehow, people think it is an Ok or good idea to suck other people into their emotional tornado of upset. Resist the urge to drag others down, and you will quickly find yourself moving through your upsets in an energetically cleaner, more responsible, more respectful, and more Loving manner. Your loved ones will reap the benefits.

It took me some time to learn how to resist the urge to dump on other people in an unhealthy way, so if you are still venting out onto anyone else in your life, be gentle with yourself and know that you can change that pattern if you set a clear intention to do so.

Use Intention to Become Aware of Your Emotional Expression

Set an intention to become aware of your emotional self-expression. You can call upon the services of your neutral observer to watch the way you express yourself. Doing so will bring your attention to your emotional energy and will allow you to begin to observe your own emotional behavior. You will first find yourself becoming aware when you are dumping on someone and will observe yourself acting out an old pattern of blaming someone else for how you feel. Soon, you will be able to cut yourself short when you observe yourself placing blame. Then you will begin to become aware directly before you begin to dump and will have a split second chance to decide to spew or to get some space to express your feelings privately in a healthier manner. You will probably spend a period of time going back and forth, doing a little of both, and will get to see how it feels to take personal space when upset instead of dumping on someone else. Pretty soon, you will be able to stop yourself from dumping on another person every time and will be able to decide how best to support yourself to emote your feelings in the healthiest, most responsible way.

An Alternative Way to Verbally Vent

If you don't have a private or remote space to vent, and you really feel the need to verbally release, you can always use this exercise: set your energies of protection, love, and compassion. From there, tap into your feelings. Feel the feeling in your body, and breathe into the feeling deeply on an inhale, breathing in as much air as you can take. Hold your breath for just a second or two, really wrapping the feeling up with your breath. Make a sound, any sound, and breathe out on that sound, exhaling fully. Repeat two more times, inhaling deeply as you feel the feeling in your body, holding your breath for just a few seconds as you wrap your breath around the feeling, and then breathing the feeling out of your body on the sound. When you have done this breath three times using the same sound, check in with your body to see how you feel. If the emotional energy is still strongly present, you can do one more cycle of three breaths, possibly changing the sound if you are so guided. This usually releases some of the stored energy, allowing you to feel more centered inside until you can explore that feeling more fully.

The sound you make when you exhale can be anything. Just be spontaneous and allow whatever sound you make to be alright. It may be an 'Ahhh', 'Aaah', 'Uhhh', or another vowel sound. It may be a hard consonant sound like 'Dddd' or 'Kkkkk'. Or, it may be a combo of sounds like a 'Bbbuzzz' or 'Gggaaakkk'. Whatever it sounds like is fine. The idea is not to make some great-sounding noise but to get the emotional energy up and out of your body.

If you are at work or in a public setting when a strong emotion surfaces, you might consider taking a restroom break to do the above breathing exercise, just to get the energy moving up and out of your field. Be sure to acknowledge the feeling and to let yourself know that you will work with the feeling later when you have the appropriate space and privacy.

Other Healthy Ways to Release Emotional Energy

In addition to verbally venting and doing write & burn, I have released my feelings through physical movement such as dance and yoga, and through creativity by painting and singing. I have friends who use running, cycling, or other types of strenuous exercise or physical exertion to release stored energy.

Sex can also be a great way to release emotion. If it is done with clear intentionality to transmute emotional energy into Loving, you will literally be 'making love' as you engage sexually with your partner. This is an incredibly powerful form of spiritual alchemy. Many people have used drumming, piano playing, and songwriting as a highly successful outlet for emotional release. One of my former partners writes poetry, which is often very intense and highly charged.

Know that if you put your emotion into a creative endeavor, such as music, art, spoken word, writing, film, or any other form of art, your work will contain the energy of the emotion. This is a much healthier way to release the energy than verbally dumping it on someone else's head. With a creative outlet, other people have the freedom to view the art or listen to the music or poetry without taking on the energy of the piece. The information of the emotion can be transmitted to others in a way that allows them to choose whether to receive it neutrally or to be touched by it on a feeling level, either positively or negatively. In this way, art can be used as a catalyst or trigger for other people's growth. Art that resonates with people will encourage them to look deeper into their own feelings and issues, which can be in the highest good of all concerned.

These are some methods of expressing emotional energy

in a healthy manner, and there may be other methods that work as well. Be willing to experiment to discover what the best ways are for you to emotionally express your feelings when they arise. You are the only one who can know what is in alignment for you in regards to your own emotional expression.

Compassion is the Key to Releasing Stored Emotional Energy

Remember, however you decide to go about releasing your emotional energy, compassion is the key to allowing the emotion to move up and out of your energy field permanently. This may be the most important point in this entire book, so it bears repeating; the energy of compassion is the key to allowing the emotional energy to fully release, moving up and out of your field once and for all. The reason compassion works to help release the energy is that compassion *takes the place* energetically of the emotion that was just released.

Understand that energy has volume; what this means is that the feeling you are holding is energetically taking up space inside of your energy field. Your emotional body is layered over your mental and physical bodies and literally permeates your physical body right down to the cellular level. This means that the energy of your stored emotions is filling up the apparently empty space inside of your cells – that space that is in between all of your subatomic particles. Since the universe abhors a vacuum, the space inside of your cells must be filled with some sort of energy all the time. If you do not replace the emotionally discharged energy with something higher, you will simply suck it back inside. This is why many people often will vent out their feelings of anger, resentment, or frustration, only to take them back into their cells to reuse again at a later date.

Have you ever known someone who continually spews the

same feeling out over and over again, simply recycling it for the next outburst? Have you ever recycled a feeling or held on to a feeling of anger, resentment, or a grudge, and told your story repeatedly with feeling? I have definitely done this many times in my past. In fact, I can recall at least a dozen or two stories that had a high emotional charge for me that I told and retold a number of times over a period of years, each telling containing just as much suffering as the actual experience. This is because I didn't vent my emotions in the presence of compassion; I only vented from the limiting level of the initial feeling of hurt, anger, resentment, and suffering.

When we vent our anger, and we listen to ourselves from a place of that anger, we keep the energy of anger swirling around in our own energy field. Listening with sympathy for the emotion keeps us stuck in the same emotion. Asking for or seeking sympathy is like sucking someone else down into your upset. If you get someone else to resonate with your icky feelings of upset, it is like the nurse freaking out over the injured patient. Now two people are upset and in need of healing; the amount of upset has just been doubled. Venting emotion in the presence of calm, clear, rational compassion allows us to heal.

You can liken a healthy emotional vent in the presence of compassion to pouring the poison out of your cells and then refilling your cells with the healing, soothing balm of compassion. In actuality, compassion is pouring in as the emotion is releasing – it happens simultaneously. The more compassion you can apply, the easier and faster the old, emotional energy will lift and release. When compassion is present, and a Loving intention has been set, the toxic energy will completely transform, transmuting into the Loving as it leaves your energy field for good.

Releasing Old, Stored Emotions

As you move forward into learning how to express in the healthiest possible way, know that when you are highly triggered in-the-moment, it is usually an indication that there is old emotion stored along that particular vibrational line or tone of energy that needs to get released. This is why our feelings in-the-moment can often seem out of proportion to whatever is currently happening in real-time.

Have you ever seen someone have a much bigger reaction to something than the situation seemed to warrant? Have *you* ever had a strong emotional reaction to something that seemed smaller to you in retrospect? I can think of dozens of times this happened for me, and in every case, I was able to go back and feel the root cause of the stored emotion and allow it to release once I made the time to listen to my feelings. But, life is in session, and sometimes we will be highly triggered in-the-moment even when we have the awareness that the feeling is an old, unresolved feeling from our past. If this happens, this is an excellent opportunity to begin to practice your healthy expression of feelings.

If you feel highly triggered while in a public situation, I would encourage you to avoid saying anything from a feeling-place, if at all possible, if you think you might direct it out onto others. Just continue to validate the feeling inside of yourself, acknowledging and hearing the part of yourself internally that is feeling upset. If you have to engage verbally, do your best to keep your statements neutrally languaged, or make 'I-statements' if there is an emotional charge to your words.

To Express Emotion in Front of Others, Use I-Statements

What this sounds like verbally is that you will use only 'I-statements' when verbalizing your feelings in front of another. Avoid using the word 'you', and avoid any finger-pointing, naming of a scapegoat, or any other form of blame or denial. Example: Say you were exploring your beliefs around your patterning as a child, and you discovered that you had been walking around on eggshells for years, unable to express how you really felt for fear of making other people upset or angry. The very next time you found yourself acting out that pattern of walking on eggshells, you might feel some big feelings bubble up to the surface. To own it fully and responsibly, you might say something like, "Ugh! I feel so mad that I acted like that again. I can't believe I did that! I am feeling so angry that I put everybody else's feelings above my own. Grrrr!" So, nowhere in there are you directing any energy of blame or againstness toward anyone else; you are fully owning your own feelings without blaming your parents, your partner, your friend, your boss, or anyone else you may have tiptoed around for your emotional upset. This gives you the empowering opportunity to hear yourself, release the emotional upset, and then move into process to free yourself up from the old, unhealthy pattern of behavior.

Nonverbally, you would limit your expression of body language, facial expression, and emotional discharge to your own immediate space if other people were present when your feeling arose. If your face felt like you were scowling, you could direct your gaze away or down, or even close your eyelids rather than direct a dirty look or glare of anger towards anybody else. If someone else happened to be close by, and you felt your feelings would spill into their space, you could excuse yourself and go find more space somewhere else until you were centered again. When you keep your verbal and nonverbal expression of emotion within your own energy field and fully own every drop of it, energetically, it will release up and out, without touching anyone else.

When you consciously release your old emotional energy up and out, with clear intentionality in the presence of compassion, the energy will be transmuted into Loving as it releases from your field.

If you are unable to use 'I-statements' in the moment and observe yourself saying blaming statements or otherwise directing your emotional energy towards someone else, resist the urge to beat yourself up over it afterward or make yourself bad or wrong in any way. Allow it to simply be a learning opportunity. Apply compassion to yourself, saying something like, "Wow, I noticed how I just spewed anger all over my co-worker. That's Ok. I am learning and growing. I am learning about healthy communication right now. It didn't feel good to do that, so next time I will do my best to own it more fully."

You may have someone who has patterns of healthy emotional expression in your current life, and you may not. If you have a role model for healthy emotional behavior, consider yourself very blessed and use the modeling in service to your own growth. If you do not have a current role model for healthy expression of feelings, you will need to use your imagination to visualize healthy expression until you can re-pattern your behavior. Either way, know that it is absolutely possible to change the way you respond to your emotional energy for the better, letting go of all judgment towards emotion and simply using it as a tool for your personal growth and evolution.

All Emotions are OK from the Loving Perspective

The truth is that all emotions are Ok. All emotions are just feeling-energy, and that feeling-energy is neither good nor bad, nor right or wrong. It is simply information for us to use as we are learning and growing. Our feelings are a barometer for how we are doing at any given moment. The more you can learn to check in with your feelings throughout the day to get the information they are providing you with, the more connected and steady you will become emotionally.

Emotions May Surface for Healing – This is Normal

As you get more comfortable tuning into your feelings, acknowledging your feelings, and venting emotional energy in a space of compassion, you may find that many old emotions – maybe things you've never consciously felt before – will begin surfacing and clamoring for your attention. Don't panic and think you've suddenly turned into an emotional basket-case. It is natural and normal for the suppressed energy to want to come up and out. Imagine your feeling energy, having been denied, squished down, repressed, and ignored for years upon years saying, "Yeah! Finally, she is listening! Hallelujah. Now I can get a move on and do what I came here to do." Let the feelings up and out as often as possible. Note the information the feeling is here to share with you. Don't judge your feelings in any way; just allow them to surface and place your awareness on them in a detached and neutral manner as much as possible. Listen with compassion, and soon all of the excess, trapped emotional energy that has been stuck inside of your body vehicle will be moved up and out. You will experience tranquility, inner peace, and bliss as a result of letting it all go.

Letting Go of the Fear

Fear is one of the most dominant energies upon the planet at this time. Most of us are very intimate with fear-energy, having shared a bed with it our entire lives. When you become ready to reside in the Loving paradigm, it becomes vital to drop the fear and move into the infinite trust in the Loving. Fear is different from most other types of emotional energy. It doesn't get stored the same as, for instance, emotions such as shame, guilt, or anger. With fear, you don't have to express it so much as simply drop it.

I was up a creek without a paddle, out on a limb that was beginning to crack, hanging off of a cliff over an endless abyss when I finally decided to let go of allowing fear to run my life. Before I decided to align my will with the will of my soul, I was practically penniless, weaker physically than I'd ever been in my life, struggling to raise three children as a single mom, and terrified that I would lose everything if I didn't keep it together by my own sheer will. Everything I did during that period in my life was based on fear.

When I look back on that incredible time of my life, what I can see is that my personality-based will was so strong that I had to hit a rock-bottom place in order to shift. I had a very high pain threshold, so my life had to get really, *really* painful for me to decide that the fear-based choices weren't working for me anymore. I was literally afraid for my children's lives – afraid that I wouldn't be able to feed them, cloth them, shelter them. My deepest fear was that I would lose them. Nothing could be scarier for a mother, yet I had to put my desire for freedom – my desire for a peaceful, joy-filled life – above my fear of survival for my family in order to be ready to transform. At that point, I was only breathing in fear, so I had to want freedom more than I wanted to breathe.

It literally came down to a choice. I chose love over fear. From the moment I made that choice – the decision that my love and determination were stronger than my fear – my life has been moving forward in a positive, life-affirming direction, straight into the Loving, gaining momentum all the time. I have been continuing to move into more joy, into greater personal freedom, and into deeper levels of fulfillment than I've ever experienced.

What I want to make really clear right here is that the

only way past the fear for me was through it. The branch I was clinging to did crack and break. I took a freefall into the dark abyss. I lost the job I'd been clinging to out of fear. I lost the moldy apartment I'd been struggling to keep, and I lost nearly every single belonging I had except for the clothes on my back. Worst of all, I felt like I might lose custody of my children. But because I'd made the decision to trust in the Loving, I'd put my faith in the Loving 100% and made the decision to simply observe the fear yet not feed it... amazingly... miraculous things began to manifest in my life almost instantaneously.

Yes, I was suddenly homeless with three children... and I was guided to reach out for help. A beautiful, generous, and compassionate friend opened her home to us, where we lived for six months with her and her three children until I could financially support a new apartment. Yes, I was completely broke... I prayed for support, and then a friend recommended me for a teaching job out of the blue at a new community charter school. Suddenly, I went from working for next to nothing to holding an inspiring, meaningful, and lucrative job. Yes, I was physically sick and depleted from living in a moldy environment... I visualized health for my family, and with the new job and a free roof over our heads, I was able to spend the majority of my income for the next several months supporting my own physical healing as well as supporting my children to heal and detoxify the mold from their bodies. Yes, we had lost all of our clothing and belongings... I asked for support, and we immediately received donations of clothing from friends in our beloved community. Yes, I ended up having to go to court to retain custody of my youngest child... I faced my scariest, darkest fears as both the court and Child Protective Services investigated my ability to be a fit mother for my child. I surrendered the outcome over to God's will;

that ended up being a moment of incredible power and success for me as I stood in my truth, allowing my guides and my soul to support me. In the end, my children and I were able to stay together.

As I faced each of my deepest, darkest fears – homelessness, poverty, illness, failure, loss of material things, and the bone-deep fear of losing the right to raise one of my children – the fear simply dissolved before my eyes as I fell deeper and deeper into the abyss. Like a mist lifting, what was revealed was the truth and beauty of the strength of the Loving. By placing my trust in the Loving and facing the deepest depths of my fear, I was able to see the irrationality of my fears, and my own connection to Source was strengthened.

When I finally decided to stop running from my fear and to face it head-on, I felt authentic power flowing through me freely, flooding my very veins with energy. I felt pulled on-course by my soul and aligned with nature and all beings. I was suddenly able to see clearly, and able to take right-action despite any presence of fear-energy. Initially, the fear-energy was still there, but it was as if it couldn't sway me any longer. Every decision, from the moment I decided to align my will with God's will and follow the will of my soul, became crystal clear. I was so divinely guided that I felt safe even as I left behind the home that we lived in and the material possessions I'd collected over a lifetime.

Not only did I feel safe enough to finally take the leap away from everything I'd been so desperately struggling to keep, I knew deep down that things were only going to get better once I let go. And they did.

After diving into my fears, eventually, I landed in a beautiful valley that contained my entire past laid out before my eyes. Each step I took led me past a moment in my childhood, showing me clearly how I'd arrived at whatever fearful belief I'd been using to manifest my fear-based world. I walked past each event with a sense of curiosity and awe, as each step revealed the origin of my current fear-based thinking. I was instantly able to see the irrationality of my fears, and I was able to clear dozens – make that hundreds – of irrational, fear-based beliefs on every subject that had been shaping my life up until that point. I walked across the valley at the bottom of my personal abyss of fear with eyes open, the sun shining brightly on every detail, and I alternately laughed with delight and cried with heartfelt relief as I poured love and compassion upon my most painful memories.

Here in the valley of my fears was where I identified and embraced all of the parts of my personality I'd been doing my best to ignore or deny. Here was where I cleared years' worth of self-judgment and rewired my belief system to reflect my new Loving reality. It was some months of wandering the valley of my past before I was healthy and strong enough to begin the upward flight into my present level of freedom. Every single moment spent in that valley examining and clearing my fears was a moment well-spent. I know that I could not be where I am now without first going there to face my fears, heal my past, and integrate all of my spiritual awareness and understanding into knowing and being. This was an integral part of my journey.

What Fears are Keeping You Small and Stuck?

Everyone's path is unique. Not everyone has to fall into an abyss of fear in order to heal and come into alignment with their soul's purpose, but most people do need to face their fears in some way and heal from their past somewhere along their own personal path. What fears are keeping you small and stuck? What are you clinging to out of fear? Is there something you are afraid to face? Are you hanging on to an unfulfilling job, an unhealthy relationship, an unhealthy lifestyle, or a limiting living situation out of fear of letting go? Are you settling in any way for less than what you truly want in life? Be willing to answer honestly.

Most people I know are settling out of fear in some way. They are staying stuck in an unhealthy relationship out of fear of being alone. They are holding lackluster jobs out of fear of not having enough money. They are terrified of doing what they really yearn to do out of fear of failure. They are clinging to credit-card debt and mortgages that are too high out of fear of not having a certain type of lifestyle or out of a need to uphold a certain superficial appearance. They are afraid to move to the place they really want to live out of fear of losing the familiarity of their current life. They are clinging to harmful habits like drinking, smoking, drugs, or overeating in order to dull the pain they are afraid to face if they ever lose the numb. They are going through the motions of the rat-race every day, filled with stress and fear that something may happen to throw off the delicate balance they've struggled to achieve – some accident, illness, or unanticipated obstacle may occur – and 'then what?!' Yes, then what. "What would happen if…" is one of the most commonly repeated fear-based thoughts to flit through most of humanity's collective mind. In my experience, we cannot get to where we most want to go until we face our' what if' fears to reveal that they are an illusion.

From the place of fear, people respond to my suggestion to dive into their fears with something like, "What?! Are you *crazy*?" How can you expect me to actually let go of my comfortable _____ (example: job, relationship, home, habit, addiction, etc.) How could I *do* that without being sure of what is coming next?" My response after doing just that is, "How can you *not*?" What I know to be true is that the new cannot come in until we let go of the old. We cannot get where we want to go unless we are willing to step away from where we currently are. If we stay small, safe, and comfortable too long, we will literally stagnate. Speaking from painful personal experience, I physically, mentally, emotionally, and spiritually *molded* from standing in place for too long out of fear of moving forward. It is much easier to keep moving than to deal with the pain that results from stagnation. When we don't use it, we lose it. This goes for muscle, brains, talent, gifts, health, inspiration – everything. We need to keep growing, or we begin atrophying and dying.

How can you willingly choose to start atrophying just because you are afraid? Yet this is what most people do. They get to a certain level of success or satisfaction with their life, and then they are simply finished facing their fears. Rather than continuing to stretch themselves, they decide that it is easier to just rest comfortably at whatever level they have thus far attained in life, rather than have to push through more fear. They suppress or deny their true heartfelt dreams, convincing themselves that they need to settle for whatever they've currently got. This is when they will begin dying. In cases where people have actually followed their dreams and have continued to stretch in career or relationship, they remain robustly healthy until their source of livelihood is taken away. How many people do you know who have declined in health or wellbeing the moment they have officially 'retired'? I can think of dozens offhand. Suddenly, they can no longer run around the way they used to move. They have joint pain, hip pain, a bum knee, back pain, arthritis – you name it – to keep them from getting out as much. If we stop growing and cease to live meaningful, purpose-filled lives where we are contributing to the betterment of mankind in some way, we will immediately begin to atrophy and cause ourselves tremendous pain and suffering.

What I have discovered through great personal experience is that the level of pain and suffering caused by stagnating is *much* greater than the momentary suffering caused by facing fear and continuing to expand and grow. The incredible thing about facing fear is that the moment you step into the fear, the suffering dissipates. Remember how the darkness just dissipates the moment you turn on the light? Facing fear is the same principle; when you shine a light on the fear by looking at it directly, shining your attention and awareness on it fully, the fear-energy just dissipates. What you are left with is whatever information was hiding under all of that fear.

I can recall looking around my life with a detached sort of amazement after I took my leap despite my fear, leaving my period of stagnation and moldy house behind. "Oh, look at that… I thought my children would end up naked and starving, and what I see now is that we have lots of people who care about us who won't let us go without food, clothing, a roof, or whatever else we may need. That wasn't so scary…" and, "Oh, look at that. I thought that the only way we could survive is if I clung to that low-paying job… Now I know that I can actually be supported even *better* than that by doing work that fulfills me deeply. Wow…" In fact, when I finally decided to take the leap, the relief I felt from the suffering was enormous. I immediately just knew that things would get better and better. And they did. It was so worth taking the risk.

Since that first initial leap of faith out of my stagnated, fear-based life, I have taken many other leaps of faith as I've gone higher up my learning spiral. In order to do what I'm here to do, I had to quit my day job and hang my shingle as a healing facilitator. This leap was quite scary; it took me several years to stop clinging to my safety-net and really let go and leap, and yet the minute I did, I had clients to support me to keep going. I have been self-employed ever since.

To move on to the next level of teaching to a wider audience, I had to face my seemingly-horrific fear of public speaking. First, I was guided to join a local Toastmasters club. In the beginning, the prospect of getting up and speaking in front of a group of people I barely knew was so intimidating that I can recall sweating profusely, having shaking knees, feeling light-headed, having such a dry mouth that my lips stuck together, and more. But once I did it a few times and survived, the level of fear my body experienced began to lessen. By my third speech, I was already feeling a lot better about the whole thing, and by my sixth speech, I was even beginning to develop a new feeling of self-confidence. It was totally liberating.

After giving speeches at my club for a few months, I was guided to join the board to develop my leadership skills. A few months later, I was stretching myself again in the role of club President. I was responsible for holding the energy of an entire group and had to learn how to hold the integrity and vision of the club's mission over individual wants and needs. Just a few months later, I was asked to be an area governor, another stretch into a higher level of leadership. Here, I had to work with many other leaders and to learn how to support people to lead in their own way. I moved through dozens of new fears. The following year, I was guided to run for the office of division governor, an elected role that presented a whole new set of challenges and fears to face. The following year, I was appointed to the district board and worked with the organization in an even larger capacity, where I had the opportunity to work through even more fears. By the time I finished those three years of district leadership, I felt capable of managing a board of my own, felt confident speaking in front of huge audiences, felt confident delegating to others, had much improved my problem-solving skills, and felt fully able to put on large events such as workshops and retreats. I couldn't have arrived at my current level of leadership without moving through the fears that arose at each stage of my growth.

Moving Out of Your Comfort Zone Brings Up Fear

Understand that with each and every up-leveling you will ever take in your life, there will likely be some initial fear involved. This is because your fear-based personality and subconscious mind are always seeking the comfort and security of the familiar. Every time you attempt to expand in any way, fear will surface and attempt to hold you back. The temptation to settle out of fear will ride in the wake of your fear. Your sub-personalities will begin screaming, 'No! You can't possibly do *that*!' Every irrational thought that is currently standing on the platform of your life will have to surface for your awareness in order to get on board the train before you can reach your next destination. But guess what? You can feel free to leave the fear on the platform and board the train without it.

Imagine instantly releasing the fear and filling all of your cells with energies of trust. As you fill yourself with trust, the fear will dissipate. The parts of your personality that are still stuck out in the dark, still residing in fear and suffering, will do everything in their power to sabotage your growth, to prevent you from getting on that train and taking the leap to the next level. Know that your will is stronger than your fear. Get on the train despite your fear. Take the leap despite your fear. Take the risk of facing your fears over and over, and you will begin to have the experience of living fearlessly. This has been one of the most liberating stages of my own journey – to experience living free of fear.

Another opportunity to leap presented itself in the area of finances when I initially began writing this book. I had to decide whether to focus on my clients and students or to place my trust in the universe to support me while I focused on writing. My soul had been urging me to get the book done, but I'd been hesitant because I'd had some fears about how my family would manage financially. After dragging my feet awhile, I took the leap of faith that if my soul wanted me to write a book, then the universe would certainly support me to do so. The moment I made the decision, I felt fearless about it. I moved into my writing in the space of calm, clear, rational thinking, in complete alignment with the will of my soul. As I spent more time immersed in my writing, I stopped teaching classes and workshops, and gradually my client hours began dwindling as well. My income decreased dramatically. There was a moment where I had a choice; I could entertain fear again, or I could simply reside fully in the trust of the Loving. I chose to reside in trust.

The things that happened for me over the course of that year financially were what many would call 'miraculous'; I received numerous tithes from students and clients, most of which came right before my rent or bills were due. I received random checks in the mail for rebates, class-action settlements of which I didn't even know I was part, payments for services rendered from clients that had long-standing past-due balances, and surprise gifts of money from friends and family. Gifts of food were brought by, friends offered to take us out to dinner, and, most remarkable to me, I had old clients schedule sessions with me out of the blue – clients I had not heard of in four or five years were suddenly making appointments, right when the support was most needed. It was amazing to me that I had to put out almost no effort to support my family during that year – I was able to focus on my writing with just enough healing sessions sprinkled into my week to keep a roof over our heads.

One month, we ended up a little short on rent money; I found myself checking in with my guidance, asking, "Should I put together a class? Try to round up new clients?" Spirit told me to stay focused on completing the book, so I decided not to worry and continued writing. That month, a woman who I hadn't heard from in over six years contacted me to do a pencil drawing of her newest child since all her other children had had one done. Portrait drawing was an old business I'd done in the past that had never fully supported me, and now, here it was coming in out of nowhere to support me to continue to focus on doing the work of my soul. What a blessing!

Each time the refrigerator was empty, I told my family to trust and just asked the universe to send us some food or grocery money. Then my older daughter would call to take us to lunch, a friend would have produce from her garden to share, someone would randomly give us food – in one case a piece of freshly-caught tuna fish – or a check would arrive immediately, either getting dropped through our mail slot by a client or arriving through the mail. In one remarkable instance, my son called out, "Mom, there's nothing for dinner." I sent a blast of light out into the universe, blessing my family with prosperity, affirming that all of our needs were met. About two seconds later, the phone rang. It was our local grocery store, letting me know that I'd won a drawing for free groceries. Bemused, I told my son that I didn't even remember entering any drawing. He laughed, sharing he'd filled out several forms in my name the last time we'd gone shopping. He'd manifested his own dinner! In the past, if I'd been operating with an empty refrigerator or with a zero bank balance, I would have been freaking out with fear and panic, desperately trying to figure out what to do. Now, I know that I can simply relax and trust that my soul has everything handled. The universe supports me completely to do the work of my soul.

Dropping Fear Takes Forward Momentum

The thing about dropping fear is that all it takes is simply a decision to do so and then a forward-making motion. Moving forward creates momentum, so the more decisively you are willing to move, the faster you will drop the fear and adjust to a higher vibration of freedom. Don't allow yourself to grow complacent and comfortable – at whatever level you land – because becoming comfortable will make it harder to move on again from there.

I can clearly remember being about eight years old the summer I first went off the high dive at our local pool in the small town where I grew up in Pennsylvania. It was a solid platform rather than a springboard dive; I don't know how tall it was, but it felt miles high and took me forever to climb up the ladder. I waited my turn, climbed up that torturously long ladder – knees knocking, palms sweating, dizzy from looking down – and I finally got to the top. Holy crap it was scary to me. It was so far up in the sky, the other kids looked about the size of ants. The pool seemed like a little rectangular plastic take-out container filled with light-blue water. I felt sure that if I jumped, I would miss the water and splat all over the deck. I began to hyperventilate. I couldn't breathe. If I hadn't just emptied my bladder a little while earlier, I am certain I would have peed in my bathing suit. I felt terrified. I finally decided I couldn't do it and made to climb back down the ladder. Instantly the lifeguard began blowing his whistle, telling me, "No! That's against the rules!" The deal at that pool was this: if you were brave enough to climb up, you were brave enough to jump.

There was no backing down (now I understand what that

saying means). My only way out was to jump. Yet, I just stood on that platform, paralyzed with fear. Whistles were blowing, people were screaming, "jump, jump!" my older siblings and their friends were booing me and screaming insults like, "you stupid idiot, just jump!" my mother was scolding, "Cynthia Lynn Lamb, you are holding up the entire line. Get down here right this instant!" It was the absolute scariest, most humiliating moment yet in my eight years of life. In the end, after about probably five or ten minutes of standing on that high dive in a state of excruciating fear, panic, anxiety, dread, with sweat pouring, bile churning, adrenaline pounding through my veins, I finally stepped up to the edge, held my nose, and jumped. I landed safely in the water about 4 seconds later, free of fear.

Lesson learned? It is the waiting to leap that is scary. It is only the anticipation of the movement that frightens us – the actual move beyond our comfort zone is always liberating. The second, and I mean the very instant you decide to make a move, and you move into action, the fear dissipates. Remember that having the courage to act doesn't mean a person doesn't feel afraid; courage is the quality of acting *despite* the presence of fear. If I had only been willing to courageously run down that cement platform straight off the edge, I could have saved myself from experiencing seemingly endless agony.

The longer you stay in one place, the tighter the subconscious mind will cling out of fear to the known comfort zone, and the louder the fears will scream when you get ready to move on. Keep moving and growing. I encourage you to be willing to first decide to make the forward motion – whatever that may be in your life – and then move forward decisively and purposefully. Making the decision to face and move through a fear purposefully can be likened to running into the ocean even though the water is cold. If you just run into the water and dive under the first wave, you will soon adjust to the water temperature. Suppose you are one of those people who likes to move into the ocean of your fear very tentatively, dipping in one little toe at a time, squealing and backing up again. In that case, you will still be experiencing the suffering of the freezing cold water splashing against your stomach years from now. Meanwhile, the ones who used their forward momentum will be out there blissfully swimming with the dolphins.

Moving decisively and purposefully means the opposite of running from your fear in a blind panic. When you act decisively, your goal and intention will be very clear. Your attention would be focused on the first step toward your goal. Your movements would be smooth, deliberate, fluid, and in the flow with nature and the Loving. You will be listening to and in attunement with your divine guidance, and will act accordingly as you take the steps toward accomplishment of your goal. With each and every step you take, your old fears that had been holding you back in the past will simply fall away behind you, leaving you liberated.

I've faced the fear of having my children starve, and I know it is an illusion. I have faced the fear of homelessness, and I know it is an illusion. I have faced poverty, and I know it is an illusion. I am so well taken care of, it is almost ridiculous. I feel like laughing out loud with the joy of it every day, knowing that it is my trust in my divine connection that supports us. I went totally out on a limb to write this book with next to no income coming in, and yet it was what I was guided to do. When I follow my guidance, I am acting in full alignment with the will of my soul, and that is when I can trust that all is well. I have complete faith that my family and I will be taken care of, that all of my rent and bills will be paid with grace and ease, and that more money will begin to flow into our lives as the energy produced by all of my writing is released out into this world.

Trust That You Are Divinely Supported in Every Moment

This is how faith works. We simply place our trust into God's hands and know that we are divinely supported every step of the way. With each leap of faith I have taken, I have less fear and more trust since I've now had repeated experience of the amazing grace that happens when I drop the fear, surrender to the divine flow, and simply do as I am guided to do.

Know that you are *always* supported when you decide to face and move past your fear to reach your heartfelt dreams and goals, whatever they may be. Learning to trust in your guidance and aligning your will with the will of your soul is an adventure and one well-worth the exciting ride.

Living Free of Fear

There are some who will say that you can never live free of fear – that fear is a necessary emotion that keeps us safe. Those people simply haven't yet arrived at the level of consciousness where they live free of fear. Understand that all emotion is energy and that at a certain level of being – at the level of peace, to be specific – you can receive the energy as pure information without feeling any fear attached to it. My first experience of this phenomenon happened in 1996, the year I trained as an Integrated Etheric Healer.

After spending all day up in Agoura Hills attending the healers training, around ten p.m., I began the drive back home to Los Angeles. I was in a high state of consciousness from a day of working in the etheric realm, feeling calm, centered, and peaceful while driving southbound on the 101 freeway. As I neared the connection ramp for the southbound 405 freeway, I started to apply the brakes. I felt an instant prickle on the back of my neck. In the past, I would have perceived this warning prickle as fear and would have tensed up; in this case, I didn't experience any fear at all. I felt a *sensation* of energy, which I perceived as a warning signal of some kind. I simply tuned in and listened to the warning neutrally. It said inside of my head, "Hold steady." I held the accelerator steady as I entered the curve of the freeway interchange ramp – now, here, I do have to admit that I was driving just a few miles over the speed limit; it was ten-thirty at night, the freeway was practically empty, what can I say? I held at 75mph for several seconds until I received the next signal, "now accelerate… keep accelerating." My speedometer reflected my increase in speed, the needle pointing to 80, 82, 84, 86 then 87 as I flew around the curve. Approximately twenty yards before I merged onto the 405 freeway, a dark colored sedan came out of nowhere, flying in mid-air, hurtling up, up over the guardrail of the 405 freeway in front of me off to my left in my peripheral vision. Time slowed down. I watched with detached fascination as it flew in the trajectory of the freeway ramp I was currently driving on…. and I observed myself calmly drive directly toward it, trusting in the Loving and my divine guidance to guide me and protect me. Time slowed to almost a stand-still as I sped safely under it. Just barely. I looked in my rear-view mirror as the flying car hung over my trunk for a nano-second then fell with a tremendous 'thwump', crashing to the pavement directly on the ramp within millimeters of the back bumper of my speeding car. I physically felt the 'whoosh' of it, as if the wind of it falling propelled my car forward even faster. It was like a well-orchestrated stunt in an action film. Practically unbelievable.

    I know, without a doubt, that if I had bought into the idea that the initial prickle of warning alerting me to pay close attention and listen up was fear, I would have braked. I might have been going slower as I rounded that curve and could have driven head-on into that car as it crashed. Or, I could have panicked when I saw the car flying towards me and swerved, flying off of the freeway ramp myself, otherwise crashing my car or getting squashed like a bug by the other car. The cars behind me were much further back and would have had time to brake to avoid a collision, but because my soul knew that the other car was coming in that instant, I was given the necessary information to protect myself without the energy of fear that would have clouded my thinking and caused me to have a potentially life-threatening fear-based reaction.

Since then, I have been gradually moving into living in total freedom – which is a place of absolute trust that exists free from fear. The longest I have resided in total trust is a period of nine months between 2008-2009, and that was the most expansive and liberating period of my life thus far. When I went to uplevel from that space again, I had some new fears come up as I anticipated the move out of my comfort zone. These were fears I'd never dealt with before, such as fears of appearing on camera and fears about getting a book published. For the past few years, up until this past year, I've been able to go several months between fears cropping up, and it is a delightful, joy-filled experience to be able to live so free of fear. My goal is to live fear-free, completely in the trust in the Loving, where I receive all precautionary warnings as information. I absolutely know it is possible.

I encourage you, wherever you are in relationship to fear in your own life, to know that you can drop the fear and still be safe.

Understand that dropping the fear does not in any way mean that you ignore your own intuitive warning-energy and act heedlessly, carelessly, or possibly put yourself or someone else in harm's way. By dropping the fear, I simply mean that you do not need to feel scared in any way. You absolutely *do* need to listen to the message that gives you the initial warning. In-the-moment type of warning-energy has a definite purpose, which is to keep you alive and well, so it is imperative to heed.

For instance, when I was eight, climbing to the top then standing up there on the top of a ridiculously-high platform dive, my fear served the purpose of getting me safely to the top and directing me to aim for the pool. I could just as easily have jumped – or fallen – from the ladder side and landed on the cement; my fear was directing me to stay focused on the ladder, hold tight, pay attention, place my foot carefully, and be alert to the potential danger of my situation.

Spot the Difference Between Irrational Fear and Useful Fear

The fear I felt climbing that ladder is the type of fear that I consider useful, relevant, and healthy fear. It is the kind of fear that serves a purpose, acts as a warning, and guides us to keep us safe and alive. Most fear, however, is not this handy in-the-moment kind of message, but a pervasive feeling that has permeated our entire world and infected all of its inhabitants with constant worry, lack-thoughts, limiting beliefs, and self-doubt.

Once you have cleared much of the latter – the useless and disempowering kind of fear – you will easily be able to spot the relevant type of fear as merely a warning and heed it. When you know the difference between irrational fears based on passed-down, familial, or societal fears, and the in-the-moment, 'heads up' warning signal of useful fear, you will quickly be able to begin to get the message from your relevant fear-energy without feeling scared in any way. The clearer you can get from old, limiting, fear-based beliefs, the sooner you can become liberated from fear entirely and move into trust.

In my own experience, here are some of the useful types of fear-warnings that I have received fearlessly: I have been warned to cross to the other side of the street when walking alone at night. I have been cautioned to 'wait' at an intersection after I received the green light, even when cars were honking behind me to go, only to have another car run the red light speeding in the opposite direction. I have been instructed not to eat a certain burrito – which was very challenging because I was hungry and it smelled very good – I didn't heed that particular instruction, and one tiny bite of it gave me food poisoning. I have been instructed to drive a different way, avoiding accidents and traffic jams on numerous occasions. I have been warned about certain uncomfortable circumstances before entering a room or a public setting, which allowed me a moment to center myself and mentally prepare for a challenge. I have been cautioned not to attend certain events, to find out later that something unpleasant or even disastrous happened that I gratefully avoided. And I have been instructed to lock my car, park my car in a different space, and take my purse out of my car or shopping cart on numerous occasions. These are just a few examples of messages that have come to me on the line of 'head's up' energy I formerly identified as fear. Now, when that energy gets my attention, it is simply an indication for me to become very present, to pay close attention, to keep my eyes wide open, and to tune in to my guidance for clear instructions.

When you are conscious, tuned in, and listening to your own thoughts, you can quickly receive the underlying message or instructions that are riding on the 'head's up' warning energy without feeling upset or panicky in any way. Then you can begin to drop your fears by moving out of your comfort zone into your next level of growth. The more you do this, the quicker you'll see how much better life gets. As the quality and conditions of your life improve, you will begin to see that fear has no power over you, that most fear is just an illusion of darkness, that the sun is always shining – even when it is raining, snowing, sleeting, hailing, etc. – the light of the Loving is strong enough to dissipate all fear. Within your connection to the Loving, you have access to infinite intelligence, so you can get the information you need from relevant warning energy without any fear-energy present in the message. You can live in trust, flow, and alignment as you fulfill your soul's purpose upon the planet.

The power of living fearlessly, residing in a state of peace with complete trust in the Loving is enormous. From a place free of fear, your intuition will be heightened, you will have better control in dangerous situations, you will be able to remain cool, calm, and collected in emergencies, potential harm can be avoided, and, most of all, trusting just *feels* better. The list of benefits is endless.

Drop your fears, live in the trust of the Loving, cultivate healthy patterns of emotional self-expression, and move into emotional freedom from within.

Exercise: Claiming Emotional Freedom

Begin by saying a protection prayer, setting conditions of love and light, and invoking spirit's presence.

Place your hands on your heart. Set an intention to access the highest vibration of Loving available. Breathe in the Loving and fill your body with Loving energies from head to toe. Then, set an intention to access the highest level of compassion. Breathe in compassion and fill your body with compassion from head to toe.

Repeat out loud any of the following that resonates, changing the phrasing as needed to reflect your own beliefs:

"I forgive myself for buying into the irrational belief that expressing my emotions is _____ (bad, unsafe, weak, sissy, etc.)." "My new updated belief is I now know that emotions are just energy that needs to be expressed in order to be released from my body. It is absolutely Ok and healthy for me to express my emotions in a safe, responsible manner."

"I forgive myself for buying into the irrational belief that if I allow myself to express my emotions, someone will get hurt." "My new updated belief is, I now know how to express my emotions safely. I now own my feelings fully, and vent them in a healthy, responsible manner – by listening to myself, validating my feelings, venting with a write & burn, using 'I'-statements, or some other healthy way of moving the energy."

"I forgive myself for buying into the irrational belief that it's not Ok to feel and express my anger." "My new updated belief is, I now know anger is a normal and natural emotion. It is simply one emotion in a whole range that my feeling-barometer uses to signal when something is off-course for me. I now know that anger is simply information, and if I give it a voice, I can hear what it is trying to tell me. I can emote the anger safely, then use the information it gave me to course-correct. It is now safe for me to feel and express my anger in a responsible manner."

"I forgive myself for buying into the irrational belief that my feelings have the power to _____ (overwhelm, destroy, hurt, depress, kill, etc.) me." "My new updated belief is, I now know I am not my feelings. I am a soul in a body, and my feeling-barometer inside my body-vehicle is simply a tool that lets me know if something is on or off-course. My feelings themselves cannot harm me. I can emote the energy safely, transmute it with Loving, and simply use the information as guided to take action and transform my life."

"I forgive myself for buying into the irrational belief that I have to always tell other people how I feel." "My new updated belief is, I now know my feeling-barometer is my own, internal indicator of where I am at any moment in relation to the will of my soul. My feelings actually have nothing to do with anyone else. It is absolutely Ok for me to keep my feelings to myself and vent my emotional energy in private or with a trusted confidant. My feelings are my own business, and from now on, I trust my discernment before expressing my feelings publically."

"I forgive myself for buying into the irrational belief that I need to try to get sympathy or to get someone else to agree with or support my feelings." "My new updated belief is, I now know my feelings are my own, and the highest and most responsible way for me to emote is to keep my energies 100% contained in my own field until I transmute them with compassion. I now know that eliciting a sympathetic response simply adds to the sum total of suffering, and I chose to alleviate world suffering by owning my feelings fully, allowing others to remain at peace when I feel suffering."

"I forgive myself for buying into the irrational belief that if I don't share my feelings or elicit sympathy, I will go unheard and unsupported." "My new updated belief is, I now know I am my own source of listening. I am my own source of support. I now know that I can hear myself from a place of compassion. I can validate my own feelings, respond to my own feelings, and support myself to transmute my feelings by applying compassion within my own consciousness. Healing is an inside job, and I am sourced from within."

"I forgive myself for buying into the irrational belief that because other people around me are feeling _____ (angry, upset, scared, terrified, sad, etc.) that I need to feel that way, too." "My new updated belief is, I now know the healthiest response I can have to someone else's _____ is to hold in neutrality, to stay separate, and to simply allow them to feel however they are feeling from a place of peace or compassion. I am of greatest service to myself, the other person, and the world if I hold in Loving in response to other people's suffering."

"I forgive myself for buying into the irrational belief that it serves me in any way to allow my fears to hold me back." "My new updated belief is, I now know the fear is in the anticipation – fear only lasts until I make the decision to act. I now know that I am free to move forward, knowing that the moment I take the leap that the fear will simply dissipate. I now know that I can use forward momentum to keep me moving through my fears with grace and ease."

"I forgive myself for buying into the irrational belief that I will always have to have fear in my life." "My new updated belief is, I now know healthy fear-energy is simply information, a warning to stay alert, be diligent, or to act carefully in any given moment. All other fear-energy is irrational, coming from an old story, or passed down my familial line. I now know that I can simply drop the fear, take the information it is sending me and move forward freely. I now trust that the universe supports me to live in peace and freedom."

Close your process by acknowledging yourself, expressing gratitude to spirit, and fully grounding your energy. Drink plenty of water.

CHAPTER TEN
Cultivating New Healthy Patterns of Behavior

As you go about making the paradigm shift into Loving, you will become aware of specific unhealthy patterns of behavior that are no longer serving you. In my experience, changing an unhealthy pattern of behavior is challenging if you have not done the prep work of working with your beliefs, judgments, disowned aspects, and old emotional energy first. Once you have had some experience working your process around all of the above, you will find that changing an old, unhealthy pattern of behavior for a more supportive pattern to be simply a matter of making a clear intention to change, making a commitment to yourself, and maintaining persistence as your behavior begins to shift for the better.

Patterns are Like Bridges with Columns of Beliefs for Support

The first step to changing a pattern is to dive deep and uncover all of the irrational beliefs that have been holding the pattern in place. I like to picture patterns as long bridges with many concrete columns supporting the weight of the bridge. The columns are like the pillars of beliefs that hold the bridge of behavior up. To take down the bridge, first, you must take down the support system.

When you take down the old support system, it is vital that you understand that your intention is not about eradicating the old bridge but rather building a newer, better, stronger, healthier bridge in a different place *first*. Sometimes people try to knock down the old bridge before constructing a new one, and this can lead to snarl-ups during rush hour. So, the idea is to get the new bridge in place, fully supported by strong, healthy pillars of beliefs, and then the old bridge will naturally collapse and fall in its own timing.

Examine Your Pattern of Behavior Thoroughly

Look at the pattern of behavior that you wish to change. Identify the action or conditioned response – your bridge. Now, look underneath the pattern or bridge to see what has been holding it in place. Be willing to look deeply and fearlessly at your own consciousness to thoroughly examine your old behavior pattern.

Let's take an example. Say the pattern is cigarette smoking. The pattern of behavior is that every hour or so, a person reaches for a cigarette, lights up, and smokes the whole cigarette. The bridge of behavior is pretty straight-forward – habitual smoking of cigarettes. Looking deeper, why does the person reach for the cigarette? Habit, you might answer. Ok, yes, that is true, but what I want to know is why did the habit develop in the first place? How did it begin? In order to look deeper, the person might need to go back to the very inception of the habit. What were they thinking when they first began smoking? Ideas like 'this is cool', 'I'll fit in better', 'all of the really tough kids are doing it', 'I look good with a cigarette in my hand', 'smoking is sexy', etc. might have been present at the very beginning of the habit. Next, what thoughts followed these initial ones after the behavior had been going on for a while? The person may recall thinking things like 'I really enjoy smoking', 'now I fit in', 'smoking makes me feel better', 'I get to relax when I take a smoke break', 'smoking is comforting, soothing', 'smoking eases my stress', 'smoking calms my nerves', and so on. Only the person examining their own consciousness can know what beliefs are holding the pattern in place.

When it comes to your own patterns, only *you* will be able to determine why you developed your particular pattern of behavior in the first place. Everyone has their own reasons and experience. One person may have started smoking to fit in, another may have begun because their father smoked, a third may have thought tobacco smelled great, and a fourth may have been intimidated or dared to do it. Whatever the reasons, once you know your initial motivation for beginning the pattern of behavior and have examined the beliefs that have supported you to perpetuate the habit, you are ready to begin to build a new bridge.

Looking back at the beliefs the person made to support the behavior of smoking, you can see that the person labeled the cigarettes as their source of enjoyment, relaxation, comfort, soothing, calming, and so forth. The truth is that those cigarettes are a very poor, temporary substitute for the real thing. As whole, complete spiritual beings, our needs are all met from within; everything we have ever needed comes from our source of Loving, which we can only access from inside of ourselves. The ticket to clearing any pattern is to determine what need we attached to the pattern – what we thought it did for us – and take full responsibility for that need, and bring it back inside to our Source.

Take Time to Visualize a New Pattern of Behavior

Before beginning to work a process to update your beliefs around the old behavior, I would suggest spending a few moments visualizing the new pattern of behavior. A person wanting to quit smoking could ask themselves, "What do I want to do instead of smoking to meet my need?" I suggest making the new pattern simple, easy to do, and highly effective to meet the need at the level of Source. A complex pattern is not likely to work out well, no matter how healthy the new pattern may appear. For instance, if the new pattern a person decides to adopt instead of smoking cigarettes to meet the need for comfort and relaxation is something like 'to meditate for ten minutes in a quiet room with incense burning and soothing music playing', how likely is that to actually happen? Not very. What happens when the urge to smoke hits while the person is at work? What about if it hits while the person is driving? I am sure you get the picture. The new behavior has to be *doable*, anytime and anywhere, above everything else.

A new behavior to meet the need that used to be met through smoking may be as simple as breathing in the energies of peace and comfort, saying inside, "I am my own source of comfort. I am at peace." If you are a visual person, you could add a visual element, such as getting surrounded by loving arms like a warm hug. If you are a sensory person, you might add a feeling of getting wrapped in a fuzzy blanket of warmth or feel the warmth of the sun shining Loving down upon you. However, you decide to meet your need in a new way, be sure that it is something simple enough that you can and will remember and be able to readily access whenever the need arises. Breathe in Loving Source-energy until the need is met fully from within. This is just one example of creating a new pattern of behavior that is rooted at your Source.

Whatever new behavior you decide to put into place, come up with your new, healthier pattern of behavior *before* dropping the old one. This is important because remember, you may have been driving down that same 'ol bridge for years. If you attempt to take down the bridge before erecting a new one, how will you cope when your mind says it's time to drive in that direction again? How will the person who has been smoking for twenty years deal if they don't have an alternative in place when in a stressful situation where the urge strikes to take a break and go have a cigarette? When people don't have a healthier pattern in place, they will usually quickly rebuild the old bridge in frustration – often adding a few extra supports in the process such as 'I can *never* stop smoking', 'quitting doesn't work, so I may as well just live with it', and so on.

Or, if a person has not yet decided upon a new pattern of behavior, yet is committed to change, they may grab the nearest substitute and simply transfer all of the old, supporting beliefs onto another unhealthy habit. A common example is a person who quits smoking and immediately starts gaining weight – they have just substituted eating for smoking.

And, sometimes a substitute doesn't work because the person can't meet the need through the substituted behavior. Lots of ex-smokers say, "Just chew gum", "Chew on a toothpick instead", or whatever. But what if the gum/toothpick doesn't make the person feel comforted, relaxed, soothed, cool, sexy, mature, de-stressed, and so on? What if chewing gum makes them feel childish or immature when one of the old beliefs is about looking cool? If the supporting beliefs cannot be transferred and the underlying need does not get met, the substituted behavior simply will not stick, no matter how hard a person tries to stick with the new habit of behavior.

Substituting Less-unhealthy Behavior is a Short Term Solution

Substituting a less-unhealthy behavior is a short term solution for becoming truly healthy and sourced from within. Swapping another less destructive external habit for an unhealthy habit is not a bad thing; it can sometimes ease the suffering temporarily and help a person transition towards healthier living. It will not, however, bring a person ultimate joy or freedom. Only Source-energy can provide that. For someone who has substituted another addictive behavior, there will usually come a time in that person's growth when they will become ready to be free of *all* unhealthy habits, and they may not know how to proceed.

I have heard dozens of recovering alcoholics say, "I can never stop _____ (drinking coffee, eating cookies, smoking, chewing gum, etc.) because that's what I do instead of drinking." That idea is limiting and doesn't have to be true for them. Any pattern of behavior can be changed. Spending some time visualizing and imagining a newer, healthier pattern of behavior where the support comes from within is the key to meeting whatever need you have had associated with any particular behavior.

Working Your Process to Establish a New, Healthy Pattern

Once you have spent some time visualizing a new, healthy pattern of behavior clearly that is easily doable, is approved by your aspect, and meets your needs from within, you are ready to work your process to update your supporting beliefs and build a new bridge of behavior.

Follow the three stages from chapter six, under updating

your belief system, clearing any and all irrational beliefs that were acting as pillars that were holding your pattern in place. When you feel like you have cleared all of the beliefs surrounding your pattern, make a forgiveness statement around the pattern itself, and update the pattern to reflect your new, healthier pattern of behavior. The verbiage to update a pattern is:

"I forgive myself for buying into the irrational belief that *it serves me in any way to perpetuate the pattern of* _____ (state old pattern of behavior)." "My new pattern is that I now _____ (state new pattern of behavior)."

For example, the person changing the pattern of smoking might say:

"I forgive myself for buying into the irrational belief that it serves me in any way to perpetuate the pattern of smoking cigarettes." "My new pattern is that I now breathe into my source of Loving, taking in full, deep, healing breaths of compassion, repeating 'I am my own source of comfort and relaxation. I am at peace' whenever I feel the need to feel comforted, soothed, relaxed, or de-stressed. I am sourced from within, and my new pattern is to breathe right into my Source-energy to get my needs met."

Watch for an Aspect Connected to an Unhealthy Pattern

When working your process around an old, unhealthy pattern of behavior, understand that there may be a sub-personality attached to the particular behavior. This part of your consciousness may be holding onto dozens and dozens of irrational beliefs that are supporting the unhealthy pattern of behavior to perpetuate. Be willing to explore yourself deeply. Why does this aspect of you need to engage in this behavior? What does this part of you get out of it? How does this part of you feel about it? You may need to work with the aspect first before this part of you is healthy and strong enough to let go of an unhealthy behavioral pattern. Understand that disowned aspects will cling to unhealthy patterns out of fear until the level of trust, compassion, and Loving is stronger than their fear.

If you discover an aspect that is in charge of a behavior that is resistant to change, get diligent; spend time listening and attending to this part. Reach out to this part with loving arms, no matter how unhealthy you deem this aspect's behavior. Build rapport and establish trust. Apply more compassion until this aspect feels your infinite love and acceptance. Persevere until this part of you moves into your light.

Once you integrate the sub-personality fully into your heart, it will be an easy matter to change the old, unhealthy behavior into a healthier, self-supporting behavior. Before moving into process around the specific behavior, approach your aspect respectfully and ask this part if it's ready for a promotion. If there's any resistance, keep working with your aspect, applying more compassion until this part feels ready for an upgrade. Once your part is on board with the behavioral change, you can imagine giving that part a new job description, a new title, and a healthy raise. Just be sure that you keep the aspect in a role that supports meeting the same underlying need behind the original behavior.

Watch for Old Emotions Attached to Your Unhealthy Behavior

There are often strong emotions attached to a behavior. Even though there are likely just as many negative emotions related to the behavior coming from other parts of you, it is important to identify the positive feeling-energy associated with the behavior so that you can be sure your new behavior meets your needs and creates the most positive feelings attached to the old behavior. For example, the majority of the personality of the person trying to quit smoking may feel emotions such as bad, guilty, ashamed, sick, depressed, or hopeless in relation to cigarettes. The aspect or part that is perpetuating the habit may feel good, calm, safe, protected, satisfied, self-righteous, better-than, and so on. You might examine the positive feelings surrounding an unhealthy behavior and realize that there is a better way for you to feel 'good, calm, safe, protected and satisfied'. You might like to clear the irrational beliefs that create feelings of 'self-righteous, better-than, etc.' as these are feelings that are based solely on thoughts and beliefs that are stuck in right/wrong ideas of inequality since it no longer serves you to support this type of thinking.

Watch for Judgments Surrounding the Unhealthy Behavior

There will also be judgments associated with the behavior; again, just as with feelings, a certain line of judgments will be coming from the aspect in charge of the behavior, and another set of judgments will be coming from other parts of you that are in favor of stopping the behavior. The parts that want to quit may have judgments like 'I hate smoking', 'smoking is bad', 'smoking is unhealthy', 'I stink', 'my bad breath is disgusting', 'my teeth look gross, ew yuck', 'my stained fingers are revolting', and 'I am pathetic, stupid, weak, and disgusting for smoking'. Conversely, the part that is invested in continuing to smoke may have judgments like 'smoking is good', 'smoking is cool', 'I am cool', 'I look good', 'I look grown-up', 'I look mature with a cigarette between my fingers', 'smoking tastes great', 'cigarettes smell wonderful', and more. Because all judgments are locked into fear-based, right/wrong thinking, I would encourage clearing and forgiving yourself for holding *all* of the judgment and bring the whole thing into the neutrality of the Loving.

Exploring the beliefs, feelings, and judgments around your pattern will give you the information and insight you need to change your pattern for good. Because let's face it, you were unconscious when you began this pattern.

To unconsciously begin an unhealthy pattern of behavior means that you likely lacked awareness about yourself when your unhealthy pattern of behavior began, which in turn means that you were not really fully awake or aware of what you were getting yourself into at the time. Because you weren't aware of what was present for yourself at that time, you missed the opportunity to take a higher course. In order to get back on track with the will of your soul, you will now need to go back to that time where you decided to adopt that particular habit or behavior and apply your new awareness – your full, undivided, focused attention – to determine what inspired your choice to engage in that behavior in the first place. And then apply compassion for the suffering you experienced. Only by doing so can you become free of it.

Sometimes people balk at going back to look at themselves, saying things like, "I don't know why" or, "I can't remember what I was thinking; it was too long ago" or whatever excuse they can come up with to avoid looking deeply. And yet, if they persist and keep talking about it, a memory or a feeling will pop in that will provide invaluable insight into their decision. Even if the only memory is saying something as simple as, "I just went along with the crowd. It was what all of my friends were doing, so I did it, too", this is still *very* valuable information. You could then ask yourself questions like, "How does it serve me to 'just go along with the crowd'?", "Is it in my highest good to follow others blindly, or is it Ok for me to think for myself?", "How do I feel about always following the crowd now?" and, "Do I want to continue to think that way?"

When you pose these kinds of questions, listen carefully to what your aspect says in response. For instance, you may think from your higher self's perspective that it's Ok and wise to be an independent thinker. But when you check in with this part of yourself who has adopted a specific habit of behavior to fit in or 'go along with the crowd' and ask if it is Ok to think for yourself, that part may answer quite differently. It might bring up old, dormant fears or things you heard during your childhood. Messages like, 'you stupid idiot – you don't have a brain in your head', 'you can't think worth a darn', 'you are too young to decide', or my favorite of all of my childhood messages, 'if you had a brain, you'd blow up'. Once you listen carefully to what the aspect has to share about why it is better or safer to go along with others and identify the irrational beliefs, you will probably be ready to update those beliefs to new ones that serve you better.

Two Examples of Creating a Healthy Pattern of Behavior

Here is an example of a pattern that I changed in my own life – my pattern of avoidance and procrastination. I'd struggled with avoidance and procrastination for many years, attempting to change my patterns many times with poor results before I learned the skill of identifying and integrating disowned aspects of my personality. Before I went to shift this particular pattern, I spent some time with an aspect of myself, which I had named 'the Avoider'. I explored this part of myself thoroughly. This sub-personality would pick up a book anytime I wanted to avoid doing something that I thought I didn't want to do. This pattern of behavior caused me some serious suffering over the course of my life as I spent the majority of my time reading. As a result, I then had to fly around in a panic to get anything else done on time. As a student, I did sloppy, last-minute homework. I never felt good about any of my assignments because I never put in enough time to give anything my best. As an artist, I did sloppy, last-minute drawings or paintings and always had the excuse of saying, "I did this very quickly," just in case someone didn't like my work. As a mother, I did sloppy, last-minute clean-ups before friends came to visit or quick last-second runs to the grocery store for lunch foods on the way to school, often causing my kids to be late – which they hated and still complain about to this day. In my career, I avoided advertising my workshops because I didn't feel confident about how to do the marketing. Was my flyer lame? Was that picture too dumb? I avoided writing for years because I felt afraid of what might happen if I attempted to publish a book. What if nobody read it? What if they *did* read it and criticized me? This pattern of avoiding everything made it so that I was accomplishing very little in my life, and finally, I decided that it was time to change.

Because my pattern of procrastination directly led me to pick up a book, I identified my bridge of behavior as 'picking up a book to avoid doing something else'. Next, I identified the beliefs that were supporting the unhealthy behavior. Mostly, they were beliefs about protecting me from pain, failure, hurt, criticism, and rejection. I had experienced a good deal of rejection and criticism as a child, so as a defense mechanism, if I didn't create or accomplish anything, I figured that there'd be nothing to criticize. 'I didn't have time to do my homework' became easier in my mind than turning in something that might be judged as a failure. So, I had beliefs attached to reading and avoiding that said things like, 'just read and don't worry about that, you can do it later', 'reading is safer', 'that other stuff doesn't matter anyway', and other ideas that encouraged me to read instead of facing my fears. All of these beliefs were preventing me from living in the flow, from accomplishing my goals, and from giving my best to the tasks that were my responsibility to handle.

Once I identified my behavior and took a thorough look at the beliefs that were supporting it, I was able to ask myself, 'what would I like to do instead?' I determined that what I really want to do was to feel free to go ahead and get things done. When we need food, go grocery shopping, promote my workshops when I have a workshop coming up, write a book when I'm guided to write, or accomplish any other task or goal with grace and ease. I decided that I want to move forward toward my goals fearlessly, and fluidly. The need that was being met by the old behavior was a need for safety and protection from pain. Therefore, I decided that my new behavior would be to surround myself with Loving, state that my safety is in the Loving, and that it is now safe for me to get things done. I checked in with my aspect, the Avoider, to make sure this part was ready for a promotion, got the green light, and gave this part of me a new job title, the Doer. I worked my process, updated my beliefs, and established my new pattern of behavior.

Shifting this particular pattern of behavior was interesting because, unlike something like smoking or any other unhealthy addiction, I think reading, in and of itself, can be an Ok thing. I didn't actually want to quit reading; I only wanted to quit avoiding and procrastinating and start getting things done. Therefore, initially, whenever I had the urge to pick up a book, my new pattern had me ask myself the question, "Do you really want to read, or is there something else you could be accomplishing right now which you are attempting to avoid?" I would get an immediate sense of whether or not I was reaching for the book to avoid, or if I really just wanted to read for the pleasure of reading. If I felt any 'avoiding' energy present, I would surround myself with Loving, state that my safety is in the Loving and that it is now safe for me to accomplish things. This met my need for feeling protected. As a result, I can now easily discern what needs doing and just do it. I no longer reach for my kindle throughout the day. I freely go grocery shopping whenever the need arises, clean my house, do laundry or dishes, write books, draw with genuine effort, and in general apply myself fully to whatever I decide to do in any given moment. And, I still usually read for about an hour or two before bedtime or sometimes read to shift gears after a client session without feeling like I am avoiding doing anything else.

Creating this new pattern of behavior has allowed me to accomplish more of my goals in the past five years than I have ever completed in the past. It's supported me to go from sloppy, mediocre performance to giving things my best – definitely a change in service to my highest good. This is just one of many patterns I have shifted for the better.

Another example: Kirsten was a thirty-year-old woman who was struggling with extra weight and body image issues. After spending some time working with several of her disowned aspects and applying lots of compassion, she was ready to address her behavior of eating too many sweets. Kirsten labeled her behavior as 'reaching for sugar when I want to feel better'. Kirsten explored the inception of her sugar habit thoroughly. She remembered a mostly-painful childhood punctuated with brief moments of lightness that had always included sugary treats. The highlights of her life were celebrated with candy on holidays, cake on her birthday, sweets at other people's birthday parties, and the occasional treat such as an ice cream cone on the boardwalk or cotton candy at the fair. She came to the awareness that she had made a determination inside herself as a young person that sugar in any form – candy, cake, cookies, brownies, chocolate, pie, ice cream, etc. – was her only source of happiness in life. As soon as she had money of her own as a teenager, she began the habit of buying a candy bar to feel better, to feel happy for a little while, in her otherwise unhappy life. This pattern escalated when she was in her twenties to include weekly binges of all her favorite sugary foods. When she felt bad enough about her body size, she would have periods where she would go cold-turkey and refuse to buy any sugary foods for a while to attempt a healthier diet, but then something stressful would come up, and she'd go right back to binging again. She was ready to change the behavior for good this time, so to do that, she needed to go deeper to find the underlying beliefs.

She was easily able to label the beliefs that were supporting the unhealthy pattern of behavior, some of which were: 'sugar makes me feel better', 'I only feel good when I eat sugar', 'On a bad day, sugar is my only consolation', 'It is good for me to treat myself when I feel bad', 'sugar is what makes me happy', and 'If I give up sugar, I won't be able to cope'. Kirsten saw how she had labeled the sugar as her source of happiness – this was her unmet need she was attempting to get met by consuming sugary treats. Since she was now connected to her internal source of Loving, she could see the irrationality of viewing sugary foods as her source of happiness.

Kirsten was able to connect inside with her true source of joy, so she decided to use 'joy' as her new pattern of behavior. She decided she would simply remind herself that she had all of the joy she ever needed or wanted right inside, and that happiness was an inside job. She could choose to breathe in joy at any moment. She took it even further, knowing that she was both connected to her Source and one with her Source; she declared, "I AM the joy!"

She then went into process, applying infinite compassion for the aspect of herself that was in charge of the habit of eating sugary foods who she'd been calling 'Sweetie Pie' – a little girl who'd felt so unhappy and disconnected from her source of joy and Loving. She loved up that younger part, renaming her 'Joy', until her aspect felt fully connected to joy and melted into her heart. She then updated all of her beliefs, creating supportive beliefs that kept her sourced with joy from within. Her new beliefs were empowering, giving her the ability to access her pattern of being the joy anytime, anyplace, taking the power off of the sugar and placing it all in her own hands at every moment. She was able to neutralize the sugary foods, to see them as simply one choice in a whole range of food choices, and she began to choose healthier options to feed her body, such as fruits, vegetables, healthy fats, and proteins. Kirsten affirmed her power to choose joy daily, anytime, anywhere, and her life went from bleak to wonderful in a matter of weeks.

Since connection with her soul had really been what she'd always been seeking, being filled with her source of joy daily was so much more satisfying than eating sugary treats had ever been. It was, therefore, fairly easy for her to let the sugar go and to simply be the joy whenever she needed to feel better. She was tested a few times under stressful situations, and each time she went for the sugar she was able to uncover more beliefs that were tied to the old habit. She diligently applied compassion and kept committed to her new pattern, persistently updating the limiting beliefs, clearing the judgments, and continuing to move toward her goal of vibrant health. With perseverance, Kirsten began to honor herself, eat healthy foods, exercise, and care for her body daily as an expression of Loving, and to live in a consistent state of joy. She soon became radiantly healthy and fit as a result of her new pattern of behavior.

Changing an Unhealthy Behavior Can Take Time and Effort

Changing unhealthy behaviors can take some time. Be patient with yourself, and keep working your process about whatever comes up as you are changing your pattern. It is essential, with any behavior, to find *all* of the irrational beliefs that are keeping the old behavior in place. What this means is that you might do some updating around a behavior, and cultivate a new replacement behavior that better meets your needs. And, you might even be able to do the new behavior a few times, but then you may find yourself inadvertently engaging in the old behavior again. This is normal. It doesn't mean that the effort you put in didn't work; it simply means that there are more irrational beliefs supporting the old behavior to uncover or that the aspect running the behavior has not yet fully integrated. If this happens to you, and you suddenly find yourself acting out in the old pattern of behavior again, first and foremost, go easy on yourself. Resist the urge to beat yourself up and instead choose to view this as an exciting opportunity to gather more information about the old behavior. Go back into it and look deeply again.

This time, when you check in with the aspect in charge of the behavior, you will very likely get different information or discover different feelings or different reasons for why you need to keep doing this particular behavior. After you get the new information, be sure to make time to work your process around it, applying compassion, updating all of the new beliefs you discovered, and repeating the process of updating your pattern each and every time:

"I forgive myself for buying into the irrational belief that it serves me in any way to perpetuate the pattern of _____." "My new pattern is that I now _____."

Keep listening to yourself, keep updating your beliefs, keep clearing judgments, and keep cultivating the new, healthier pattern of behavior. If you continue working your process around an unhealthy behavior, you will absolutely be able to shift to a new, healthier pattern. Persistence is the key to success when it comes to changing habits for the better.

Know that you can shift any pattern you wish for the better. Your intention to shift will act as your guiding light, so keep a strong commitment and intention to change in your thoughts as you go about this process. You are worth having healthy, supportive, and empowering habits of behavior. You always have free will choice, so choosing your behavioral patterns is part of your experience while you are in Earth-school. Choose radiant health and well-being. You are so worth having the healthiest patterns of behavior you can visualize. Go for it!

Exercise: Cultivating New, Healthy Patterns of Behavior

Begin by saying a protection prayer, setting conditions of love and light, and invoking spirit's presence.

Place your hands on your heart. Set an intention to access the highest vibration of Loving available. Breathe in the Loving and fill your body with Loving energies from head to toe. Then, set an intention to access the highest level of compassion. Breathe in compassion and fill your body with compassion from head to toe.

Repeat out loud any of the following that resonates, changing the phrasing as needed to reflect your own beliefs:

"I forgive myself for buying into the irrational belief that I will always be stuck with my unhealthy habits; that I can never change." "My new updated belief is, I now know that I can change any habit or pattern that I desire to change. I know that I can simply figure out what need was being poorly met, and I can decide to meet that need in a better, more Loving, more supportive way. My will and my ability to look deeply at my beliefs and motivations around the old behavior are much stronger than the temptation to settle for unhealthy patterns."

"I forgive myself for buying into the irrational belief that it will be too hard or difficult for me to give up _____." "My new updated belief is, I now know I can choose grace, ease, and joy as I change my unhealthy pattern of behavior for a new, more supportive, healthy pattern of behavior. I am not my behavior. I am a divine soul in a body, and my soul supports me to move into alignment with radiant health and well-being in every way. I can do it!"

"I forgive myself for buying into the irrational belief that because I've been doing _____ for so long, it means that it will take a long time to change." "My new updated belief is, I now know I can change as rapidly as I can update my beliefs to create new, more supporting beliefs for my new pattern of behavior to take hold. If I go back to the old behavior, I know that simply means that there are more beliefs for me to update, and I can keep working my process around the behavior until I have fully embodied the new, healthy pattern fully."

"I forgive myself for buying into the irrational belief that if I lapse back into my old, unhealthy pattern of behavior, it means I'm a failure." "My new updated belief is, I now know that if I revert to an old pattern or habit, it simply means that there is still some information for me to gather around the behavior – some more irrational beliefs, judgments or a disowned aspect that is calling for my attention. I can be gentle with myself, knowing that there is no such thing as failure – only lack of doing – so I can keep moving forward and working my process until the new, healthy behavior is fully anchored in my reality."

"I forgive myself for buying into the irrational belief that if I let go of my old, familiar, unhealthy pattern of behavior, I won't be able to cope when I feel stressed." "My new updated belief is, I know that I can cultivate a new, healthy, self-supportive behavior before I let go of the old, unhealthy one. By having a healthy behavior in place, I can easily make the transition and begin to meet my own needs from a higher perspective of Loving. I am so worth having the healthiest habits!"

"I forgive myself for buying into the irrational belief that I need to fear that if I change my unhealthy habits for healthier ones, my _____ (spouse, friends, family, coworkers, etc.) won't want to be around me anymore or won't like me." "My new updated belief is, I now know I want to be around me, and I like me. I am my own source of liking, and as long as I love my own company and like myself, other people will like me, too, and will want to be around me. And, if these particular people don't want to be around me anymore, it's Ok because I can easily attract people who do. I can cultivate new, like-minded friends who accept me and support me as I support myself. My inner reality creates my outer reality."

"I forgive myself for buying into the irrational belief that if I change my old, unhealthy habits of behavior for healthy ones, I won't have any fun or be any fun." "My new updated belief is, I now know my source of joy is internal. I have instant access to the energy of joy through the Loving, and I can have as much fun as I wish in every given moment. Joy is my birthright, and my joy exists independently from any outer habits or behaviors. I declare that I am joy-filled and have the delight of a child."

Close your process by acknowledging yourself, expressing gratitude to spirit, and fully grounding your energy. Drink plenty of water.

CHAPTER ELEVEN
The Integration Process

So what does the path of healing and integration look like once you have the necessary tools required for lasting change? Your ongoing path will look uniquely individual, as each person's clearing is distinctly different from everyone else's. There are some general guidelines that you can follow to support yourself, yet for the most part this is going to be an instinctive process where only *you* are going to be able to determine what you need to do in any particular moment to best support yourself to integrate a higher level of truth and transform your life.

You Have All of the Necessary Tools to Resolve Your Issues

If you have read this book thoroughly and followed the forgiveness exercises at the end of each chapter, you most likely have a basic understanding of the tools that are required for healing and resolving your issues on an ongoing basis. In any given situation when an issue arises, you now have a whole toolbox of ways to respond to your issue that will support you to resolve your issue fully, in your own highest good. Let's look at these tools:

- Self-observation using your neutral observer to gather information
- Identifying your issue
- Taking 100% responsibility
- Listening to your feelings
- Acknowledging your feelings
- Compassionate self-talk
- Identifying a disowned aspect or sub-personality
- Listening to an aspect of yourself
- Applying love and compassion inside yourself
- Listening to your inner guidance
- Checking in with your internal feeling-barometer
- Discerning your truth
- Identifying irrational beliefs
- Updating irrational beliefs
- Working a 3-stage process: preparing the space, working a process of self-forgiveness, closing with gratitude
- Owning a projection of judgment
- Clearing self-judgment
- Emoting your feeling-energy in a healthy manner
- Creating a new pattern of behavior

With these tools in your personal toolbox, you now have the ability to respond to yourself in the healthiest of ways when you feel triggered, upset, or out of alignment within yourself in any way. Now, it is just a matter of committing to becoming your highest self. Make a commitment to complete your spiritual curriculum and work your process around anything that disturbs your peace on a regular, ongoing basis. If you do this, you will rapidly move out of fear and into the Loving.

Examples of Working Your Ongoing Spiritual Process

Here are some examples of what working your spiritual process may look like as you go about your everyday life:

Issue: Bob is at work and finds himself becoming upset when a coworker does something that he thinks is incorrect.

Process: Before addressing the coworker, Bob goes into working his internal process. First, he *checks in with his feeling-barometer and identifies the feeling* as 'angry' – anger means something is off-course inside, locked into right/wrong thinking. Bob *acknowledges the feeling* of anger by addressing it directly, "I hear you. You feel really angry." Next, Bob *listens to the feeling*, allowing it to express why he is feeling angry in order to *identify the irrational beliefs and judgments*. Bob's anger replies, "I'm angry because Sheila did it wrong. She should have done it this way. She should know by now because she's been here for over a year! She's an idiot!" Bob *acknowledges the feelings* again, "I hear that. I hear you think that Sheila did it wrong and that you think she's an idiot…" Bob *applies compassion* inside, "It's Ok… it's alright to feel angry; I can just let that up and out…" Bob breathes the feeling out on a sigh to *emote it in a healthy manner.* Bob thanks the feeling for sharing then *updates the irrationality, applying love and compassion* inside. "I forgive myself for buying into the irrational belief that there is only one right way to do something and that everyone 'should' know how to do it by now. My new updated belief is, I now know there are many ways to do things; it's Ok to do things differently. It's Ok for people to make mistakes; mistakes are how we learn. I forgive myself for judging Sheila as an idiot. She's a soul in a body, just learning and growing, doing the best she can." Bob is feeling much more centered. He can now go back to work knowing he can address Sheila from a calm, respectful, compassionate place rather than dump anger, judgment, and criticism on her head. If Bob is diligent, he will *write down the triggering beliefs and judgment* and work more deeply later, *applying compassionate self-forgiveness, updating irrational beliefs* about right/wrong, 'should's, and *owning the projection of judgment* of 'idiot' energy.

Issue: Sarah is a mom of three highly energetic boys. When she asks them to do something, and they do not listen, she finds herself becoming extremely frustrated and upset.

Process: Sarah now has the awareness and the tools to handle her upset when it occurs. First, her *neutral observer alerts her to her feelings* when she begins to feel frustrated or starts to yell at her children. She is able to *identify the feeling* of frustration. This feeling is familiar and leads her to *identify a disowned aspect or sub-personality* that she has just recently identified as 'poor me' – a part of herself that has felt unheard, unwanted, unsupported, and unloved. Now she can *listen to the aspect*, taking note of what it has to express: "Nobody ever listens to me. What I have to say doesn't matter. Everybody else's needs are more important than mine. Nobody cares about what I need or how I feel." Sarah *acknowledges her feelings,* "I hear that you feel unheard and unimportant. That what you say doesn't matter and that no one cares about you." Sarah then *applies love and compassion* internally, wrapping her 'poor me' aspect in her truth, "The truth is that I care about you, I love you, and I am here to listen to you. What you have to say is very important. You are important. Your needs matter." Sarah's feeling of frustration immediately transmutes as *compassion is applied internally*, and she is able to cheerfully call out the limit again to her children from a clearer, more self-supported position inside of herself. Her children hear her as a result and respond more positively to her request. Before she forgets, Sarah jots a quick sticky note – *identifying her issue* – about the triggering upset and sticks it on her nightstand as a reminder to keep working with her 'poor me' aspect and to keep clearing and resolving this issue. Later that night, once the boys are in bed, Sarah *works her process, using the three stages to prepare her space, update her limiting beliefs* to create strong, supportive and empowering beliefs, *clear her judgments* of 'unheard', 'unsupported', 'unimportant', 'insignificant', etc. and *close her process with gratitude*. She also spends some time *listening to and nurturing her 'poor me' aspect* in her heart, giving that part of herself all of the love and attention she missed out on as a child.

Issue: Keesha gets triggered up every time she hears a love song on the radio or sees something that reminds her of her ex-boyfriend.

Process: Keesha has already claimed her source of Loving on the inside, and she is still working on integrating that concept into knowing on every level. She *identifies her issue* as whenever she thinks about him, she feels very sad, lonely, and despondent, and she puts it all out on missing her old boyfriend. She *gets the message from her neutral observer* and catches herself missing him, thinking if she just had him back, she would feel better, and everything would be different. She *listens to the feelings* and acknowledges the feelings, "I hear you really feel sad and miss him," then immediately reminds this part of herself about her updated beliefs, "And I now know that my boyfriend has never been my source of Loving, my source of attention, my source of happiness, or anything else. All of that is inside of me already. I am a whole, self-contained being, and all of my needs are already met. All I need to do is breathe in whatever I feel I need in any given moment." She sits with that for a moment, then hears an irrational part saying, "But I can't be happy without him!" There is a lot of energy behind this thought, so Keesha first *acknowledges the feeling;* "I hear that. You think you can't be happy without him." The part responds, "He made me happy. I was only happy while we were together." She *applies compassion* until the feeling calms down, "I hear that it's Ok. I hear you really think that." She moves into *self-forgiveness and updates her beliefs*, "I forgive myself for buying into the completely irrational and fear-based idea that my ex-boyfriend is, was, or ever has been my source of happiness. My new belief is that I may have felt happy at times when we were together, and my happiness always came from within me. He didn't give it to me; we only shared it. My happiness is my own choice. Joy is my birthright, and I can choose to feel joyful anytime, anywhere. I am totally responsible for my own level of joy and happiness." She feels the strength of her updated belief and steeps in it for several minutes, then keeps *working her process* about the few other *irrational beliefs* that popped up. "I forgive myself for buying into the irrational belief that my ex broke my heart. My new updated belief is, I now know I am whole; my heart is whole. I forgive myself for buying into the irrationality that I'm not Ok without my ex, that I'll die or something. My new updated belief is, I now know I am 100% whole, Ok, well, and complete. I am sourced from within, and I have everything I need to thrive inside of me. I am self-supported from within." Keesha moves into *clearing her self-judgments* and *owning her projections of judgment*, "I forgive myself for judging myself as lonely. The truth is that I am surrounded by my guides and angels and fully connected to all that is. I forgive myself for judging myself as sad. The truth is I am joy in a body! Sad is just a temporary feeling and not who I really am. I forgive myself for judging myself as despondent. The truth is that I am whole, well, radiantly healthy, and alive. Everything happens for a reason, and I can trust that all is well – that this is in my own highest good. I forgive myself for judging my ex as responsible for my feeling of heartbreak. The truth is I am solely responsible for my own feelings, and he is only responsible for how he feels. I forgive myself for judging myself as responsible for screwing up my life. The truth is that it is all Ok. I can't screw anything up – I am just learning and growing, doing the best I can. It is all good." Keesha feels better and spends a few minutes inputting reminder messages on her phone calendar to support herself for the next few days. She continues to practice *Loving self-talk* each and every time her feelings get triggered up about her ex until she integrates the knowing that joy, love, support, and more are all inside of her.

Issue: Daniel frequently catches himself getting defensive and is over feeling this way.

Process: Daniel has *identified the feeling*; he is aware that he has felt defensive for most of his life. He had highly critical parents and developed a pattern of shielding and deflecting blame at a young age. He is *working his process* daily to *cultivate a new pattern* of staying open to receiving feedback from a neutral position internally. Daniel is too busy at work to work his process deeply, so he has come up with a plan to gather information all week long and spend several hours by himself each weekend to heal this issue and change this pattern of behavior. He uses *compassionate self-talk* internally to get through the day at work without feeling bad about himself. When his boss demands to see him, his old, defensive feelings are triggered up. He *checks in with his feeling-barometer* and notes he is feeling bad, wrong, guilty, and worried – all before he's even had a chance to hear what his boss has to say. As he walks down the hall toward his boss' office, he responds inside of himself with *compassionate self-talk*, "It's Ok. Everything is alright. You've never done anything wrong. You are just learning and growing all the time. Everything that happens is Ok from my soul's perspective." He is calm and neutral by the time he arrives and is able to simply stay open and hear whatever his boss has to say without becoming defensive in any way. He jots a note to himself about the upset in his personal notebook, *identifying the issue.* Throughout the day, he continues to jot notes to himself, when he thinks the waitress at lunch doesn't like him, when a coworker makes a sarcastic remark, and when his wife asks him to move something he left in the hallway. By the time the weekend arrives, Daniel has several pages of notes of all of his upsets. He gets pen and paper, reads over the reminder notes, and lets his feelings pour out onto the page in a *write & burn:* "Why is everything always my fault why do I feel so bad all the time I hate myself I never do anything good enough for anyone I'm such a loser no wonder my mom hates me nobody likes me I'm not good at anything why do I even bother trying" writing until he eventually comes to a natural conclusion. Daniel carefully burns the pages in a metal bowl as soon as he has finished venting. He then gets out his healing journal and *identifies his irrational beliefs* based on all of the thoughts that were creating all of his feelings. There is a long list. He works the *three-stage process, preparing his space, updating his limiting beliefs,* "I forgive myself for buying into the irrational belief that I need other people to like me in order to like myself. My new updated belief is, I now know the source of my liking is inside of me. I like myself. I'm the only one who needs to like me in order for me to feel likable inside. I forgive myself for buying into the irrational belief that every other person's upset is my fault – that I am to blame for everything. My new, updated belief is that there is no such thing as 'fault' or 'blame' from the Loving perspective. It is all Ok, and each one of us is 100%

responsible for our own feelings – including our own feelings of upset. If my boss, the waitress, my coworker, or my wife is feeling upset, it is their responsibility and really has nothing to do with me. I can remain neutral." And so on. When Daniel is finished updating his beliefs, he updates his pattern again, "I forgive myself for buying into the irrational belief that it serves me in any way to perpetuate the pattern of blaming or defending when someone gives me feedback. My new pattern is that from now on, I remain open, receptive, and neutral when someone tells me something. I can simply hear whatever they need to say without taking any of it personally. I know I am innately good, and I like myself no matter what." He *closes his process with gratitude and grounds himself.* As a result of spending an hour or two with himself each weekend, Daniel is happier and more productive at work, is becoming more connected with himself, is more at ease in his own skin, and is rapidly becoming more intimate with his wife and family members.

These are just some samples of how you might go about working your process. The best way to move into a healing process in any given moment is to work with whatever is most pressing first. You will begin to see a natural order of operations as you become more familiar with these healing tools and spend more time coming into the rationality of the Loving. For instance, if you have big feelings of upset present along with some clear irrational thoughts and judgments, you will feel compelled internally to vent your feelings first before you will be ready to update your irrationality or clear your judgments. If you have a very strong judgment present, you may need to spend some time in self-forgiveness to transmute the judgment energy with compassion before you feel ready to look at the underlying irrational beliefs that were attached to your judgments. If you have a stubborn pattern that seems resistant to change, you may need to work with a disowned aspect before focusing on creating a new pattern of behavior. If you are stuck in your head, thinking about a certain issue, you might go straight into identifying, clearing, and updating your old irrational beliefs.

If you cannot summon the energy to work your process at all and notice you are feeling tired or defeated, you may decide it is time to take a conscious break. If you can ask yourself what is most presently occurring in your own awareness, you will quite naturally begin to be able to figure out what tool to apply as you go about your ongoing process of transformation. Most importantly, as you go about working your ongoing process, be kind and gentle with yourself; your ultimate goal is freedom, and in order to keep moving toward your goal, it is vital that you do your best to be encouraging to yourself.

Self-Acknowledgment is Crucial to Stay Motivated

Working your process is a learning experience, so, just like with anything else that is new for you, be patient with yourself as you explore how best to support yourself on your path to freedom. The gentler and kinder you can be with yourself inside of yourself, the easier your process will feel, and the more likely you are to keep going forward. To the degree that you can acknowledge yourself and encourage yourself, you will feel inspired to keep your commitment to your growth and make time to work your process.

Take the time to really acknowledge yourself after each and every session you spend working your process. By taking the opportunity to move through your issues and complete your spiritual curriculum, you are giving yourself the greatest gift of learning that there is – the gift of self-realization. There is truly nothing more important that you can give yourself in the grand scheme of things, so give yourself the credit you deserve when you make the time in your busy life to focus on what is most important – your spiritual growth.

Even if you feel very humble, understand that there is a part of your consciousness that needs to hear that you appreciate yourself and that you acknowledge yourself for what you are doing to better yourself. You will only be able to hear it from within. Your acknowledgment needs to come from you to you. Until you have received self-acknowledgment on the inside, you will not be able to hear it from outside, even if people are singing your praises up and down all day long – you could be receiving compliments, happy face stickers, blue ribbons, trophies, social media 'likes', or whatever – none of that will sink in or even matter if you are shut down from accepting credit.

If receiving acknowledgment for your efforts is a challenge for you, I suggest you make a point of honoring yourself in some way every day until you feel open and comfortable receiving a 'well done' from yourself. Understand that you do not need to get an A+ in a class or invent the cure to give yourself credit. Acknowledgment for your efforts can be given for doing just about anything, even something as little as brushing your teeth, making your bed, or sitting with your feelings for five minutes. You could say inside of yourself, "Wow, I really did a great job brushing my teeth just now. I honor myself for caring for myself so much." Or, "I appreciate myself for being willing and available to listen to my own feelings. My feelings are important, and I am worth being heard. I really acknowledge myself for taking the time to hear myself." If you really do this consciously, at some point, something inside of you will shift, and you will be open to receiving your own love, recognition, appreciation, and support to a degree you could never have even imagined. You will simply feel wonderful inside of yourself, every day.

Once you are comfortable showing appreciation for yourself from within, it becomes very easy to add self-encouragement. Giving yourself encouragement can be as simple as saying, "Come on! You can do it!" inside of yourself whenever you feel afraid or challenged in any way. Feel free to add whatever else you need to hear. Only you can know what it is that would make you feel encouraged, whether it is, "Keep going, you are almost there," "You are looking better and better every day. Way to go! Keep it up because you are so worth it", or "You know this fear will pass as soon as you step forward. Go ahead and make the move; you'll see." Whatever you need to hear to lift yourself up or keep yourself headed toward your intentions, make a point of saying it. Just make sure your words are based in Loving rather than the old fear-based model of motivation. This can make the difference between giving up and settling for less than what you truly desire and going for achieving everything your heart desires. So encourage yourself to go for it.

When you consistently speak encouragingly and appreciatively to yourself in your own mind, your very thought-patterns will begin to change. Instead of responding to your own thoughts critically or with more negativity, self-doubt, or worry, you will begin to be programmed to respond with encouragement, excitement, approval, joy, appreciation, gratitude, and other love-based qualities. When your self-talk becomes mostly positive and self-supporting, your whole quality of life will become more joyful, healthier, and more satisfying in every way.

Integration Requires Desire, Commitment, and Perseverance

The path of healing and integration is an ongoing process, not an event. I often hear people cry out in frustration, "I did that already! I can't understand why this _____ (issue, thought, feeling, judgment, pattern, etc.) keeps coming up. I should be over this by now." People give up all the time, just because they get down on themselves for not being able to do it better, faster, or easier than what they perceive they 'should'. Understand that the quick fix, pill-taking, fast food, instant gratification mindset of our current culture is not going to apply to your process of self-realization. For true enlightenment to happen, you must be willing to do whatever it takes, for however long it takes. Your heartfelt desire, your dedicated commitment, and your willingness to persevere – no matter what – are qualities necessary to achieve whatever level of growth you desire.

In my personal experience as a healing facilitator, I have found that most people have never applied the level of compassion necessary to fully heal and resolve their issues and move into total freedom. Most people do their spiritual work in tiny dribbles to simply feel better, and the moment the initial terrible feeling passes, they go back into complacency. Even people who have been attending personal growth seminars for years, doing yoga, attending regular spiritual services, cultivating ongoing meditation practices, journaling their feelings, attending recovery meetings, or visiting their therapist weekly usually only have a mental-level awareness of their issues. Most people have not yet done the work of actually healing and resolving their issues permanently. The good news is that awareness is about 95% of the work, so people who have spent years on the path of personal transformation are often quite ready to learn these tools and apply them liberally. I encourage you to grab onto these tools and run with them. Get determined! Become adamant about your transformation. Be willing – be eager even – to do whatever it takes to become fully and truly liberated.

You Have to Want to Transform Above All Else

I needed to feel like I couldn't stand my suffering for one more minute before I was really ready to do whatever it took to heal and integrate. I felt totally sick of my own sob story. I had tons of self-awareness, yet I was so tired of knowing what I knew but not being able to walk my talk and actually *live* what I knew. I felt desperate for change. I felt *so* ready by the time I got serious about my spiritual curriculum. I was literally willing to do almost anything – I wanted to transform more than I wanted anything else.

I love that Sufi story about the young man seeking a teacher. It goes something like this: A young man hears about a guru in the mountains in the Far East. He travels to the local village, asks for directions, hikes up the mountain, finds the guru's cabin, and knocks on the door. When the door is opened, he says, "I am here seeking enlightenment. Master, will you teach me?" The teacher curtly replies, "You are not ready yet." and slams the door. The young man's shoulders slump, and he goes back down the mountain. A year later, he returns and asks again, "Master, will you teach me?" He receives the same reply, "You are not ready yet." He leaves and returns six months later, asking, "Am I ready now?" The teacher shakes his head and responds, "You are not ready." This time, the young man stays on the mountain and begins to follow the teacher around, asking over and over, "Am I ready yet?" One day, as the young man is following the teacher down a path near a stream, asking, "Am I ready now?" the teacher suddenly stops, grabs the young man by the back of the shirt, throws him down into the stream, and holds his head under the water. The young man is stunned for a moment, then begins thrashing and fighting for his life, finally fighting hard enough to break free. He surfaces, gasping for air as the teacher says, "When you want enlightenment as much as you wanted to breathe just now, *then* you will be ready."

Everyone I have ever known who has achieved any level of freedom or enlightenment has had to want it, fiercely and beyond anything else. Personally, I had so much fear in my life that I had to be willing to face my worst fears and say, "So what if that happens. I want to grow, so I'm willing to take the risk." My process was all struggle, all fear, and all suffering until the moment I decided that my desire for freedom was stronger than my fear. I had to decide that I wouldn't give up this time, that I would persevere no matter what, and that it didn't matter what I had to face to get there.

Are you ready? Do you want to transform more than anything else? What has been holding you back from seeking the level of freedom you truly desire in your life? Whatever it is, I encourage you to make a commitment to work your process around it and go for freedom. You are worth risking it all for your ultimate joy and fulfillment in life. Once you make your commitment to move forward no matter what, you will be amazed at what begins to happen in your life. As you work your process around your spiritual curriculum on an ongoing basis, you will begin to see everything in your life coming into alignment with your soul's purpose. Synchronicity will occur on a daily basis. You will find yourself living in the flow more and more often. Issues will still arise to disturb your peace, yet you will have the tools at hand, ready to clear any irrationality and judgment in order to get back to your peaceful center.

Each time you work your process around any particular issue, you will feel clearer, more centered, and more whole. The level of joy you have access to will become greater. At some point, once you have been residing in joy and compassion for a while, you will feel contentment seep down into your cells, and this feeling will stay with you even when another issue arises for clearing. For me, this was when life went from being really, really good to beyond extraordinary. For once, I had that feeling of contentment inside all of my cells; it was as if I had passed some invisible boundary where enough of my consciousness resided in the Loving that there was no going back to right/wrong, fear-based thinking.

This meant that even when I had an issue arise, which was seriously lodged in right/wrong thinking – I could feel very upset about the issue – I also simultaneously felt a deep sense of contentment throughout my body. My body felt relaxed as if all of my cells were saying, "It's Ok… you are alright. Everything's just fine. You can relax as all is well. This is just a temporary feeling of upset which you can clear up as quickly as you desire." This pervasive feeling of 'everything is Ok' would allow me to get through my process with grace and ease, knowing that whatever had caused my feeling of upset was just an irrational idea or old, unresolved issue that didn't really have the power to shake my peace and wellbeing. My sense of wellbeing became a given, even when a part of me felt upset.

Your Birthright is to Reside in Joy, Peace, and Loving

If you can persevere through your clearing for long enough, you, too, will reach the state where you know beyond all doubt that everything is always Ok in your world, that there is nothing bad or wrong with whatever is coming up to upset your peace, and that you can quickly resolve your issue and get back to feeling total peace and contentment. This is my deepest wish and intention for you – that you will apply and use these tools shared in this book in your own highest good, that you will clear your baggage, pain, suffering, irrationality, judgment, and so forth to the point that you reside in the radiant peace and joy of the Loving paradigm. This is your birthright. Joy is who you are. Love is who you are. Peace is who you are. You are ready to up-level into the Christos, to *be* the change upon the planet, heal the planet and all of humanity in order to create peace on Earth. Now is the time. You and only you can do it for yourself. Claim your source of Loving, claim your intrinsic worth, claim full 100% responsibility, claim your authentic power, claim your free will choice, and claim your innocence. Apply compassionate self-forgiveness inside of yourself liberally, wherever it is needed using the tools in this book, and move into freedom.

> *"Out beyond ideas of wrong-doing*
> *and right-doing, there is a field.*
> *I'll meet you there."*
>
> ~ *Rumi*

Exercise: Claiming your Integration Process

Begin by saying a protection prayer, setting conditions of love and light, and invoking spirit's presence.

Place your hands on your heart. Set an intention to access the highest vibration of Loving available. Breathe in the Loving and fill your body with Loving energies from head to toe. Then, set an intention to access the highest level of compassion. Breathe in compassion and fill your body with compassion from head to toe.

Repeat out loud any of the following that resonates, changing the phrasing as needed to reflect your own beliefs:

"I forgive myself for buying into the irrational belief that I should have gotten this already." "My new updated belief is, I now know everything occurs in its own unique divine timing, and I am upleveling all the time. My integration will happen in my own readiness, and there are no 'shoulds' from my soul's perspective. It is all Ok in the Loving. I can relax and trust that my process is unfolding in divine-perfect order."

"I forgive myself for buying into the irrational belief that I need to push myself to grow." "My new updated belief is, I now know I can grow with grace and ease. I now know that if I push against something, it will push back, creating friction and againstness. My best way to move forward is to speak lovingly to myself inside of myself and use gentle encouragement. As I support myself from within, I will be supported from without to change and grow."

"I forgive myself for buying into the irrational belief that it is too challenging to be so self-aware or to work my ongoing process." "My new updated belief is, I now know that the universe never gives me more than I can handle. If I am experiencing lots of stuff coming forward for my attention, it is an indication of my readiness to resolve my issues and complete my spiritual curriculum. I am up to the challenge, and I can set conditions of grace, ease, joy, laughter, etc., as I work my process."

"I forgive myself for buying into the irrational belief that I need to fear getting overloaded or overwhelmed if I awaken my neutral observer." "My new updated belief is, I now know that my neutral observer is a part of myself that responds to my needs. I can ask my neutral observer to tone it down, go slower, or to focus on one particular area of learning or issue at a time, as needed. I also know that I can take conscious breaks if it feels like I've been working too hard or getting too serious about working my process."

"I forgive myself for buying into the irrational belief that I don't really need to do anything about all of my 'stuff', that if I just ignore it, maybe it will go away." "My new updated belief is, I now know that I have a spiritual curriculum to complete, and I will need to look at it now or later. I now know that the fear only compounds over time, so it will feel easier to me if I simply move forward now and keep moving forward, completing my curriculum with grace, ease, and joy as I move into alignment with my soul's purpose here upon the planet."

"I forgive myself for buying into the irrational belief that I should give up or just throw in the towel when things don't seem to be getting any better." "My new updated belief is, I now know, self-realization is an ongoing process. I may feel challenged at times, yet I can simply keep persevering, keep renewing my commitment to myself. I am worth doing whatever it takes to become personally liberated."

"I forgive myself for buying into the irrational belief that the planet doesn't really need my support or cooperation to heal – that somebody else can do my part." "My new updated belief is, I now know I am the one and only one who can do my part. For the planet to heal, for humanity to create peace on Earth, I need to step up, take responsibility for my part, and begin to work my process regularly to be the change I want to see in the world and express myself to my own highest divine potential. I am an important piece, a divine piece of the whole that is God/the Loving."

And so it is. So be it. And it is so.

Close your process by acknowledging yourself, expressing gratitude to spirit, and fully grounding your energy. Drink plenty of water.

CHAPTER TWELVE
The Framework of Loving

This book has taken you through the foundational principles of creating a mindset based on spiritual truth, as well as introduced specific tools for you to use to move out of the fear-based, right/wrong paradigm into the joy and freedom of the Loving paradigm. For clarity and deeper integration, let's review what we've covered:

Chapter One: Our Source is Love

The first, most basic step toward making the paradigm shift is claiming that your source is Loving and that you are, in fact, sourced from within. You are a soul in a body having a human experience. You are made up of over 99.99% space/source energy/God/Loving/Collective Consciousness – whatever you choose to call your divine source of 'being' energy. Your essence is divine. Your Source is not outside of you; God is within you. You are one with your Source of consciousness; you are one with God/the Loving at the absolute level.

Chapter Two: We are all intrinsically worthy

The next step is claiming your intrinsic worth. You were born worthy, you are currently worthy, and you will continue to be worthy long after your body dies and you pass on to the next stage of your journey toward oneness with all that is. You are equally as worthy as every other being ever born. You are a unique, priceless, one-of-a-kind divine being, worthy of everything your heart desires. You are a whole being, completely sourced from within; you contain all of the inner resources necessary to reach your fullest potential. All of your needs are met from within. There is nothing to do to prove your worth; your worth is a given. You are innately worthy. Claim your intrinsic worth, your equality, your uniqueness, and your wholeness.

Chapter Three: Viewing Life from the Paradigm of the Loving

Moving from a fear-based, right/wrong reality into a Loving reality requires a shift in paradigm from viewing all things as either good or bad to viewing all things from a neutral, infinitely accepting position. From the Loving perspective, mistakes are Ok and simply opportunities for you to learn how to complete your spiritual curriculum and move into alignment with the will of your soul to fulfill your destiny, which is the goal. You have an internal guidance system to assist you to come into alignment, which is made up of three parts: your inner guidance, your internal feeling-barometer, and your natural discernment. To the degree you use these tools, you can learn to quickly course-correct when you go off-course to get back into the flow with all that is. Your perception of truth is relative to the place you are currently residing in consciousness – the higher you go, the more you can 'see'. As you journey up the spiral of consciousness, your awareness will rapidly expand to include higher and higher levels of truth. Absolute truth resides at the level of God/infinite Loving; you are always guided toward this, yet none of us are there yet. Therefore, use your discernment to decide what does or doesn't ring true for you.

Chapter Four: We Each have Free Will Choice

Humans are gifted with free will choice, which means every moment becomes a deciding moment. Through your inner guidance, you will be urged to follow the will of your soul, to move forward through your spiritual curriculum, and into your life's purpose here upon the planet. Your subconscious mind will be urging you to give in to the temptation to stay small, safe, and secure within the fear-based limitations of your current comfort zone. Your free will choice is always stronger than the temptation to settle for less than what you truly desire, so you can simply learn to say 'no' to temptation and move forward. Your strength of will will probably be tested several or even many times before a particular temptation will pass. Therefore, you will need commitment and perseverance to keep moving forward. If you willingly go against your own internal guidance system down a path you know to be off-course, you may end up in a hell of your own making. Getting out of hell requires compassionate self-forgiveness and saying 'no' to the current temptations that led you there. Getting into the state of heaven requires completing your curriculum, moving into alignment with the will of your soul, and moving into Christ Consciousness, the highest level of consciousness currently available to humans upon the planet. Christ Consciousness, the Christos, includes residing in qualities of joy, grace, acceptance, peace, compassion, and innocence. Once enough humans have evolved to the clarity of the Christos, heaven on Earth will be mutually created from a place of peace, joy, innocence, and unity between God, humanity, and nature. Religion is a form; spirituality is based on essence. The creation of heaven on Earth has nothing to do with religious affiliation and everything to do with aligning yourself with the will of your soul, coming into your own, unique divine essence's purpose, and continuing the upward journey on the spiral of consciousness into the Christos. Forgiveness is your birthright. Everyone is already forgiven and redeemed from their soul's perspective – each simply has to claim it and apply compassion internally to move into freedom.

Chapter Five: Taking 100% Responsibility

You are 100% responsible for yourself in every given moment. You are the only one who has the ability to respond to your circumstances in every instance. You are fully responsible for your own thoughts, feelings, and actions. You have the ability to choose your own response; no one can make you respond a certain way without your consent. There are no victims and no perpetrators from the perspective of Loving, only humans with equal access to authentic power acting out roles of stronger/weaker. By claiming full responsibility for yourself, claiming your authentic power, you will drop the shame, blame, guilt, and powerlessness of victim mentality and begin to create the life of your dreams.

Chapter Six: Making the Paradigm Shift by Updating Your Belief System

You have a mental belief system that reflects your current perception of truth, whether it is actually rational or irrational. Viewing life from the right/wrong perspective causes irrational, fear-based beliefs to form, which creates a life filled with pain, suffering, and disappointment. Rational beliefs are based on Loving and free of fear; when you decide you have had enough struggle and suffering, you can choose to change your beliefs to reflect rationality, which will create a life of joy, harmony, and success beyond your dreams. Informative files inside of your belief system cannot be deleted; they can only be updated to contain a higher level of truth. Your limiting, fear-based beliefs can easily be identified and updated into more Loving, self-supporting beliefs. If you awaken the part of your own consciousness that functions as your neutral observer, you can monitor your own thoughts to watch for irrational thinking. You can follow your thoughts to your irrational beliefs, which will include verbiage such as black & white thinking locked in right/wrong or good/bad; negatives like 'I can't'; comparisons of better than/less than; absolutes like 'must', 'should', or 'have to; extremes such as 'never', 'always' or 'only'; judgments like 'stupid', 'crazy', or 'ugly'; and any subtler, fear-based thoughts that don't follow any of these rules yet are still limiting. You will be able to use your discernment to tell you if a thought is based on an irrational belief because the thought will make you feel off-course when you check in with your feeling-barometer. Irrationality is limiting, disempowering, unsupportive, weakening, and brings you down. Rationality is freeing, empowering, supportive, strengthening, and lifts you up. By writing down any limiting, irrational beliefs that you observe throughout your day, you can work your process using the three stages – preparation, processing, and closing – in your own timing to update your old beliefs to create new, healthy, empowering beliefs. Your inner reality creates your outer reality, so as you update your belief system, your life will miraculously change for the better.

Chapter Seven: Judgment - A Natural Outcome of the Right/Wrong Reality

Judgment is neither bad nor good; judgment is the byproduct of getting born into a fear-based, right/wrong paradigm. You can learn to use judgment as a useful tool to see where in your own consciousness, you are still locked into right/wrong thinking. Judgment will present itself to you in two forms: self-judgment and projections of judgment onto other people, situations, or things. By owning your own judgment, you can quickly shift from limiting, black/white thinking into the infinite acceptance of Loving, seeing all things as Ok from a neutral perspective of learning and growing. You can clear your judgment as it arises using the process of self-forgiveness, and you can also clear judgment in conjunction with updating your belief system using the three-stage process from chapter six.

Chapter Eight: Embracing Disowned Aspects of Self

As children born into the right/wrong, fear-based paradigm, parts of our personality that are severely judged or criticized will split off from our main personality in order to protect us from feeling bad. This is a normal, natural act of self-preservation that is unconscious on our part when we are young. Parts that have separated can be viewed as aspects or sub-personalities. Your various parts will need to be identified and brought into the light in order for you to reach a higher level of self-awareness and integration. All of your sub-personalities are innately good and lovable, regardless of their beliefs, thoughts, feelings, and behaviors. To feel whole and radiantly healthy on every level of being, you can integrate your sub-personalities by identifying them, listening to them, meeting their unmet needs internally, updating any irrational beliefs that are no longer supporting you, and clearing any judgments they have been holding. You can also apply compassion to any memories that may surface and view everything through eyes of acceptance and Loving. When you are finished working with a sub-personality, you can make a sanctuary within your own heart and bring that part of yourself into your Loving heart. You can visit your aspect inside of your own heart, applying compassion liberally, until your aspect melts into the whole of your beingness and ceases to exist as separate. The goal here is to achieve total integration with all of your parts, coming into oneness and peace within.

Chapter Nine: Releasing Emotional Energy

Emotions are information that comes to us on a particular frequency of feeling-energy. To get the information, all you have to do is listen to what the feeling has to tell you. When you listen to your feelings from a space of compassion rather than attempt to stuff, suppress, ignore, deny, or negate them, you are allowing them to emote, which means to move up and out of your energy field. You can safely express your feelings by owning them fully and taking full responsibility for them, by using any of the following: using 'I statements' when speaking from a feeling place; venting in a healthy manner using write & burn, venting privately, venting with a trusted confidant; emoting out through a creative or physical process such as art, dance, music or exercise. Fear is the one exception of an emotional energy that does not need to be expressed; fear energy can simply be dropped. At any time, you can drop your fear about literally anything by simply choosing to move into an attitude of internal trust. Moving into the trust in the Loving is like turning on the light in a dark room – the fear will dissipate in the presence of the trust. When you have dropped fear and chosen to reside in trust, useful warning-messages will begin to come to you as energetic' heads up' alerts, drawing your focused attention to any potentially harmful situation without the energy of fear present. Living free of fear-energy is actually safer, as you will be able to stay calm, rational, clear-headed, and completely connected to your guidance in the event of danger or an emergency. You have the ability to become radiantly healthy on every level of being, including having healthy emotional expression.

Chapter Ten: Cultivating New Healthy Patterns of Behavior

Once you have identified and begun to work with your various aspects or sub-personalities, you will be ready to shift any unhealthy patterns of behavior into healthy patterns of behavior. You can identify the pattern of behavior you wish to change then explore the underlying beliefs around the pattern which have been keeping the behavior in place. Determine what need is being poorly met through the behavior and create a better, more supportive, more Loving way to meet that need. Imagine your new pattern of behavior thoroughly, making sure to keep it simple, doable, and sourced from within. Once you have come up with a new pattern of behavior, you can work the three-stage process to update your beliefs in support of your new behavior and clear all judgments surrounding the old pattern. Then update the pattern of behavior itself, giving the aspect in charge of that behavior a promotion. If you fall back into the old pattern, it just means that there is more to process. Keep visualizing your new pattern, and continue to work your process until your new pattern feels natural, easy, and fully established. You will know when you are done working your process around a new behavior when the temptation to dip back into the old habit ceases to arise.

Chapter Eleven: The Integration Process

Now you have the tools that are necessary to make the paradigm shift out of the right/wrong, fear-based perspective into living fully in the joy and freedom of the Loving. The complete tool list is yours. In order to make the shift, you will need to apply these tools to your daily life by working your spiritual curriculum in an ongoing process. There are several examples of what this looks like. Each time you find yourself out of alignment with your spiritual truth, take the opportunity to make a note of your trigger or upset. What disturbed your peace? Identify your upset, and work your process to restore yourself to your natural state of being – the peace and joy of Loving. You are love in a body, and your deepest desire is to experience your connection to Source-energy in every moment. By coming into peace internally, you are doing your part to create peace on Earth. It is an inside job, and the only way to realize yourself is by committing to your ongoing process of evolution.

Embodying the Framework of Loving

If we put the transformational information from these chapters together, we come up with some of the basic principles necessary for creating a life lived from the Loving paradigm – what I call the framework of Loving:

The Basic Framework of a Spiritual Belief System Based on Loving

- We are unfathomable, divine beings having a human experience on Planet Earth.
- Our souls are immortal. We existed long before we came into this body, and we continue to exist long after we leave.
- We are sourced energetically from within. Each divine being has an internal connection with 24/7 access to their soul – free access to the source of Loving and all that is.
- The source of Loving (AKA God, Goddess, The Infinite, Universal Mind, Divine Creator, Cosmic Consciousness, All that Is, etc.) is boundless, infinitely Loving, and accepting.
- Within the source of Loving, there is infinite access to the qualities of joy, peace, wisdom, beauty, gratitude, acceptance, compassion, grace, authentic power, freedom, approval, appreciation, and many more.

- As divine beings, we are all equally worthy of anything and everything. Our worth is a given; worth is intrinsic – each of us is born worthy.
- Within the source of Loving, there is no judgment. There is no such thing as right/wrong or good/bad, only true compassion and love for the learning opportunity. We are here to attend Earth School, and all forms of learning are equally acceptable.
- In Earth School, mistakes are how people learn. Each divine being has an internal knowing of what is in alignment with their own soul. Earth School provides an opportunity for us to learn how to become aligned from within ourselves in a physical-level reality through a process of trial and error. It is important to the learning to accept the process.
- Each divine being is a self-contained system, whole and complete. We each have all of the inner resources needed to complete our lessons and reach our soul's goals for this lifetime.
- Our inner reality creates our outer, physical reality. As divine beings, we are co-creators of our human experience, each 100% responsible for our life's circumstances. There is no such thing as a victim in the Loving.
- We can change our outer, physical reality by changing our inner; inner reality includes our spiritual level (state of beingness, the strength of connection to the source of Loving, degree of self-loving), mental level (Beliefs, thoughts, judgments) and emotional level (feelings, patterns of emotional response).

These concepts are foundational to living in alignment with spiritual truth. Right now, these may just be new, mental-level ideas for you. In order to transform your own life to begin experiencing higher levels of joy and freedom, I encourage you to do whatever you need to do to integrate these basic ideas from the mind-level of simply understanding them to the cellular level of knowing them as your reality. Embody these ideas fully. Do this by working your process around each new concept, updating any old, irrational beliefs that oppose these ideas, and affirming these new ideas as your truth. Clear any old judgments related to each of these ideas from your consciousness, stating your new truth loud and clear to transmute the energy stored in the judgment into Loving. Work with any subpersonalities that are nay-saying or resistant to accepting a higher level of truth; reel them into your loving heart and get them on board so that you can move forward freely. Repeat your updated beliefs often until these concepts resonate as your truth down into each and every little cell of your entire body.

When you can read the above list matter-of-factly, just nodding your head 'of course' to each point, without any resistance, fear, nay-saying, or upset in any part of your consciousness, you will know that you have claimed this new framework of Loving and are well on your way up the spiral of learning into higher levels of truth. Keep going. Your adventure of enlightenment has only just begun to unfold.

Enlightenment is an Ongoing Journey of Self-discovery

Moving up the spiral of consciousness into higher and higher levels of awareness is an ongoing journey of self-discovery. If these ideas are new to you, it may take some time to fully integrate them into your cellular knowing. At first, you may experience a mental-level understanding of this information, but there may be certain parts of you that don't agree, don't grasp the concepts fully, or keep forgetting them. This is normal and natural when assimilating a higher level of knowledge, so if this occurs for you, do not worry. Understand that your personality may be operating from many different aspects, and these various aspects of yourself have had some issues connecting with your higher self in the past. All of this can shift once you are aware of what is keeping these parts of yourself separated from your highest self. That can only occur by working your process – listening to these parts of yourself, hearing what they have to say, finding out where they are stuck in pain and suffering, and then applying compassion to the places that have felt wounded, isolated, separated, criticized, abandoned, abused, scared, and so forth. By reaching out to each part that has resistance to moving forward with loving intention and updating your belief system, you will be able to heal and repair the connection with these parts and bring them into your heart for good. From there, moving forward will be as natural as breathing.

You Are a Divine Being; Claim Your Birthright

You are indeed, a divine being. Now is the time to claim your birthright. I encourage you to do whatever it is that you need to do to move into alignment with the will of your soul. Integrate the parts of your personality that have felt separate, and come into peace inside. As you do so, your outer reality will begin to transform before your very eyes.

Your world is transitioning. There has been so much hype, so much prophecy about these times, leading up to this time in our planet's evolution. Yet, for most people, the next phase in our human development has been seen as separate, like something that will 'happen to us' as if something outside of us is going to simply be different; we'll suddenly wake up in a new world – heaven on Earth will have magically appeared overnight while we were sleeping. Guess what? It isn't going to happen that way at all. We have to wake up first; we actually have to build the new world together before it will appear. Spirit gave me this analogy: creating heaven will be like getting an incredible present that comes in a box – when you open it, it looks nothing at all like the much-anticipated picture on the front and has thick instructions that say 'some assembly required'. To get to live in peace on Earth, to get back to the garden, to create the abundant, joy-filled vision of heaven on Earth, our participation is required. Peace requires cooperation. Peace is a collaborative effort, as opposed to the fear-based method of separation and againstness that has been perpetuated for thousands of years upon this planet in the name of God.

To build heaven on Earth, war mentality must be healed, and all againstness toward others must cease. Not just the outer-level violence must cease, but all antagonism, hatred, envy, self-righteousness, superiority, racism, separation, pity, lack-thought, and so on must be healed and transformed on the inside. Each and every one of us must move into compassion for all beings, acceptance for all beings, rejoicing for life and learning, celebrating our diversity, embracing uniqueness, seeing God in every human. Seeing God in every cat, dog, goat, fish, insect, and spider. Seeing God in every tree, rock, river, and grain of sand. When people begin to heal as individuals, unity will begin to be cultivated in pockets around the planet. Eventually, with enough participation, the unity will spread to enfold all who are ready for oneness, and peace on Earth will become a reality. We are it.

We are the builders, the construction workers, the architects, the designers, and the landscapers of peace on Earth. What do you want the new Earth to look like? What do you want it to feel like? Are you willing to do your part? If so, embody the framework of Loving in your life, apply the tools shared in this book liberally to work your ongoing process of transformation, and bring yourself into alignment with the will of your soul. Many blessings of joy and light ahead towards your journey into the Loving.

Peace be with you.

"World peace must develop from inner peace.
Peace is not the absence of violence.
Peace is the manifestation of human compassion."

– The 14th Dalai La

Acknowledgments

This book has been a labor of love spanning more than a decade. I would not have been able to bring this body of work into writing without the consistent support of my guides, who were urging me on every step of the way. The first few drafts were written over a four-year period from 2009-2013. Big thanks go to Bryan Donohue for early edits. Shout out to Danielle Lovett and David Banks for title ideas. Heartfelt thanks to Galina, Lisa, and Kitty for contributing to my publishing fundraiser. And lots of gratitude to Marc for bringing me tea while I wrote.

The manuscript sat unpublished for seven years. Special thanks to Vilhelm Kruse for giving me a much-needed kick in the ass to dust it off and put it out there. Gratitude and deep appreciation to Elise Hamilton Ferguson, book midwife extraordinaire, for the unwavering support with rereading, revisions, and editing. Many thanks to early reader Marta Rodriguez-Karpowicz for suggestions and proofing. And big thanks to Florian Zimmer for the incredible cover art and design.

Thank you to all of my clients and students for sharing the journey with me. Your incredible strength, courage, and soul-deep healing experiences have inspired every word.

Last but not least, thank you to my family. To my beloved mom, for being my greatest teacher and biggest fan, and to my three children for putting up with my writing immersions and supporting me to follow the will of my soul.

I love you and dearly appreciate all of your support.

www.ingramcontent.com/pod-product-compliance
Lightning Source LLC
Chambersburg PA
CBHW072141100526
44589CB00015B/2026